IMMIGRATION AND CITIZENSHIP IN THE TWENTY-FIRST CENTURY

IMMIGRATION AND CITIZENSHIP IN THE TWENTY-FIRST CENTURY

Edited by
Noah M. J. Pickus

ROWMAN & LITTLEFIELD PUBLISHERS, INC.
Lanham • Boulder • New York • Oxford

ROWMAN & LITTLEFIELD PUBLISHERS, INC.

Published in the United States of America
by Rowman & Littlefield Publishers, Inc.
4720 Boston Way, Lanham, Maryland 20706

12 Hid's Copse Road
Cumnor Hill, Oxford OX2 9JJ, England

British Library Cataloguing in Publication Information Available

Library of Congress Cataloging-in-Publication Data

Immigration and citizenship in the twenty-first century / edited by
    Noah M. J. Pickus.
        p.   cm.
    Includes bibliographical references and index.
    ISBN 0-8476-9220-5 (cloth : alk. paper). — ISBN 0-8476-9221-3
(pbk. : alk. paper)
    1. Immigrants—United States.   2. Naturalization—United States.
3. United States—Emigration and immigration.   4. United States—
Emigration and immigration—Government policy.   5. Citizenship—
United States.   6. Democracy—United States.   7. Political
participation—United States.   I. Pickus, Noah M. Jedidiah, 1964–   .
JV6465.I4727   1998
325.73—dc21
                                                            98-27248
                                                                  CIP

Printed in the United States of America

∞ ™ The paper used in this publication meets the minimum requirements of
American National Standard for Information Sciences—Permanence of Paper for
Printed Library Materials, ANSI Z39.48–1984.

For Nisan and Anna-Lecee, Max and Rose
For Pick and Sara
And for Micah and Linkon
From the nineteenth century to the twenty-first century

Contents

Acknowledgments

For generous financial support, I am grateful to the H. B. Earhart Foundation, the Jockey Hollow Foundation, the Josiah Charles Trent Memorial Foundation, the North American Studies Program at Duke University, and the vice provost for academic and international affairs at Duke University.

I owe a tremendous debt of gratitude to Betsy Beinecke Shirley and Barbara Smith, who believed in this project well before they had any evidence it would succeed.

My colleagues at the Terry Sanford Institute of Public Policy offered good advice and a congenial place to work. Phil Cook, Joel Fleishman, Bruce Kuniholm, and Fritz Mayer especially made it possible to organize the Duke University Workshop on Immigration and Citizenship and to produce this volume. I owe a special debt of gratitude to Jay Hamilton, who willingly answered all of my questions, great and small. I also received valuable counsel from Alex Aleinikoff, Linda Bosniak, Paul Donnelly, Martin Ford, John Griffin, Jennifer Hochschild, Michael Jones-Correa, Robert Keohane, Elizabeth Kiss, Susan Martin, John Miller, Robert Pickus, David Rosenberg, Peter Schuck, Suzanne Shanahan, Peter Skerry, Peter Spiro, Dan Tichenor, and Scott Wong.

I would like to express special appreciation for the fine work of Troy Dostert, who coordinated the Duke workshop, labored tirelessly and with good humor to corral thirteen authors and fashion this book, and offered excellent intellectual contributions. Special thanks are also due to Maura High for her superb editing skills; Teddie Brown for lending her remarkable talents to making the Duke workshop successful; and Steve Wrinn and Lynn Gemmell at Rowman & Littlefield for their patience and encouragement.

Trudi Abel initiated and nurtured this entire project. Without her, nothing would have been done.

Foreword

Rogers M. Smith

Politicians create citizens. To be sure, as Marx said of history, they do not do so under conditions of their own choosing. But in thinking about the topics of immigration and citizenship, which mean so many things to so many people, it is important first to remind ourselves that for better and worse, it is politicians who establish the rules legally defining who is a citizen and of what sort. Politicians make the laws that make some people officially citizens of one country, other people citizens of different ones, still others not citizens at all but rather "subjects" or "nationals" of this or that regime. And sadly, politicians make laws that leave some people bereft of any state or territory willing to recognize them as its own. The laws made by politicians also define much of what citizenship means to people—the rights it entails, the duties it imposes, its gradations and conditions, who can get it or lose it, and how they can do so.

In the United States at the close of the twentieth century, all these features of citizenship law are controversial once again. Is the United States letting too many immigrants come, or the wrong kind, and is it good or bad for them to seek to become citizens? What rights should citizens have to government programs like food stamps, unemployment, health care, education, public employment, and officeholding that noncitizens should not have, if any at all? What can we properly demand of those who seek to become or those who are already U.S. citizens—must they know English? Give political allegiance solely to the United States? Display appreciative knowledge of American culture and values more broadly? Under what conditions can the United States get rid of would-be citizens if they don't seem to be working out too well?

These are questions to which American politicians now must give answers, one way or another, like it or not; and again, not under circumstances of their own choosing. But they do have real choices nonetheless, and so do all of us who play some role in shaping the conditions under which politicians choose. The choices American politicians are making today are likely to have tremendous significance for the lives of many millions of people, and for the future of the United States and many other countries, throughout the next century.

To think well about what those choices are and how they should be made, we therefore need to think about politicians and the circumstances under which they choose. We need to think about the politics of citizenship. We need to ponder both the general conditions that lead politicians to create citizens and the particular challenges facing American politicians today. The essays in this book are excellent starting points for doing so.

To see why, let us begin with the big picture. The choice to create citizens really involves several linked but distinguishable issues. One issue is whether most members of a political community should in fact be designated as "citizens" at all, as members entitled to share in governing, instead of something else such as "subjects" or "nationals." In the United States today the answer to this question seems obvious, but it was not always so. The term "citizen" is a venerable one, stemming from the ancient Greek city-states and the Roman republic, but those regimes faltered and "citizenship," as opposed to "subjectship," then almost vanished from the face of the earth. It was revived first in Renaissance Italy, then in very different forms by the political efforts to build large national republics that began in northern Europe during the Enlightenment of the seventeenth and eighteenth centuries. Those efforts had their first great triumph in the creation of the United States. Yet even in the United States, historically many people have been "nationals" but not citizens, including slaves, Native Americans, and many inhabitants of the colonies acquired in the Spanish-American War. Today the United States still governs some such nationals residing in unincorporated territories like American Samoa, as well as many U.S. citizens with somewhat limited political rights (such as territorial, commonwealth, and D.C. citizens) and many permanent resident aliens with few political rights at all.

Should all such persons eventually become U.S. citizens? Should others? The question of who should be a full member of the United States or any other country ultimately turns on political choices that go beyond the issue of the type of government a certain country should have. That issue is only one facet of broader and deeper questions, including whether a given country should actually be a distinct political community at all and what kind of community it should be. These questions matter greatly to politicians, for politicians are persons who hope to govern certain populations. Hence they very much want those populations to believe that they constitute a political community, a "people," and a people who are properly governed by those selfsame politicians.

Fostering an appropriate sense of "peoplehood" is, however, usually a difficult, contentious task. Even though the world has always been divided into particular political communities, some now quite old, no community is simply natural. No political society in the world today has existed as such from time immemorial. All existing communities are products of long, contested histories that have left deep marks on their current members. Some feel profoundly loyal to their countries, but others feel milder or mixed allegiances or even deep alienation. Think, for example, of Scottish, Welsh, and Irish nationalists in Great Britain, Basque separatists in Spain, many immigrants with dual nationality throughout Europe and in the Americas, as well as Chicano, black, and Native American champions of self-determination for their groups in the United States today. Even among those who feel allegiance to a particular political community, there are great differences about the sort of community it should be. Both Pat Buchanan and Jesse Jackson are in their different ways genuinely patriotic Americans, but their ways are very different indeed.

One major way politicians not only express but actually craft senses of "peoplehood" is by enacting laws of membership that determine who is in and who is out and what their respective rights and duties are. An America governed by Jesse Jackson would probably be more eager to attract Zulu immigrants and to sustain majority minority districts than an America governed by Pat Buchanan, for example. Those policies would in turn greatly affect what America and Americans would be like in the future. But if that contrast makes it clear that the choices politicians make concerning immigration and citizenship rights matter greatly, it's now time to take note of the constraints politicians also face.

Neither Pat Buchanan nor Jesse Jackson is likely to govern the United States in the near future (though Buchanan may have a better chance). To gain power, candidates need to win the support of populations that already have well-established senses of what America has been and should be. If their visions of nationhood vary too greatly from the accustomed ways, the established interests, or the ideals and aspirations of the great bulk of those they wish to lead, they will lose to more conventional politicians. Though Buchanan and Jackson can each play important roles in reshaping prevailing senses of American nationhood more in directions that would support their own rise to power, neither seems likely to shift enough Americans in his direction to win any time soon.

Their examples suggest that in crafting a politically successful sense of nationality or peoplehood, in creating citizens, politicians must speak to both the inherited identities and the contemporary values of those they would govern. Potential U.S. leaders must be concerned both with history, what America has been, and with theory, what Americans think it should be. They must provide accounts of each that many Americans find persuasive. Those requirements constrain what politicians can say and do successfully; and worse, they can contradict each other. History and theory do not always point in the same direction in their implications who should constitute a people and what their principles of political community should be; yet neither can be ignored.

In various ways, the authors in this book confront this tension. Some appeal chiefly to American history in order to discern what they take to be the authoritative theories that should guide our conceptions of American nationality. Others instead appeal chiefly to theory and contemporary values to judge what in American history merits preservation and continuation and what requires rejection or correction. The resulting views of American history, political theory, and the proper connections between them vary greatly. But all these inquiries and debates are inescapable aspects of the task of crafting a successful sense of peoplehood, the task of creating citizens, in the United States or any other political society.

In America, however, politicians engaged in fostering an appropriate sense of national identity and citizenship also face at least one special circumstance and a special challenge. On the eve of the Revolution, Thomas Paine proclaimed that the cause of America was in large part the cause of all mankind, and many Americans since have always seen their nation as a great vehicle for furthering the rights and well-being of all humanity. Yet most Americans have also always wanted to feel somehow more obligated to their country than to humankind at large, and most American leaders have wanted them to feel that way, without renouncing their more universalistic values. How can this be done? How can cosmopolitan principles and aspirations be combined with a sense of particular nationality vivid and distinctive enough to command the degree of loyalty needed for any society to survive the troubled times that every society sooner or later faces? This is the issue that several chapters in this volume ponder, both in terms of basic conceptions of American nationality and in the very practical context of decisions concerning the notions of American identity that naturalization processes should be designed to express and strengthen.

So far I've suggested that the general challenges of forging a sense of peoplehood and the particular challenge of combining a sense of American distinctiveness with universalistic values have faced American nation-builders throughout U.S. history. But today, American politicians also face some quite new circumstances. Progress in communication and transportation systems and growing economic interdependence mean that people today can move back and forth between two or more countries with amazing frequency and can pursue many activities in one country even while dwelling in another. These same developments mean that relatively affluent nations like the United States, long magnets for immigrants, now have many resident aliens who have no desire to sever most of their extensive ties and interactions with their homelands. As a result, in the United States and elsewhere, many more people are seeking to be recognized as dual citizens, as members of more than one nation. In the United States and elsewhere, issues of the rights of immigrant resident aliens are becoming more pressing and complex than they have been for generations. The concluding chapters explore these new issues of dual or multiple citizenship and immigrant rights. These emerging issues reflect trends that call into question basic notions of national sovereignty. As such, they have the potential to transform the relationship of the American political community to the rest of the world's population more radically and fundamentally than ever before in U.S. history.

Even so, it is likely that in one way or another, politicians will continue to create citizens, to form and define political communities, and they will continue to do so in ways they expect to serve the interests and ideals they favor. That is a reality that has endured and is likely to endure for a very long time. But it matters that politicians do not act wholly under circumstances of their own choosing or making. For one of those circumstances is the existence of thoughtful, informed opinion on how politicians should proceed. At best, such opinion can constrain and guide politicians, helping make their choices wiser and more beneficial for all humanity. That is why the complex and fascinating topics addressed in this volume are vital ones for all of us to consider. The conclusions we reach may play an important role in defining what America is and who Americans are as they step into the dawn of the twenty-first century.

Introduction

Noah M. J. Pickus

As chair of the U.S. Commission on Immigration Reform, Barbara Jordan called for a revival of programs that Americanize new immigrants. She claimed that Americanization "earned a bad reputation when it was stolen by racists and xenophobes in the 1920s." "But," she added provocatively, "it is our word and we are taking it back."[1] The Commission on Immigration Reform, in its 1997 Report to Congress, *Becoming an American: Immigration and Immigrant Policy*,[2] reminded us that the country has paid little attention to programs that integrate immigrants into American society and civic culture. The report pointedly asked, "What do we expect of the immigrants we admit? How will we receive them?"[3]

These issues have concerned immigrants and ordinary Americans for some time. Recently, policy analysts, who have focused more on the economic aspects of immigration, have also begun to look at the broader themes, asking how immigrants become citizens and a part of American society.[4] There is, however, much disagreement on the most fundamental questions: What is America, and what should an American citizen be?

Jordan's strong words on Americanization suggest why elected officials and policymakers have avoided confronting these questions until now. The very terms of membership in the national community are hotly contested: for some, Americanization, like assimilation, is a dirty word; for others, Americanization is essential to immigrants' and the nation's wellbeing. "Immigration," observed Shirley Hufstedler, the last chair of the commission, "is about who and what we are as a Nation."[5]

From October 30 to November 1, 1997, thirty-seven men and women representing government, universities, and nonprofit organizations gathered at the Terry Sanford Institute of Public Policy at Duke University to undertake the first major analysis of the commission's 1997 report. The controversial question of Americanization, which lay at the heart of the report, focused discussion on the role of rights, culture, and civic identity in the incorporation of immigrants into America. The papers presented at the workshop are collected in this volume (in some cases in revised versions), along with the commentators' responses, which are based on the original rather than the revised essays.

The workshop concentrated on the second of the commission's two themes, *immigrant* policy (what happens to immigrants in America), rather than on *immigration* policy (how many and what kind of immigrants are allowed entry). It examined recent controversies over citizenship and the incorporation of newcomers into American civic and social life, specifically controversies over the commission's Americanization proposals, as well as naturalization, dual citizenship, and welfare reform.

Such controversies raise critical questions about immigration and naturalization and about the meaning of American nationhood in an increasingly multicultural and transnational age. What does Americanization mean today? What should a revised naturalization examination look like? How should the United States regard dual citizenship? How much should a person's citizenship count for in a democratic society?

How we answer these questions will shape our understanding of American citizenship in the twenty-first century. Are we on the verge of developing new notions of citizenship and community, ones that successfully weave together our multiple allegiances from the local to the universal? Should the notion of individual membership in a single nation-state be replaced by an emphasis on group representation, cultural rights, and membership in multiple countries? Or would such new notions of transnational and multicultural citizenship threaten basic principles of American democracy? Will the shared civic identity that makes both self-governance and the protection of rights possible suffer if these changes come to pass? Perhaps democratic politics depend on some degree of cultural homogeneity, shared affinity, or political loyalty that operates at the national level. Or perhaps democracy works best within a framework of multiple, overlapping, divided memberships and identities.

Answers to these questions are so very important because they impinge on broader debates about race, multiculturalism, globalization, and national unity. The introduction of newcomers into our society invariably has implications for the way we understand issues of collective identity and the responsibilities we owe toward one another. Newcomers can strengthen or undermine a shared sense of citizenship. They can reinforce the importance of having a distinctive American identity, or they can encourage citizens to conceive of themselves as members of a subnational group, a transnational association, a global community, or some uncharted combination of these identities. Whether we conceive of American identity as something singular or, on the other hand, variegated and diverse, will also have a significant impact on what benefits are available to newcomers; how many immigrants become citizens and under what conditions; what newcomers learn—and teach—about the meaning of citizenship; and whether Americans regard newcomers as intruders or as partners with whom they share a common fate.

America has not faced such widespread reconsideration of its immigration *and* citizenship policy since the 1910s and 1920s. In that period, the movement to Americanize newcomers coincided with the Dillingham Commission's recommendation that Congress reduce the overall level of immigration.[6] The debate over immigration and citizenship policy in the Progressive era also intersected with a broader argument among Americans over who they were as a people. At that time, the dispute focused on whether to increase the power of the federal government and, if so, to construct a more felt sense of national identity. Today we face similar questions on a global scale.[7]

In a nation of immigrants, conflicts over the meaning of citizenship are especially complicated. These conflicts are dominated by emotionally charged, polarized arguments and drastic solutions: either we end all immigration or we open our borders to virtually anyone; either we eradicate all subnational ethnic identities or we reinforce them at all costs. It is increasingly difficult to hold a thoughtful discussion among Americans who disagree on the relation between immigration and civic identity but who fall between the extremes of the debate.

The contributors to this book represent a variety of disciplines, including political science, philosophy, history, and law. All of them pay attention to current controversies in public policy. They also press us to recognize the ways in which our politics is itself structured by deeper and more constitutive issues and demonstrate that efforts to fix policy without careful attention to those issues will result in bad policy and in bad theory. Their approach reflects the conviction that conceptions of citizenship shape the way in which public policy controversies are framed and that careful reflection on the intersection of theory and practice can illuminate, and help resolve, some of those controversies.

Part I of this book addresses historical and conceptual quarrels about the meaning of American identity and the implications of these quarrels for the incorporation of immigrants. Part II analyzes the implications for public policy of contemporary disputes about the character of nationhood in an age of multiculturalism and globalization. Part III considers the proliferation of membership statuses among nations and within nations.

I. The Meaning of Americanization

How should we tell the story of American citizenship? Is it a noble chronicle of liberty, a shameful tale of domination, or a narrative too complex to reduce to any one account? The answers to these questions inform competing visions of citizenship for the next century.

In his essay, "The Promise of American Citizenship," Charles Kesler rejects multicultural and transnational conceptions of citizenship. He regards them as threats to the slow, difficult process of aligning political practice with the founding principles of the United States. Cosmopolitan notions of citizenship, he says, particularly ones that involve regional or transnational governance, "strain the limits of human affection and self-interest" while creating bureaucratic structures unaccountable at the local level. He argues that multicultural notions of citizenship encourage individuals to think of themselves as members of subgroups within a polity and thus reduce politics to the contest of power and identity rather than opening it up to the play of reasoned arguments. Kesler worries especially that the combination of multicultural and transnational conceptions of citizenship will undermine the notion of self-government, of a political community based on consent and natural equality, as well as the love of country needed to preserve those values.

In Kesler's view, the gap between our principles and our practice has led many scholars to reject those principles. Yet, he argues, racist traditions in American history are not as legitimate or authoritative as the founding principles of liberty and equality. Moreover, he contends, the view that history *is* theory makes it difficult to explain which part of our history we should strive to advance. It rules out any standard that itself transcends history. It also castigates us as hypocrites because it doesn't measure political life in terms of pragmatic steps toward achieving our aspirations.

Kesler is impressed by the difficulty of sustaining a political order that takes popular will and the rule of law seriously. Self-government, he notes, requires a constant effort to "consolidate public opinion behind [broad] principles, to persuade popular majorities to govern in the interest of minorities too, to encourage citizens to strive for the common good." He therefore emphasizes the importance of cherishing a distinctively American conception of citizenship, one that encompasses American habits of mind and conduct, the Protestant work ethic, a common language, an affection for the Constitution and the Union, and a sense of national spirit.

Kesler acknowledges that some citizens do not feel accepted as Americans. But he denies that they are, in fact, not welcome. He rejects the notion that narrow cultural definitions of belonging, which would limit who can become a citizen and be accepted as an American, reflect the founding heritage. Hence, rather than altering what he believes America stands for, Kesler stresses that new citizens should become full members of the polity by consenting to the principles that animate the Declaration of Independence. This consent links them to other Americans by what Abraham Lincoln called an "electric cord" of equality.

In his response to Kesler, "Citizenship in Theory and Practice," Kwame Anthony Appiah calls the linchpin of Kesler's theory of citizenship in the United States, consent, a "pious fiction." Most American citizens, Appiah points out, were born into their status, rather than having actually consented to become citizens. Kesler insists that this fact "overlooks the importance of America's consciousness of itself as a founded (indeed, a revolutionary) society and an immigrant society." Appiah believes that it requires us to find the foundations of American peoplehood in the liberal tradition of political thought embodied in thinkers like John Locke and John Rawls.

This tradition, he emphasizes, urges us to allow citizens the liberty to forge their own future. For Appiah, himself a recently naturalized American citizen, the United States can ask newcomers to understand something about liberal political principles before becoming citizens. We need not, however, ask anything more of applicants for naturalization. In contrast to Kesler, who is concerned about multiculturalism, Appiah regards the pressure to assimilate as a powerful force in American life. He worries, instead, about the threat to individual freedom and to the liberal tradition that arises from constraining newcomers in areas they should be left alone to freely choose or reject.

Juan Perea's chapter, "'Am I an American or Not?' Reflections on Citizenship, Americanization, and Race," echoes and builds on Appiah's concerns. Perea argues that Americans have, for most of U.S. history, failed to consistently adhere to the principles of liberty, democracy, and equal opportunity. Kesler's view of American history as a heroic struggle to put its principles into practice relegates discrimination against minorities to a mere footnote instead of making it the main story. This view detaches political theory from history by regarding failures to live up to the principle of equal treatment for all as mere deviations from the norm.

In fact, Perea believes, those failures constitute alternative, competing conceptions of membership based on subordination. Kesler, he charges, slights the experience of minorities and disregards the struggle necessary for overcoming inequality. Perea regards current efforts to end birthright citizenship as clear evidence against the argument that America has slowly, but steadily, moved toward greater equality. He believes that these efforts demonstrate how the value of citizenship is contingent on race, because the main group affected by such attempts will be Latinos.

For Perea, the Commission on Immigration Reform's emphasis on Americanizing new immigrants exemplifies the broader problem with separating theory from history. The attempt to separate the concept of Americanization from its historical moorings is bound to fail, he says, because the excesses of Americanization are intrinsic to that concept. Perea views the early twentieth-century Americanization movement as an unredeemable blemish on U.S. history; a spasm of xenophobia to be invoked only with a proper sense of national shame. It aimed not to inspire immigrants to share in the political principles of America, but rather to coerce Anglo cultural conformity. In contrast to Kesler, he is deeply dubious about Americans' willingness to accept newcomers.

In Perea's view, the discrimination newcomers face today constitutes the major problem to be eradicated, not their lack of knowledge about, or commitment to, America. We should therefore focus less on immigrants as the cause of America's troubles and more on the need for American citizens to fully embrace the principles of tolerance and respect for diversity. In Perea's view, it could be said, Americanization means that while immigrants should learn about their new country, citizens need to make the greater effort in embracing newcomers and protecting their rights.

The dispute over how to interpret the relation of principles to practice is also an argument about what those principles are and how the methodological fight will affect the incorporation of newcomers. John Miller, like Kesler, worries that the founding principles of liberty, democracy, and equal opportunity are being replaced by radically different content. In his response to Perea, "Reviving Americanization," Miller contends that nativists don't think immigrants can become Americans and multiculturalists don't think immigrants should become Americans. He praises the Commission on Immigration Reform for emphasizing that immigrants can and should become patriotic Americans. Like Kesler, Miller argues that immigrants can bond with native-born citizens by identifying with the American story. That story, in his view, tells of a people who have successfully struggled to live up to the core principles of liberty and equality articulated by their Founders.

For Miller, Americanization means that immigrants should adopt the American civic culture and that citizens are responsible for helping immigrants through this process. This help cannot be coercive; it must be based on consent. Unlike Perea, Miller praises the commission for its faith in the good will of Americans to honor this injunction. If carried out properly, he believes, a renewed Americanization movement could help secure a common understanding of America and of why America is special. Miller does, however, hint that the commission's emphasis on shared values masks the fact that Americans deeply disagree on how to realize those principles. While many Americans believe that our values oblige us to provide group entitlements to new immigrants, many Americans regard such efforts as the betrayal of those same values and as a disservice to immigrants.

II. Nationalism and Citizenship

The dispute over Americanization is itself part of a larger quarrel about the connection between national identity and citizenship. How do the particular claims of the nation relate to the claims of a citizenship accessible to all based on liberal principles?[8] The second part of this volume analyzes nationalism in the United States in terms of that broader debate. It focuses on the meaning of American national identity, especially the principles of individual autonomy and communal self-government, in an era when the claims of multiculturalism and cosmopolitanism are becoming increasingly powerful.

David Hollinger ("Nationalism, Cosmopolitanism, and the United States") and Noah Pickus ("To Make Natural: Creating Citizens for the Twenty-First Century") construct versions of liberal nationalism that see the American nation as the best vehicle for advancing a commitment to cosmopolitan values. They emphasize especially the possibilities for combining individual rights and national identity. While there are important differences between Hollinger's and Pickus's understanding of American identity, each begins from the position that Americans are deeply divided over what it means to live up to the principles embodied in the U.S. Constitution.

Hollinger criticizes a singular, uncontested conception of American identity. He is suspicious of attempts to draw group identity too tightly on the basis of nationality. Yet he advances a vision of American nationalism, what he calls a cosmopolitan nationalism, in contrast to the ideals of multiculturalism and universalism. He sees a sense of shared American purpose as necessary if we are to redistribute resources within the United States, help minorities achieve greater equality, and expand the circle of humans whom Americans care about and feel responsible toward.

Hollinger emphasizes that the United States occupies a special, if not entirely unique, position among nation-states. The presence of so many ethnic and racial identities, he asserts, makes the dangers of nationalism less pronounced. The U.S. commitment to liberal political principles means that loyalty to America can coexist with a commitment to the broader human community.

For Hollinger, the United States is more than a set of institutions, procedures, and abstract liberal values. It is also a finite historical entity. Unlike Kesler and the Commission on Immigration Reform, Hollinger rejects the notion that American identity is defined by a timeless, static set of civic values. Instead, he contends that our common citizenship should be based in a dynamic conception of a historically significant people, a people committed to an ongoing debate over their collective identity. American national identity, in Hollinger's work, serves common purposes without obscuring our differences. He believes we can accomplish this difficult task by recognizing that we share a past that consists of quarrels about the meaning of American identity as well as a common project of expanding human freedom.

In his chapter, Pickus emphasizes how difficult the task is of creating citizens who share common values. The very virtue that most characterizes liberal constitutional orders, the capacity to entertain and even encourage multiple identities and conflicting allegiances, can threaten those polities if those identities and allegiances are not sufficiently integrated. Paradoxically, the United States must support that which most threatens it. It is precisely because multiple identities and conflicting allegiances are so important, and yet can prove so explosive, Pickus emphasizes, that a national sense of identity should be forged carefully.

Pickus sketches a vision of constitutional citizenship that consists of three elements: consent to a set of abstract political values; emotional attachment to the polity; and the capacity and dispensation to deliberate over the nature and purpose of a people's commitments. He acknowledges that there are obvious tensions among ideology, emotion, and interpretation as components of American citizenship. But, he insists, they are tensions that appropriately reflect the delicate balance of civic goals: creating a shared sensibility, sustaining democratic principles, preserving self-governance, and protecting rights.

Pickus's chapter focuses on the controversy over naturalization policy in the United States. He argues that the models of citizenship that have shaped that controversy emphasize culture, rights, civics, and participation. These models all fail, he contends, to even try to sustain the balance among the different aspects of citizenship. As a result of this failure, our naturalization policy does not generate a sense of mutual commitment among naturalized and native-born Americans. Pickus proposes instead to build a naturalization process that more adequately reflects a constitutional conception of citizenship. Naturalization, in his view, could be an instrument for fostering immigrants' identification with their new and complex identity, a link between old and new immigrants, and an opportunity to encourage both native-born and naturalized citizens to explore the meaning of their shared identity.

For Hollinger and for Pickus, Americanization might be understood as a process of reciprocal or mutual exchange. Immigrants may change what it means to be an American, just as they are changed by the process of becoming American. Such an interpretation raises crucial questions about the relation of immigration to self-government, constitutional politics, and national identity. Most fundamentally, is a commitment to shared quarrels, or to interpretation, sufficient to bind a heterogeneous population? Put a different way, what, if any, limits are there on a transformative conception of national solidarity, one in which citizens may believe in new principles and ideals and the nation may be reconfigured?[9] These broad conceptual questions require answers, and not simply as a matter of political theory. Why should Americans, who think they know what values and sentiments constitute U.S. citizenship, accept a definition of membership that suggests those values and sentiments might be replaced or transformed?

A related issue turns on the question of the process by which the American nation might be changed. Will it, for instance, come as a result of elite politics, of international courts and bureaucracies imposing a set of transnational rights? Or will Americans, as a self-governing people, consciously decide to alter what they mean by citizenship and national identity? The answers to these questions will be crucial to determining how well any changes are accepted.

Hollinger's focus on history and on narrative hints at one possible response to some of these questions. He finds historical narrative the best vehicle for addressing both our differences and our similarities: the history of Americans as a specific people grounds, and limits, their debates; it allows them to connect to the sense that many have of belonging to the nation as well as to their devotion to broader principles and cosmopolitan commitments. Pickus emphasizes as well that critical judgment in the absence of emotional attachment is as risky as attachment without judgment. Some proposed changes might also reasonably be rejected on the grounds that they undermine self-government and violate the very premises that give a people the right to govern in the first place.

Still, Hollinger's and Pickus's approaches are riskier strategies than a straightforward attempt to inculcate new and old citizens with a specific set of values and characteristics. Both authors nonetheless clearly believe that one can render an honest picture of American history that is, all told, inspirational. Indeed, teaching new and native-born citizens that American history is an epic tale of the conflict over who we are as a nation may have great potential to inspire commitment to liberal principles and the American nation. But this project calls for a delicate balancing act between inspiration and criticism, idealism and alienation. Rather than argue about whether American history should be celebrated or censured, we might explore ways in which that balancing act can be accomplished.

Linda Bosniak ("A National Solidarity?") and Joseph Carens ("Why Naturalization Should Be Easy") insist that we should promote liberal democratic citizenship, not just American citizenship. In their view, Hollinger and Pickus place too great an emphasis on a distinctively American conception of citizenship. In doing so, they foster exclusivity and work against promoting a salutary universal vision of liberal democracy. Neither Bosniak nor Carens proposes that we establish a world state or pursue the immediate institutionalization of global forms of democratic governance. Instead, they emphasize more simply how democratic nation-states can expand liberal values by according full rights to migrants.

Bosniak challenges proponents of liberal nationalism on both empirical and normative grounds. She suggests that attempts to reappropriate nationalism on liberal terms may be patching a leaking boat rather than building a new craft for radically changed seas. Improved communication, better transportation, free trade laws, the proliferation of dual citizenship, and a prevailing discourse celebrating universal personhood and cultural difference now mean that the link between migrant and home country will persist and can even strengthen over time. As a result, the effort to build a sense of communal concord based on geographic connectedness hearkens back to the outmoded models of the nineteenth century more than it embraces the challenge of creating new forms of membership for the twenty-first century.

Moreover, Bosniak suggests, attempts to define a thicker sense of national culture on liberal terms of diversity and tolerance raise awkward questions: What, for instance, is Hollinger willing to require of newcomers with regard to naturalization and assimilation? His emphasis on national culture points toward a more rigorous process of incorporation, she contends, while his commitment to liberal principles of openness suggests an easier path to membership. Bosniak is concerned that efforts to privilege the national community, perhaps like the current emphasis on Americanization, could be used to rationalize limits on the entry of newcomers and the rights accorded legal and illegal aliens already present in the polity. In her view, we should instead cultivate greater respect for difference and emphasize the need to protect the rights of all human beings, whether nationals or not. These goals do not require pursuing the more fraught enterprise of cultivating national unity; indeed, they counsel against such an undertaking.

For Carens, a more rigorous conception of citizenship will establish an unduly high threshold of knowledge required to become a citizen; consequently, the naturalization examination will serve more as a barrier to citizenship than a rite of passage. In his view, civic knowledge does not necessarily make someone a good citizen—native-born U.S. citizens do not have to take a test. So it is unreasonable to require only applicants for naturalization to take one. In any case, tests of this sort often improperly favor some groups at the expense of others.

A polity may expect immigrants to adopt certain social behaviors and attitudes, Carens maintains, and it may hope that they come to believe in the core values of the society. But it cannot *require* that newcomers demonstrate any of these behaviors or exhibit knowledge of any of those values in order to become a full member of the polity. This is so because, for Carens, civil society is morally prior to political society. In a view strikingly at odds with Kesler's and Pickus's approach, Carens emphasizes that the web of social, familial, and economic ties that an immigrant forms by living in a country properly constitutes the basis for formal membership. Whereas Kesler and Pickus emphasize the creation of a people as a matter of politics, Carens stresses the recognition of persons as a matter of justice. For Carens, legal residence alone should fulfill the requirement for becoming a citizen. If we admit immigrants, he insists, we are morally obliged to accord them all the rights available to citizens, including the opportunity to participate in political rule.

III. Multiple Memberships?

Part III of this volume addresses the debate about single and multiple membership status head on. It examines two recent and potentially far-reaching changes, the proliferation of dual citizenship and the changes in U.S. welfare and immigration law that deny many benefits to noncitizens. As the essays by Peter Schuck and Hiroshi Motomura demonstrate, these changes have raised, in practical and very specific ways, the most fundamental questions about the relation between immigration and citizenship in the next century. The advent of plural membership statuses presents an excellent opportunity to evaluate the dizzying pace of globalization, and its effect on structures of democratic governance, by focusing on a very real change in how societies organize themselves.

The United States is likely to have more dual citizens now than ever before, for a mix of reasons, including increased immigration, marriage between individuals of different nationalities, advances in international communications and transportation, and changes in U.S. and other countries' laws. New citizens must take an oath of allegiance, but they do not have to prove that their renunciation of other allegiances is legally effective in their country of origin, nor are native-born citizens prohibited from becoming citizens of other nations. By continuing as nationals of other countries, are newly naturalized American citizens perjuring themselves? Are native-born citizens who become citizens of other nations while retaining their American citizenship violating their allegiance to the United States?

Most Americans recognize that everyone has multiple loyalties. One can be a Catholic, an African American, a member of the North Carolina Bar Association, and a supporter of Amnesty International. But does formal membership in two nations threaten the fragile sense of unity that makes possible the integration of all those other identities? And does citizenship in the United States require more than just participation in the political system? Many Americans have a visceral response against the notion of dual nationality or citizenship. Yet other Americans welcome the opportunity to formally belong to more than one nation-state and are puzzled by the harm their fellow citizens think this may cause. It is in this explosive situation that Peter Schuck's chapter ("Plural Citizenships") offers a careful balancing of the costs and benefits of plural citizenships to individuals, to nations, and to the international community.

As ties among people and institutions become more numerous and cross national boundaries, Schuck argues, we should accept that American citizens might be members of many different groupings. Dual citizenship, he says, gives individuals "additional options—an alternative country in which to live, work, and invest, an additional locus and source of rights, obligations, and communal ties." Moreover, if dual citizenship induces more immigrants to naturalize, then it strengthens democracy by making the voting population more closely mirror the actual resident population.

If there is no direct conflict between two countries, Schuck asks, especially liberal democratic ones, why object to an individual asserting one set of interests in American elections and another set elsewhere? For Schuck, the U.S. national interest consists of an aggregation of its citizens' preferences, and there is no reason why those preferences should not include a citizen's interest in supporting another country's policies. Schuck acknowledges that dual citizenship raises fundamental questions about the meaning of community and the definition of national unity. But he does not think that dual citizenship necessarily threatens a shared sense of solidarity or that only single citizenship can facilitate assimilation.

Schuck suggests that, whatever its imprecision, most Americans appropriately consider marriage and the marriage oath the closest metaphor for capturing the sense of loyalty and commitment expected of new citizens. But, he notes, neither marriage nor the marriage oath requires one to abandon all previous loyalties, only to forswear those attachments that are inconsistent with the new union. The United States need only ask that new citizens and, Schuck argues, native-born citizens as well, pledge their political loyalty. For Schuck, "the citizen's only essential duty is to observe the law . . . not to love the country."

In "Why Immigrants Want Dual Citizenship (And We Should Too)," Michael Jones-Correa reinforces Schuck's conviction, on both normative and empirical grounds, that Americans should embrace dual citizenship. American citizenship, he believes, is not about a culturally based or blood-based nationality; it is about participation in a political system. Immigrants' attachment to their country of origin, he points out, has not prevented them from acting loyally toward that system, indeed, from fighting and dying for it. Jones-Correa urges us to recognize that becoming a citizen is not an end in itself, but a key part of incorporating new members into American political life. He concludes, based on his research among Latin American immigrants in New York City, that dual citizenship will allow newcomers to become more actively involved in America. He is more certain than Schuck that immigrants who can maintain their previous nationality or citizenship will naturalize sooner and integrate faster into the United States.

In regarding multiple citizenships and American unity as compatible, indeed, even as mutually reinforcing, Schuck and Jones-Correa open up the question of the extent to which plural citizenship constitutes a crucial shift in notions of membership. This shift could alter the nation-state itself and, in doing so, reconfigure the very meaning and constitution of democracy and democratic practices. Rather than simply facilitating the integration of immigrants into an existing political system rooted in individual nation-states, it is possible that plural citizenship is a key step on the way to regional forms of governance, supranational confederations, local autonomy and secession, transnational networks of individuals and nongovernmental associations, or other systems of political organization. While it has become fashionable to herald the end of the nation-state, the reality seems more complex. Political organization and identity can be arranged in a number of different ways, each of which would have different implications for nations—peoples with a sense of common identity— and for states.[10]

To evaluate dual citizenship thus requires us to think more clearly about which, if any, of these directions we wish to move and what are the best ways to reach our destinations. The next century will likely witness new and different forms of community and governance, but there are prudent and perilous methods for extending democratic values and political rule. Plural citizenship may be one of the most prudent methods for accomplishing those goals. Might plural citizenship, however, exacerbate a process of alienation already at work within liberal democracies? Many citizens feel increasingly estranged from their governments. If largely high-end professionals and low-wage workers, both of whom regularly cross borders, take up multiple citizenships, will these groups stand in opposition to citizens attached to the principles and claims of their nation?

Other difficult questions arise from this debate: Will plural citizenship make governments more responsive to their increasingly far-flung citizenry, or will it sever the tie between representatives and citizens? If plural citizenship helps usher in new forms of transnational economic, bureaucratic, or cultural identities and political systems, what new kinds of conflict might be expected to emerge? Will these conflicts be milder or more vicious, more amenable to democratic deliberation or more difficult to control because they are not linked to nation-states? Other unanswered questions include whether there is a limit to the number and types of loyalties one can sustain and still remain sufficiently committed to any one particular loyalty. As a person's affection and commitment are divided among different interests, as is likely to happen with dual citizenship, will that affection and commitment also weaken?

Different membership statuses exist within the United States. Recent welfare reform, for instance, signals a major shift in federal policy away from providing a safety net of benefits to legal permanent residents, raising important questions about the legal status of aliens in relation to citizens. How differently should citizens and legal permanent residents be treated? Are some differences in rights justifiable, while others are not? Hiroshi Motomura's chapter, "Alienage Classifications in a Nation of Immigrants: Three Models of 'Permanent' Residence," surveys the contending conceptions of permanent residence within U.S. law and public policy.

Motomura observes that an "affiliation" model has shaped policy analysis and constitutional law when it comes to the provision of rights and benefits to noncitizens, especially legal permanent residents. In this model, legal permanent residents enjoy similar rights and benefits to Americans, because permanent residence represents a form of association with American society. The only rights that can be justifiably denied to legal aliens are those that concern certain political activities such as voting, though advocates have suggested including the franchise as well. Legal immigrants who pay taxes, the argument goes, should be entitled to social benefits in the same manner as citizens. Further, excluding noncitizens from the welfare safety net compromises their socioeconomic integration and creates a group of permanently marginalized residents. As Motomura makes clear, this model of membership expects that citizens and permanent residents will coexist with no special efforts made to change residents into citizens.

Motomura contends that we can best understand the position of permanent residents in American society, and the protections afforded them, by recognizing the influence of two other models of citizenship, one based on contract, the other on the transition to citizenship. He argues, further, that the transition model is the one that offers the strongest argument for protecting immigrants' rights, especially welfare benefits, before they are eligible to naturalize. This is so, in part, because it derives its normative and political appeal from the notion that newcomers should be afforded certain protections because they are preparing to become citizens and join the political community.

Whereas Schuck's analysis of plural citizenship supports multiple membership statuses among nations, Motomura's emphasis on the transition model of permanent residence leans toward a single notion of citizenship within a nation. What should we make of these apparently contrasting trajectories? Does protecting rights at home require singularity while expanding them on the global level require multiplicity? Is national citizenship merely instrumental to the protection of rights, or is that task an offshoot of a more fundamental project of self-governance and communal definition?

Daniel Tichenor's response to Motomura ("Membership and American Social Contracts") helps us begin to address some of these questions. He reminds us that even efforts to emphasize a singular, shared conception of citizenship can produce further multiplications of membership statuses, provide fewer protections for resident aliens, and harm efforts to achieve greater equality at home. He points out, for instance, that the contract model could itself produce multiply tiered membership statuses within the United States if permanent residents are accorded different benefits depending on when they arrived in the United States and hence when they entered into the contract. He further notes that the more prominence we give to the transition model, the more those migrants who choose not to naturalize may be stigmatized, thus raising questions about whether one values the achievement of a single citizenship status over the provision of benefits.

Motomura countenances some differentiation in membership status. He suggests that rights and benefits for permanent residents who have chosen not to naturalize after the five-year waiting period could still be protected, but they would be protected on the basis of their long-standing affiliation with American society, not because they are citizens-in-training. The key question here is to what extent these are simply different justifications for the same protections and to what extent, given an array of membership statuses and justifications, it is appropriate to provide fewer protections after the five-year waiting period for naturalization has expired.

The controversy about the rights of noncitizens is not, however, simply about their status. As Tichenor makes clear, it is also organically linked to the question of greater equality among citizens. He wonders whether expanded immigration and immigrant rights may weaken the chance to overcome economic inequality among citizens by eroding the bonds of nationhood. Like Motomura, Tichenor implicitly connects the controversy over the rights and benefits accorded to resident aliens to the debate over national identity discussed especially in Part II of this volume.

IV. Becoming American/America Becoming

What does it mean to become American in an age when the meaning of America is so very much in dispute?[11] Current controversies over immigration and citizenship offer a tremendous opportunity to confront profoundly divisive questions, to improve how the United States incorporates newcomers, and to revitalize our public life. Many of the authors in this volume favor current immigration levels and are skeptical of linking our understanding of citizenship to an overly specific American identity. Many Americans, in contrast, harbor doubts about the influx of newcomers and are firmly committed to the value of a unique, well-defined national identity. We must bridge this gap if we are to further advance discussion about immigration and citizenship.

The essays in this volume demonstrate that articulating models of citizenship, defending them, and connecting them to specific public policy conflicts is a crucial part of that task. This process offers us greater mastery over the often distant forces transforming our lives and clarifies the larger issues at stake in particular controversies. This is no mean accomplishment. It challenges all of us to engage in "reflection and choice" about key questions facing our communal future, rather than simply fall prey to the "accident and force" that this country's Founders understood was the fate of most polities. The questions raised in this book, and the choices citizens face on the brink of the millennium, are about the basic organization of political community. They are questions and choices about how we should structure the relation among economic forces, governmental authority, racial and religious identity, and political allegiance.

The contributors to this book also make clear that resolving the controversies raging at the intersection of immigration and citizenship is not simply a matter of establishing the right model. We must also think hard about the different implications and often contradictory impulses of those models; we must do so mindful of the human costs that abstractions can impose on those in the most desperate situations, and of how, together, we want to reach our most cherished ideals.

Notes

1. Barbara Jordan, "The Americanization Ideal," *New York Times*, 11 September 1995, A15.

2. U.S. Commission on Immigration Reform, *Becoming an American: Immigration and Immigrant Policy* (Washington, D.C.: U.S. Government Printing Office, 1997). For an elaboration of the intellectual structure undergirding the commission's report, see Lawrence Fuchs, *The American Kaleidoscope: Race, Ethnicity, and the Civic Culture* (Hanover, N.H.: University Press of New England, 1990).

3. Statement of Shirley M. Hufstedler, Chair, U.S. Commission on Immigration Reform, 30 September 1997, press conference for the release of *Becoming an American*.

4. Michael Fix and Wendy Zimmerman, "After Arrival: An Overview of Federal Immigrant Policy in the United States," Immigrant Policy Program, The Urban Institute, July 1993; Fix and Zimmerman, "Immigrant Policy in the States: A Wavering Welcome," Immigrant Policy Program, The Urban Institute, July 1993. See also Alejandro Portes and Min Zhou, "The New Second Generation: Segmented Assimilation and its Variants," in *Interminority Affairs in the U.S.: Pluralism at the Crossroads*, ed. Peter I. Rose, *The Annals*, 530, November 1993, 74–96.

5. Statement of Shirley M. Hufstedler, Chair, U.S. Commission on Immigration Reform, 30 September 1997.

6. *Reports of the Immigration Commission*, Vol. 1–41, printed in the *Senate Documents* of the 61st Congress, 2d and 3d Sessions, 1910–11.

7. Michael J. Sandel, *Democracy's Discontent: American in Search of a Public Philosophy* (Cambridge: Belknap Press of Harvard University, 1996), chap. 7, conclusion.

8. Martha Nussbaum, *For Love of Country: Debating the Limits of Patriotism* (Boston: Beacon Press, 1996).

9. For a helpful exploration of these questions, see Sanford Levinson, *Constitutional Faith* (Princeton: Princeton University Press, 1988), chaps. 2, 3.

10. See Noah Pickus and Suzanne Shanahan, "The Changing Boundaries of Membership," unpublished essay on file with author. See also Robert O. Keohane, "Globalization and Changes in Sovereignty," discussion paper prepared for the John F. Kennedy School's "Vision of Governance for the Twenty-First Century" Project, 10 June 1997, on file with author.

11. On this point, see Nathan Glazer, " 'A Nation of Immigrants': Is There an American People?" in *"What, Then, is the American, This New Man?": A Conference* (Washington, D.C.: Center for Immigration Studies, 1998), Center Paper 13; and responses by Orlando Patterson and Noah Pickus in that volume.

Part I

The Meaning of Americanization

1

The Promise of American Citizenship

Charles R. Kesler

> The citizens of the United States of America have the right to applaud themselves for having given to mankind examples of an enlarged and liberal policy—a policy worthy of imitation. All possess alike liberty of conscience and immunities of citizenship. It is now no more that toleration is spoken of as if it were [by] the indulgence of one class of citizens that another enjoyed the exercise of their inherent natural rights, for, happily, the Government of the United States, which gives to bigotry no sanction, to persecution no assistance, requires only that they who live under its protection should demean themselves as good citizens in giving it on all occasions their effectual support.
>
> —George Washington, letter to the Hebrew
> congregation in Newport, 1790[1]

This beautiful statement, part of George Washington's response to a letter from the Hebrew congregation of Newport, Rhode Island, congratulating him on his election as the nation's first president, reveals much that is distinctive, and noble, about American citizenship. Grounded in the natural rights of mankind and guarded by a written constitution, U.S. citizenship marked a new beginning in the world's long experience with civic membership. The American revolutionaries' self-proclaimed *novus ordo seclorum*, a new order of the ages, was in fact largely an implication of their novel understanding of citizenship; and for the Jewish community in Newport, as well as for many other Jews, Catholics, and Protestant dissenters who had fled the Old World for the New, an invaluable emblem of the new, American view of citizenship was the Constitution's simple but emphatic declaration that "no religious Test shall ever be required as a Qualification to any Office or public Trust under the United States."

Thus George Washington, celebrating in 1783 the official end of hostilities with Great Britain, thanked his soldiers for accomplishing "the glorious task for which we first flew to arms," namely, "erecting this stupendous *fabrick* of *Freedom* and *Empire* on the broad basis of Independency" and "protecting the rights of human nature and establishing an Asylum for the poor and oppressed of all nations and religions." Later that year, he addressed a similar sentiment to new immigrants from Ireland. "The bosom of America is open to receive not only the opulent and respectable stranger," he wrote, "but the oppressed and persecuted of all nations and religions."[2] In the subsequent two centuries, the United States lived up to Washington's words, admitting a larger number of immigrants from a greater variety of nations and religions than any other country in the world's history, and generously extending—to some sooner, to others later, but eventually to all new Americans—the privileges of citizenship on an equal basis with the original inhabitants.

Living up to the promise of American citizenship, however, has not been easy or without struggle. In 1790, the same year that Washington corresponded with the Hebrew congregation of Newport, he signed the country's first naturalization law, which provided that any alien who was "a free white person" might apply for citizenship after two years' residence in the United States. Naturalization remained limited to whites until 1870. Slavery was not abolished in the United States until the Thirteenth Amendment was added to the Constitution (1865); blacks en masse were not recognized as citizens until the Fourteenth Amendment (1868) and were not guaranteed the right to vote until the Fifteenth Amendment (1870)—and their right of suffrage proved unenforceable in most Southern states for most of the twentieth century.[3] The first federal immigration law, which followed hard upon these constitutional victories on behalf of black Americans, was the Chinese Exclusion Act, passed in 1882 in order to prevent a further influx from China. Immigrant Chinese (as distinguished from their American-born children, who became citizens by virtue of the Fourteenth Amendment) were not made eligible for naturalization until 1943. White American women (and black women too, after the Fourteenth Amendment) were certainly citizens, but most were denied the right to vote and gained constitutional recognition of this right only with the passage of the Nineteenth Amendment in 1920.[4]

Other examples could be cited. The salient question, however, is not so much whether the United States ever fell short of its moral and political principles—it did, of course, many times—but what those principles were in the first place, and whether they are worthy of respect and allegiance today. For the contemporary controversies that rage over the meaning of American citizenship turn, to a greater or lesser extent, on the interpretation of those first principles; they turn in particular on the question whether those original principles are so disfigured by racism, ethnocentrism, and other ills as to be unworthy or obsolete guides to our contemporary immigration and citizenship dilemmas. Many scholars argue, for example, that America's failures to live up to its formal principles of liberalism and republicanism are endemic, proving that the "failures" are not historical lapses or exceptions but are themselves the rule—or at least *a* rule, an alternative, competing vision of American citizenship, every bit as authentic and "American" as equality and liberty, perhaps more so. These "illiberal, undemocratic traditions of ascriptive Americanism," as Rogers M. Smith calls them, represent therefore not unfortunate frustrations of American citizenship's logic, much less imperfect stages of its development, but instead are essential to it. As confirmation of their intrinsic role, Smith reports that these ugly traditions live on in contemporary efforts "to maintain white supremacy, to preserve old gender roles, to uphold Protestantism in public life," and in general "to resist many egalitarian demands in liberal and democratic ideologies."[5]

If the old principles are inherently flawed, then we need new ones— friendlier to participatory democracy, socialism, feminism ("maternal citizenship"), or multiculturalism ("heterogeneous citizenship"), to mention only a few of the leading contenders.[6] At the end of this chapter, I shall take up for criticism the last of these alternative theories, which is probably the most influential and carefully worked out of the lot. But before proceeding to my main business of explaining the distinctiveness and moral sweep of the American view of citizenship, the threshold objection—that, in theory and in practice, the country's professions of equal rights were shams or, at best, half-truths—needs to be met. Otherwise, it would be difficult to take seriously any account of the philosophical or universalist grounds of our citizenship.

History and Theory

Although this style of objection comes today from the Left, its political origins in America go back to the antebellum defense of slavery, when Stephen A. Douglas, for instance, argued that the human equality proclaimed in the Declaration of Independence did not apply to all men, but only to white men. This was how the signers of the Declaration had understood it, he claimed, against considerable, indeed massive, evidence to the contrary. Nonetheless, he insisted that "this Government was established on the white basis. It was made by white men, for the benefit of white men and their posterity forever, and never should be administered by any except white men."[7] Why the contemporary Left, or important parts of it, should be embracing (as historically correct though repugnant) a view of the Constitution originally propounded by the defenders of Negro slavery is an interesting question. It has much to do with the historicist temptation, the tendency to believe that everyone is a child of his times and that, for the children of any given time and culture, "whatever is, is good." How could eighteenth-century Americans, living amid many "illiberal, undemocratic traditions of ascriptive Americanism," including Negro slavery, not believe wholeheartedly in these traditions?

This is a temptation shared by some on the contemporary Right as well. Willmoore Kendall, for example, the Yale political scientist who served as a senior editor of *National Review*, delighted in arguing that equality, as an abstract political principle, had little to do with American life as it had actually been lived from the Mayflower Compact up to the Civil War, when, in his view, Abraham Lincoln "derailed" the American political tradition by turning abstract equality into its goal. Here is Kendall on the real meaning of equality in America:

> "Every Frenchman," Charles de Gaulle has written somewhere, "wants a special privilege or two; that is how he expresses his passion for Equality." "Every American," I suppose an equally cynical observer here in the United States might say, "wants a right or two that he is by no means willing to concede to everybody else; that is how the American expresses *his* passion for Equality."[8]

American life as it had actually been lived, Kendall insisted, was a tradition of *inequality*, expressed in racial segregation, denial of voting rights, malapportioned legislative districts, local mixtures of church and state, and the like. Whereas the Left despised these "illiberal, undemocratic traditions," Kendall liked or at least defended them as examples of good, old-fashioned American constitutionalism, which he defined as "deliberative" but otherwise unprincipled majoritarianism.

On the Left and Right, then, one finds important thinkers prepared (albeit for different reasons) to baptize racist and other unsavory American traditions as authoritative expressions of American principles. One difficulty with so readily turning history into theory—identifying historical practice with organic political principle—is that it underestimates the permeability of tradition, or in other words, the ability of human beings to use their reason in order to change a tradition. Tradition itself, after all, is not a static thing; its greatest defenders have always emphasized that living traditions must slowly adapt to life's changing circumstances. What's more, tradition is never a unitary thing: Every vital tradition contains diverse, competing strands. Such diversity is necessary, in fact, in order that the tradition may survive, may adapt.[9] Diversity and changeability provide the openings for reason's critique—as well as its use—of tradition. For in order to choose among the conflicting strands of tradition, in order to decide which are *worthy* to survive, reason must have resort to some standard that transcends tradition as such.

In American life as it has actually been lived, racist and antiracist traditions (to take one example, and to simplify a bit) have coexisted and battled over many generations, but this does not make them equally legitimate, authoritative, or good. For example, the presence in the Constitution of certain compromises over slavery does not, ipso facto, turn slavery into a constitutional principle or the Constitution into a proslavery document. That these are "compromises," of course, can be known only by looking at them in the light of the Constitution's principles—of the regime principles that are more fundamental than statute or even constitutional law, because they set the ends or purposes of all such law. The brute fact of slavery's continued existence under the Constitution, in other words, does not settle the crucial question, whether slavery was regarded by the Constitution's Framers as a necessary evil or a positive good, which can be accosted only by looking at the moral principles—the ends or aspirations—incorporated in the government that they founded.

Consider the Constitution's treatment of the slave trade. The Northern and Southern delegates to the Constitutional Convention could not agree to ban the slave trade immediately, but they compromised on a provision of the Constitution (Article I, Section 9) that would give Congress the power to prohibit the slave trade beginning twenty years later, and they guaranteed the deal by making that provision unamendable (Article V). Even the Southern delegates, notice, were prepared to see this international traffic in human beings come to an end eventually, as indeed it did when Congress banned it two decades later, in 1808. This was an important compromise precisely because a vital principle was involved. James Madison, himself a Southerner and a slaveholder, made this clear in *The Federalist Papers* in his defense of the compromise:

> It were doubtless to be wished that the power of prohibiting the importation of slaves had not been postponed until the year 1808, or rather that it had been suffered to have immediate operation. But it is not difficult to account either for this restriction on the general government, or for the manner in which the whole clause is expressed. It ought to be considered as a great point gained in favor of humanity that a period of twenty years may terminate forever, within these States, a traffic which has so long and so loudly upbraided the barbarism of modern policy.[10]

This "unnatural traffic," as Madison went on to call it, ought to be prohibited for the same reason that slavery itself was reprehensible and unnatural: Slavery treated a "moral person" as a "mere article of property."[11] America's prohibition of the slave trade showed how decisively the principles of the Revolution—the basis of the new theory of American citizenship—were able to abrogate or abridge old traditions and institute new ones.

The difficulty, to be sure, is that slavery and racism were not ended by the Founders' actions. This consideration raises a second general reason why historical practice cannot simply be equated with a regime's principles, namely, that it is sometimes very difficult to live up to those principles. With republican government this is especially true. Now, with some exaggeration one might say that America began as a nation of slaveholders. Slavery was legal in each of the thirteen colonies. By the 1780s, however, slavery had been abolished in three states; by 1804, five others had adopted laws for gradual emancipation; and the Northwest Ordinance had forbidden slavery to spread into the trans-Appalachian territory from which five more states would eventually be formed. So considerable progress had been made. But the Union was left half-slave and half-free, and so it would remain until the Civil War. From a certain point of view, America's inability to live up to its principles of equality and freedom could be—often is—condemned as hypocrisy. This opinion was held by many abolitionists at the time, is held by many historians today, and could be said to be quasi-Kantian in character: If you allow your interests and circumstances to prevent you from doing what it is your categorical duty to do, the critics reason, then you are acting immorally.[12] In the case at hand, if the Founders did not abolish slavery immediately, they must not really have been against slavery. QED.

Yet political life is not Kantian. Its morality is prudential, always pitted against the weakness of human nature and mindful of the circumstances (and consequences) of human choice, and therefore usually measured by slow progress toward the good. For this very reason, hypocrisy is not the worst of all moral conditions: Hypocrisy is the tribute that vice pays to virtue, as La Rochefoucauld said famously, and thus is a recognition that virtue deserves honor. Besides, hypocrisy is not the best and certainly not the only explanation for slavery's persistence. Stephen Douglas raised the charge of hypocrisy in his campaign for the U.S. Senate in 1858. If the Founders really did believe that blacks were "created equal" and had natural rights that white men were bound to respect, why did these statesmen not immediately abolish slavery in the United States? His Republican opponent, Abraham Lincoln, responded:

> They [the signers of the Declaration of Independence] did not mean to assert the obvious untruth, that all were then actually enjoying that equality, or yet, that they were about to confer it immediately upon them. In fact they had no power to confer such a boon. They meant simply to declare the *right*, so that the *enforcement* of it might follow as fast as circumstances should permit.[13]

Once the moral end or goal was clear, the means to realize that goal would be found and employed "as fast as circumstances should permit." Prudence, not hypocrisy, governed the Founders' thoughts as they attempted to put slavery on the course of what Lincoln called "ultimate extinction"—but without extinguishing the Union and the Constitution along the way.[14]

Yet taking the Founders seriously means trying to understand their principles not simply in light of historical circumstances, but also as reasoned conclusions about the proper ends or purposes of political life. What were the moral ends or goals intrinsic to the Americans' new understanding of citizenship, and how were they justified? What was so novel about their precepts? To answer these questions, we need to begin with the ideas that served as the American Founders' own point of departure.

Citizenship and Its Discontents

Who should be a citizen? This practical question, which in moments of political founding and revolution is extremely urgent, depends for a reflective answer upon a prior, more speculative question: What is a citizen? The English word is cognate with "city," a relation that is constant throughout the term's backward etymological journey through Anglo–French and Old French to the Latin *civis* (citizen) and *civitas* (city), and finally to the Greek *polites* (citizen) and *polis* (city). The citizen is part of the city, a partner or member in the political association or community. The city, which seems to have been a Greek invention (at any rate, the Greeks were the first to celebrate and study it), was distinct from other forms of human association then prevailing—families, villages, tribes, and empires. The city came to sight as an alternative to the primitive tribes or nations then ruling northern Europe, on the one hand, and to the cultured but despotic empires of the East, especially Persia, on the other.[15]

The city or *polis* came into being as a unification or completion of the smaller kinship associations of families and villages. These kinship associations shared not only bloodlines, as we would commonly understand them today, but also ancestral gods who presided over and consecrated the bloodlines. From the standpoint of the citizens themselves, then, a standpoint brilliantly captured in Fustel de Coulanges's enduring study, *The Ancient City*, the *polis* was an elaborate religious cult: a complex structure of civic, local, and ancestral gods, centering on the sacred fire in the family hearth and forming a pantheon peculiar to each city.[16] In the ancient world, every city had its own gods, and its citizens thought of the city as the special handiwork and protectorate of those gods. More specifically, they thought their city had been founded by a divine lawgiver or by a mortal ancestor who was later promoted to godhood. The constitutional law of every ancient city was therefore a species of divine law, vouchsafed not to mankind but to a particular people who became a people—as opposed to a mere alliance of families or villages—precisely by acknowledging common gods and receiving the same (divine) law. Every ancient people was therefore a kind of chosen people, whose deities demanded not faith or belief in particular doctrines but obedience to the city's laws. The citizen was a part of the chosen people, a sharer in the divine rites, a child and servant of the laws.

This is how citizenship looked to the citizens of ancient cities, but not how it looked to Aristotle, the first political philosopher to give a thematic account of citizenship. To be sure, Aristotle preserves a place for the gods in his discussion by holding that although man is by nature a political animal—an animal suited to live in a city or *polis*—cities do not exist by nature. They must be founded, and "the one who first constituted" a city, whether "the one" was a god or a man, "is responsible for the greatest of goods."[17] Moreover, priests were a necessary part of every city, and honoring the gods was a public or political function that should be carried out by citizen-priests, preferably chosen from those citizens "worn out with age."[18] In general, however, Aristotle regards the city not as something divine but as something natural to man, even though it must always be instituted by one or more men using certain conventions, laws, and customs.

The necessity of conventions in politics means that the definition of citizenship is disputable; someone who is a citizen under a democracy would often not be a citizen under an oligarchical regime. The disputability of citizenship tells us, however, something important about it: that the citizen must speak up for his definition of citizenship, that he must defend his own partisan view of it in terms of the qualities or virtues that he can contribute to the whole city.[19] Citizenship does not mean merely living or working in the city, then, nor even possessing legal rights, and it cannot be defined simply as a birthright, because though children may in one sense be citizens, Aristotle observes, they are "incomplete" because of their inability to share in "decision and office." Accordingly, citizenship means participation in ruling the city. For all practical purposes, then, the city *is* its citizens or its citizen-body; the city of Athens was always called, in Greek, "the Athenians." But "ruling" the city, especially in antiquity, implied not only the right or duty to own land, to vote, and to hold office, but also to fight for the city as a citizen-soldier. Even today, the citizen's right or duty to fight for his country can color or influence the debate over citizenship, if only as an implicit contrast between the motives of the citizen and the mercenary soldier.

In democracies, which tend to have relaxed definitions of citizenship, children are still regarded as "incomplete" citizens because they cannot adjudicate and deliberate well. In other words, there is still a tension between being born a citizen and being *able* to be one, and the more virtues that are required of the democratic citizen, the more acute is the tension. This is a key admission, say the oligarchs, the partisans of the few; for if being a citizen means being able to rule well, then only those few who rule well should be citizens. But if this oligarchical (more precisely, aristocratic) element in citizenship were carried to its logical conclusion, Aristotle warns, then a man of truly outstanding virtue, so preeminently good and wise that he deserves to rule like a god among men, would be entitled to rule over the city as though it were his own household, and politics—and citizenship—would be altogether at an end.[20]

Aristotle moderates and improves the partisan definitions of citizenship by showing that neither being free-born (the democratic standard) nor being rich or virtuous (the oligarchic standard) can, taken by itself, secure the city's common good. In other words, citizenship must necessarily be based on a mixture of claims of freedom and claims of ability or virtue; the proportions of the mix will vary from city to city, depending on the quantity and quality of the potential citizens. Within a particular city, individual citizens will possess different skills or virtues, even as among sailors one is a pilot, another a lookout, and so forth. Still, the sailors' overall purpose is to preserve the ship, and similarly the citizens' purpose is to preserve the city, or more exactly, the regime or constitution (*politeia*) that makes them citizens and orders the city.

As there are many forms of regime (aristocracy, republic, etc.), so there are many forms of civic virtue. But the virtue of a good man (as opposed to a good citizen) is unchanging, and it is the good man's virtue that serves as the standard by which Aristotle judges the goodness of particular regimes and their definitions of citizenship. In light of this he urges founders and lawgivers to reform the "mix" of citizen qualities characterizing their own regime. Even today, how a regime treats a good man—for example, how the Soviet Union treated Alexander Solzhenitsyn—tells us much about that regime. The great difficulty in politics, needless to say, is that good men are hard to find! And so Aristotle emphasizes that, in most cases, regimes should aim not at unfettered rule by the best men but at the rule of good laws. In turn, wise laws will be able to educate or form citizens, enabling them to rule and to be ruled in turn in the spirit of obedience to the laws.[21]

Politics among citizens consists precisely in this alternation of ruling and being ruled, under law. Mere subjects, as opposed to citizens, experience being ruled but never the activity of ruling, certainly not in the exalted sense of free self-government. Thus active citizenship among a free and relatively equal body of citizens—the phenomenon described by Aristotle—is quite different from the perpetual subjectship that obtained under the absolute monarchies of early modern Europe, and even under the moderate monarchy of Great Britain in the eighteenth century. In practice, of course, most regimes with citizen-rulers (whether few or many, whether oligarchies or democracies) tend to agree that citizenship is inherited, that a citizen is born of citizen-parents. Such is, one might say, the citizen's view, qua citizen. He views the world of his city, whether oligarchy or democracy, as though it were *the* world.²² The U.S. Constitution requires, for instance, that the president be a "natural born Citizen," and we speak of immigrants undergoing "naturalization," as though they were being made citizens not by law, but by nature—as though they were about to be born again as native citizens. But the principle of birthright citizenship, if traced back far enough, contradicts itself; eventually one arrives at the very first generation of citizens, who perforce were made, not born.²³ Consider the case at hand: George Washington and the other members of the founding generation were not born U.S. citizens. They made themselves citizens by throwing off their "perpetual" allegiance to Great Britain and making, that is, founding, the United States.

The Achievement of American Citizenship

In one sense, Washington sought to establish a very different kind of citizenship, a very different kind of regime, from the types Aristotle had evaluated in his *Politics*, not to mention from the contemporaneous monarchies of Europe, each with its established church. Washington once explained why he took part in the Revolution: "The establishment of Civil and Religious Liberty," he wrote, "was the motive which induced me to the Field."²⁴ In the ancient world, "religious liberty" was not an issue because there was no such thing as "religion." The city and its gods were, in effect, one. From the citizens' point of view, there was hardly a distinction, even in principle, between politics and religion, state and church. But after Christianity had displaced paganism in the Western world, the problem of citizenship underwent a profound change.²⁵

The Christian God was the God of all men everywhere but of no city in particular. For the first time, there was an easy divorce possible between loyalty to one's city and loyalty to one's God (formerly, gods); there were many cities of men, but the City of God was one. To put it differently, whereas every ancient people thought of themselves as dwelling in the city of god, Christianity now proclaimed that the City of God was a heavenly, not an earthly, municipality. Divine law, therefore, was no longer constitutive of particular earthly cities, but offered the means of salvation to individual souls in every city and nation. Hence the problem for citizenship: If the principle binding citizens was obedience to the divine law, and cities were no longer thought to have divine lawgivers, what principle would oblige citizens to obedience? How would the various cities and their laws be justified?

So long as Rome controlled virtually the entire civilized world, the problem might be mitigated or finessed by identifying Rome with the City of God—the ancient city writ large. But even in the heyday of the Holy Roman Empire there were serious clashes between ecclesiastical and political authorities, between the pope and the emperor; and when the Empire crumbled, tensions multiplied between the kings of Europe and the church. Throw in the Protestant Reformation, and it is easy to see how the so-called theological-political problem came to dominate European politics, leading to actual or potential civil war in every part of Western civilization.

The history of the West after the establishment of the Holy Roman Empire consisted of a series of failed attempts to answer the above questions—to find a new ground for civic obligation now that the pagan gods of individual cities had been forcibly retired. For when pressed into political service, Christianity—a religion centered around belief in Christ rather than obedience to a revealed code of laws (e.g., Torah or *shari'a*)—had the distressing if somewhat paradoxical tendency both to deflate civil laws' significance and to inflate their pretensions. That is, the pursuit of true Christianity tempted some believers to desert the earthly for the heavenly city, but tempted others to commandeer temporal laws in order to enforce the faith. The one tendency sapped the foundations of citizenship; the other turned citizenship into fanaticism.

The American Founders' greatest achievement was to answer these questions and solve these problems, which they did in the name of "Civil and Religious Liberty." Civil liberty meant finding a new ground for law and citizenship that would protect decent politics from arbitrary claims of divine right. Religious liberty meant separating church membership from citizenship in order to protect the conscientious pursuit of true religion from civil or ecclesiastical tyranny. Civil liberty and religious liberty have the same root, a theoretical or philosophical insight: the doctrine of natural rights. Americans embraced this doctrine forthrightly in the Declaration of Independence: "We hold these truths to be self-evident, that all men are created equal, that they are endowed by their Creator with certain unalienable rights, that among these are Life, Liberty, and the pursuit of Happiness."

In a gloss on the Declaration that he wrote much later, Thomas Jefferson explained in a striking image what sort of equality he and the other Founders had in mind: "the mass of mankind has not been born with saddles on their backs, nor a favored few booted and spurred, ready to ride them legitimately, by the grace of God."[26] In other words, no human being is by nature the ruler of another, in the way that any human being is by nature the ruler of a horse. Horses are suited by nature to be ridden by human beings, but no human being is suited by nature to be ridden—or owned, bred, and sold—by another human being. Nor are any humans born "booted and spurred," ready to govern "by the grace of God" or by divine right. Members of the human species stand in a natural equality with one another, which means that each is naturally free of any other human's authority. From this natural equality arise natural rights to life and liberty, and to the enjoyment of life and liberty in "the pursuit of Happiness." Life, liberty, and the pursuit of happiness are nature's gifts to the human species, not merely to white males: Blacks and women can ride horses, too.[27]

As a consequence of humans' natural equality and freedom—the lack of natural or divinely appointed rulers within the human race—we must choose our own rulers. And so "to secure these rights," the Declaration continues, "Governments are instituted among Men, deriving their just powers from the consent of the governed." The new basis of political obligation among people is thus found in the consent of each individual, in the social contract that arises when a multitude of human beings consent to form a society and be governed together. On the basis of rights shared universally with other humans, these particular men erect a government for themselves; the universal and the particular are reconciled through an act of human choice, not through the problematic legal establishment of a universal religion, that is, Christianity, in a particular society. In fact, the social contract's ground in the doctrine of natural rights requires that the contract be for limited government—a government that secures our natural gifts of life and liberty—not an unlimited one that pursues the supernatural gift of salvation in the next world.

By building government on the basis of natural rights and the social contract, the American Founders showed how, for the first time since the days of the Holy Roman Empire, men could be good citizens of the City of God and good citizens of their earthly city without injury or insult to either.[28] The key to the solution was the insistence that questions of revealed truth be excluded from determination by the political sovereign or by political majorities. Indeed, majority rule and minority rights could be made consistent only on this basis. Under modern conditions, limited government thus becomes essential to the rule of law. For Aristotle, government was essentially unlimited, in the sense that it had no formal or doctrinal limits extrinsic to the regime, and the regime itself (whatever the type) claimed to rule in the name of its view of the good life as a whole. And for the actual citizens of ancient cities, the rule of law was anchored directly in divine, not merely human, authority. American citizenship departs from the classical models on these important points. But it does so, at least in part, for reasons that Aristotle would well understand: in order to restore to citizenship a moderation, civility, and responsibility that the amalgamation of church and state had threatened to destroy.

Immigration and Americanization

How then did the American understanding of citizenship affect questions of immigration and naturalization? On the American theory, rights inhere in individuals, who may exercise them by combining to form a body politic, a people. A people is not defined by preexisting ties of race, ethnicity, religion, culture, or language, though a people usually has such ties in common. In fact, the British and the American peoples shared most if not all of these traits in 1776, but nonetheless the Americans decided "to dissolve the political bands" that had connected them to the British. A people is defined, rather, by the unanimous consent of each member.[29] After a people has been formed by unanimous consent, "Governments are instituted" by majority consent to secure the people's rights against external and internal threats. But government is not charged with securing the rights of individuals who do not choose to join the body politic, much less the rights of foreign peoples. Political scientist Thomas G. West makes the point archly: "'We the People of the United States,'" he writes, "established the Constitution of 1787 to 'secure the blessings of liberty to *ourselves* and *our posterity*.'"[30]

The moral process at work here is vividly described in the preamble to the Massachusetts Constitution of 1780, drafted by John Adams: "The body-politic is formed by the voluntary association of individuals: It is a social compact, by which the whole people covenants with each citizen, and each citizen with the whole people, that all shall be governed by certain laws for the common good."[31] If the people do not wish to covenant or contract with a particular individual, or if he does not wish to covenant with them, then the contract fails and the conditions of citizenship are not met.[32] Consent is thus a two-way street: No one may justly be compelled to join a society, but society cannot justly be compelled to accept anyone, either. There must be mutual consent on the individual's and on society's part. Gouverneur Morris brought the point home at the Constitutional Convention, commenting that "every society from a great nation down to a club had the right of declaring the conditions on which new members should be admitted."[33] It may be objected that this process is ideal and that both the law and the history of American citizenship have been based on *jus soli* (citizenship by birth within the borders of the United States) and *jus sanguinis* (by inheriting the parents' nationality) much more than on the free consent of individual men and women. But this objection overlooks the importance of America's consciousness of itself as a founded (indeed, a revolutionary) society and an immigrant society—features that neither territoriality nor "blood" inheritance can explain. To put it differently, what is puzzling is not the fact that most American citizens are birthright citizens, and so never have to consent explicitly to being American. What needs explaining is why, despite that, most Americans regard their citizenship as consensual.[34]

Every society has the right to exclude whomever it wishes from immigrating; and every society has the right to regulate its naturalization laws in accordance with the common good. To be sure, this does not give any country the right to harm noncitizens' life, liberty, or property. And indeed every society has the obligation to allow members to emigrate, if they so choose, inasmuch as this is an implication of the natural right to liberty. Pennsylvania's Declaration of Rights, issued in 1776, states this explicitly: "All men have a natural inherent right to emigrate from one state to another that will receive them, or to form a new state in vacant countries, or in such countries as they can purchase, whenever they think that thereby they may promote their own happiness."[35] But if they emigrate to an already existing state, it must be one "that will receive them."

And if none *will* receive them? This is not an empty question, as we are reminded by the painful spectacle of the many German Jews who tried to flee Hitler in the 1930s but found no state willing to admit them. There are present-day examples of the dilemma, too. In some ways the problem is more acute than it was in the Founders' time, when "vacant countries" and vast amounts of frontier land were available and international land swaps and purchases were common. Despite the changed circumstances, however, the Founders' general account of the morality of a world of "separate and equal" peoples, to use the language of the Declaration again, remains valid. What is everyone's business is no one's business. It strains the limits of human affection and self-interest to imagine that a world government, or regional and transnational governments, or even a federation of governments like the United Nations, would care as much about the private rights and public good of a people as would this people themselves. What's more, the competence of such cosmopolitan governments would be in inverse proportion to their distance from the people whose affairs they were to administer. Less care plus less competence is not a recipe for good government. On the contrary, it is a prescription for maladministration, perhaps for despotism. Despite its imperfections, then, a world of "separate and equal" peoples is more liberal and more republican than any available alternative. And to the extent that liberal governments multiply in the world, there is reason to hope that the worst kinds of emigration dilemmas will diminish.[36]

That every society has a right to regulate immigration does not imply that any particular regulation is needful or wise, of course. In the American founding period, the main lines of discussion over immigration and naturalization contain some lessons on this score. To Washington, James Madison, Alexander Hamilton, and other Founders, the chief concern was to "cement" the Union, to overcome the centrifugal forces that had almost shattered the Union during the war and again in the 1780s, and to bolster and deepen the young country's sense of nationhood. In Washington's words, "We are a young Nation and have a character to establish."[37] This meant that the most urgent task facing the Founders was not to Americanize the immigrants but to Americanize the Americans. "The name of AMERICAN," Washington adjured his countrymen in his Farewell Address, "which belongs to you, in your national capacity, must always exalt the just pride of Patriotism, more than any appellation derived from local discriminations." It is "of infinite moment," he counseled, "that you should properly estimate the immense value of your national Union to your collective and individual happiness," and "that you should cherish a cordial, habitual, and immoveable attachment to it."[38]

Hamilton, Madison, and John Jay pursued a similar strategy in *The Federalist*, attacking the Anti-Federalists' preference for the simpler, smaller, more direct republicanism of the states by suggesting that the extended republic of the Union would be a better safeguard for republican liberty. "Publius," the authors' Roman pen name, sought not only to fracture majority factions into a multiplicity of interests that would check one another; he sought also to elicit a healthy majority opinion among his readers in favor of a firm Union and the proposed Constitution. A sound majority opinion would help, in turn, to enlist the people's interests and passions on behalf of the new Constitution.[39] The point is often misunderstood: The manipulation of individual self-interest through the Union's extended structure and the Constitution's clashing institutions was *necessary*, Publius argued, but not *sufficient* for securing republican government. In the end, republican government needed republican citizens who had a certain "veneration" or "reverence"—quasi-religious qualities—for the laws and the Constitution.[40] Under republican theory, the people's will was the source of all legitimate authority, and America's new Constitution and laws were creatures of that will. But why and how should the people learn to look up to, to revere, what they had themselves created?

Publius's great contribution to American citizenship was to center it on the Constitution. He exhibited in *The Federalist Papers* the wisdom inherent in the Convention's lawmaking, and so taught generations of Americans to revere the Constitution's Framers and thus to respect the Constitution not simply as a creation of popular will but as a rare and precious achievement of reason. He brought consent and wisdom to-

gether in support of the Constitution, which he defended as the embodi-
ment of "the reason of the public."[41] Furthermore, Publius interpreted
the new plan of government in a manner designed to encourage the American people to regard the Constitution as peculiarly their own (hence not
to be changed frivolously), whereas statute law was merely the work of
their representatives. One of his masterstrokes was to show that, because
the Constitution is uniquely the people's law, the people should mainly
entrust its interpretation to a Supreme Court of august, unelected justices,
rather than to their elected lawmakers.[42] By these and many other powerful arguments, Publius helped to ensure that American liberty would be
under law, and that American citizenship would involve a deep emotional
attachment and habitual deference to the Constitution.

Republican government had failed much more often than it had suc-
ceeded in the world, so the Founders were not embarrassed to admit that
it needed all the help it could get in America. This help included recruiting
or attracting the right kind of immigrants to the new land. Efforts had
been under way for a long time. One of the charges against King George
III in the Declaration of Independence claimed that "He has endeavored
to prevent the population of these States; for that purpose obstructing the
Laws for Naturalization of Foreigners; refusing to pass others to encourage their migration hither." Benjamin Franklin, while serving as minister
to France in 1784, warned potential immigrants to America that "America
is the Land of Labour, and by no means what the English call *Lubber-
land*, and the French *Pays de Cocagne*, where the Streets are said to be
pav'd with half-peck Loaves, the Houses til'd with Pancakes, and where
the Fowls fly about ready roasted, crying, *Come eat me!*" Franklin ad-
vised skilled artisans, "hearty young Labouring Men," "Persons of moderate Fortunes and Capitals," and anyone who was prepared to work and
to learn, to consider emigrating.[43]

The work ethic was important even then—"Industry and constant Employment are great Preservatives of the Morals and Virtue of a Nation,"
Franklin commented.[44] But even more important in evaluating potential
immigrants, the Founders maintained, were the political habits and principles they might bring with them. To be sure, the United States was a vast,
sparsely populated country, eager to attract more inhabitants; but it was
also a fledgling republic in a world of powerful and corrupt monarchies,
and Americans were keen to retain and purify their republican morals.
Thomas Jefferson was especially concerned about the fate of republicanism in America, and it is to him that we owe the most sustained reflections
on immigration in the founding era. In his book, *Notes on the State of
Virginia*, Jefferson began to address the topic from general principles:

> It is for the happiness of those united in society to harmonize as much as
> possible in matters which they must of necessity transact together. Civil

government being the sole object of forming societies, its administration must be conducted by common consent.

Living together in society is not an easy task, and the republican insistence that societies must be able to govern themselves by "common consent" makes the task harder still. Jefferson was therefore not embarrassed to try to find ways to make the enterprise easier and happier—by seeking for a certain homogeneity among immigrants, particularly in their political habits. This was also a purpose of the country's first naturalization law, though it, like almost every subsequent naturalization law, settled for residency requirements as the most practicable guarantee of good political habits. The 1790 act left immigration and permanent residence open to all, but restricted citizenship to any "free white person" who had resided in the United States for two years and in his state for one, and who could prove his "good character" and swear to "support the Constitution of the United States." There is no record of congressional debate on the racial restriction, and though racism or dislike of blacks undoubtedly played a part, it was also likely that, impressed with the difficulty of maintaining republican government, many congressmen voted for the restriction on the grounds that a biracial or multiracial society would only make the republican task harder by raising additional obstacles to "common consent."[45] In a country already cursed with a system of black chattel slavery, this worry took on added dimensions.[46]

But let us return to Jefferson's extended discussion of immigration, which he composed in the mid-1780s:

> Every species of government has its specific principles. Ours perhaps are more peculiar than those of any other in the universe. It is a composition of the freest principles of the English constitution, with others derived from natural right and natural reason. To these nothing can be more opposed than the maxims of absolute monarchies. Yet, from such, we are to expect the greatest number of emigrants. They will bring with them the principles of the governments they leave, imbibed in their early youth; or, if able to throw them off, it will be in exchange for an unbounded licentiousness, passing, as is usual, from one extreme to another. It would be a miracle were they to stop precisely at the point of temperate liberty.

Jefferson acknowledged that emigrants from absolute monarchies may, probably will be, fleeing absolutism as much as poverty, and hence may well be eager to throw off their monarchical principles in favor of republican ones. But his doubts embraced habits (or character) as well as principle; it is far harder to change someone's character than his principles, because character is formed gradually over a long time. Hence Jefferson's reservation that the new immigrants' embrace of liberty, while sincere, might not be "temperate"; and several years later, the French people's embrace of liberty, inexperienced and immoderate, proved his point—though for political reasons at the time, he would have been loath to admit it!

At any rate, Jefferson was not against immigration, particularly of "useful artificers," but he was hostile to offering bounties or "extraordinary encouragements" to lure unskilled laborers and farmers from Europe, bearing with them monarchical principles and habits. And like many of the Founders, he worried not only about the political but also about what we would today call the cultural effects of immigration. Again, from Query 8 of *Notes on the State of Virginia*:

> These [monarchical] principles, with their language, they will transmit to their children. In proportion to their numbers, they will share with us the legislation. They will infuse into it their spirit, warp and bias its direction, and render it a heterogeneous, incoherent, and distracted mass.

American government would be "more homogeneous, more peaceable, more durable" without so many erstwhile monarchists speaking foreign tongues.[47]

When, more than a decade later, Jefferson and his Democratic Republican party triumphed over the Federalist party in the election of 1800, President Jefferson reversed himself and proposed the immediate naturalization of foreigners, instead of the fourteen-year residency that the Federalists had put in place in 1798.[48] The new policy had much to do with Jefferson's sympathy for the French Revolution and with recent immigrants' support for the Democratic party at the polls in 1800.[49] Alexander Hamilton, his political archrival, took him to task, appealing to Jefferson's own words in *Notes on the State of Virginia*. Hamilton, himself an immigrant and a strong proponent of immigration, criticized the dropping of any residency requirements as extreme, and cautioned against too rapid immigration:

> The safety of a republic depends essentially on the energy of a common national sentiment; on a uniformity of principles and habits; on the exemption of the citizens from foreign bias and prejudice; and on the love of country which will almost invariably be found to be closely connected with birth, education, and family. The opinion advanced in *Notes on Virginia* is undoubtedly correct, that foreigners will generally be apt to bring with them attachments to the persons they have left behind; to the country of their nativity; and to its particular customs and manners. They will also entertain opinions on government congenial with those under which they have lived; or if they should be led hither from a preference to ours, how extremely

unlikely is it that they will bring with them that *temperate love of liberty*, so essential to real republicanism?

The success of republicanism, Hamilton concluded, depended on "the preservation of a national spirit and a national character," and indiscriminate naturalization threatened both.[50]

In the end, despite their partisan differences, Hamilton and Jefferson agreed on the basic principles of American citizenship, and together with other members of the founding generation, they agreed that there was no necessary conflict or contradiction between the universal precepts underlying that citizenship and the cultivation of "a national spirit and a national character" for this particular people.[51] Jefferson and Hamilton did part company, of course, on the exact character of that "national spirit" and the means to implement it—whether agrarian virtues or entrepreneurial and manufacturing skills would better serve republican liberty, whether states' rights or federal judicial review was a better guardian of American liberty, and so forth. But on the general principles of natural rights, the social contract, and the cultivation of republican and constitutional fidelity, there was a remarkable consensus among the Founders. And on the specific question of immigration and naturalization, most of the Founders also thought alike—that society had, in principle, the right to admit new members or citizens only on the basis of mutual consent, and had the responsibility to exclude new members or citizens who would endanger the preservation of republican government in America.

Dilemmas of American Citizenship

Having staked American citizenship on universal principles, however, every failure to live up to those principles, every concession to particular interests or prejudices, and every apostasy in favor of competing principles would look all the more glaring. The persistence of black slavery in the midst of a regime pledged to human freedom involved the worst and most obvious of these failures, concessions, and apostasies. But because it was in the name of equality, liberty, Union, and republicanism that slavery was condemned and overturned in the Civil War and in the Thirteenth, Fourteenth, and Fifteenth Amendments, it hardly seems fair to blame the principles for its persistence. And yet in one sense, there is blame to be assigned or at least understood. From the Declaration of Independence's truth "that all men are created equal," two conclusions followed: One was that governments exist to secure the equal rights of the governed, the other that governments must be instituted, and operated, with the consent of the governed. The bifurcation of these goals makes possible and necessary the drama of self-government: A free people, according to American principles, possesses the right and duty to govern itself. But part of drama is tragedy, and with the necessity of self-government comes the possibility that the people, or a significant part of them, will govern selfishly or unjustly. The tragedy lurking in American principles is that the two commandments of the Declaration may contradict each other if the people cannot be persuaded to govern in accordance with the equal rights of all. Despite all the "auxiliary precautions" erected by the Constitution to prevent majority and minority tyranny, tyranny is still possible if a popular faction is sufficiently strong, wily, and long-lasting.

Popular tyranny is the bastard child of self-government, but its illegitimacy must be proven over and over, time and again, case by case. This is a requirement of self-government's own legitimacy and honor. In this light, the supreme task of American citizenship is to live up to its own best principles—to consolidate public opinion behind those principles, to persuade popular majorities to govern in the interest of minorities too, to encourage citizens to strive for the common good. So the cultivation of a virtuous or responsible "national spirit" and "national character" is essential precisely in order to live up to the universal principles animating that citizenship. To put it differently, American self-government not only presupposes a national "self" but must help to shape and refine it.

So American citizenship helps to form American culture; it is not just a by-product of a preexisting or somehow more fundamental culture. In fact, there has always been something peculiarly political—call it republican or democratic—about American culture. Our first national forms of literature were the sermon and the political pamphlet, and many of the sermons, especially in the later eighteenth century, were about politics. Our novels, poetry, painting, and so forth came later, after the founding had stamped us "American." These later forms of art deepened and broadened American culture but did not change its main lines. Religion, an important part of what used to be meant, at least, by culture, is in its ultimate concerns transpolitical, and thus in most respects is properly off-limits to American politics. But even on religion, the principles of American citizenship have had a formative influence. The precepts of nonestablishment (the separation of church and state) and religious freedom are deeply ingrained in every American denomination. The Mormons are only the most recent example of a church that, for whatever inspired reasons, has gradually conformed its teachings to the moral and legal precepts of American republicanism.

So the founders labored to shape the "national spirit" and "national character" of a people who could live together as republican citizens. This demanded much more than a simple, ritual assent to formal political principles. It demanded, as we have seen, among citizens and immigrants alike, the encouragement of a common language, of the work ethic, of republican habits of mind and conduct, of a spreading affection for the Constitution and Union.[52] And after the Constitution-framing and lawmaking of the early founding period, Americans increasingly turned their attention to education—establishing in state after state a system of free "common" or public schools in which reading, writing, 'rithmetic, and republicanism could be inculcated.[53] By means of formal education, but also through civic festivals and oratory, public buildings and monuments, jury charges, biographies, histories, and the practice of self-government itself, the founding generation sought to perpetuate a republican regime. And of course the Founders' own lives and character—more impressive and capacious than any list of virtues—exhibited to their fellow citizens what it meant to be an American.

From the citizens' point of view, however, what it means to be a good American elides, almost imperceptibly, into what it means to be a good, or the best, human being. This identification is, as Aristotle realized long ago, inherent in citizenship, though it can be elicited in better or worse forms in better or worse regimes; but it is one reason why many contemporary critics reject so thoroughly the Founders' view of the matter. The closed character of even the most open and liberal society, the citizens' stubborn preference for their own and their willingness to fight for it, the inescapable limitations of public opinion itself—these are anathema to many contemporary critics of American citizenship. The most radical, and interesting, of these critics are the so-called "cultural pluralists," who argue that many groups feel excluded from American culture despite having American citizenship, and who conclude therefore that U.S. citizenship needs to be reconstructed along cultural, that is, multicultural lines.

Multicultural Citizenship

In a classic article of this genre, Iris Marion Young advocates what she calls "heterogeneous" or "differentiated" citizenship. To see what this means, it will be necessary to follow her argument for a while. In the first place, this new kind of citizenship arises from a critique of rights, of individual or natural rights as we find them in the central documents of the American Revolution. At one time, Young writes, individual rights were championed by "emancipatory groups" who wished to show that "some groups" stigmatized as naturally inferior to "white male citizens" were in fact their equals and deserving of equal citizenship. At that time, "equal rights that were blind to group differences" were "the only sensible way to combat exclusion and degradation." But that was then; today, "equal rights for all groups," that is, for "all persons" (she does not seem to think that persons really exist apart from groups) has basically been achieved, but "group inequalities nevertheless remain." In short, individual or universal rights were fine so long as they were progressive; in today's circumstances, however, they are, to use Herbert Marcuse's term, "repressive." Once liberating and leveling, equal rights now must be overcome.[54]

Why did "equal citizenship rights" not lead to "social justice and equality"? Part of the answer, she explains, is "straightforwardly Marxist." The right to acquire and own property, Marx argued, is in bourgeois society supposedly held by every man equally; but this formal equality masks the real inequality that results when men actually exercise that right. The equality of rights does not yield an equality of results. And so, Young concludes along with Marx, equal rights are deceptive, spurious, oppressive—a disguise for the rule of the rich over the poor; or in Young's vocabulary, for the rule of privileged groups over oppressed groups.[55] As a consequence of his analysis, Marx abandoned the discussion of rights altogether. But Young, following a different strand of twentieth-century social criticism, takes the opportunity to correct bourgeois rights by a new kind of rights. Because equal civil and political rights only reinforce and perpetuate socioeconomic inequality, any attempt to find "neutral" principles of law will be unavailing. So "instead of always formulating rights and rules in universal terms that are blind to difference," declares Young, "some groups sometimes deserve special rights."[56]

Young recognizes that her pronouncement might sound a bit ominous, so she takes pains to reassure her readers that "special" just means "specific," as opposed to the "general" rights that "all persons" should have. But "special" rights are not just added to "general" rights; the special rights that some persons or rather groups receive seem to come at the expense of the general rights of the not-so-special groups. In other words, "special" rights may well subtract from "general" rights. One of her examples is "affirmative action" or what she calls "preference to race or gender," which she defends on the grounds that "the development of truly neutral standards and evaluations is difficult or impossible" for females, blacks, and Latinos who are required, for example, to take college entrance tests designed by white males. This argument proves too much (will there have to be a caste system for teaching and grading once the female, black, and Latino students are at college?), but let's leave it aside. The main point is that "preference to race or gender" can only come at the expense of those who don't possess the preferred qualities; she acknowledges this when she defends affirmative action programs "whether they involve quotas or not." So "specific" rights are "special," after all. But not to worry, Young assures us; we're all special! She writes in a footnote: "in certain contexts and at certain levels of abstraction everyone has 'special' rights."[57]

In the end, everyone may have to have "special rights" because no one will be left with "general" ones. At least this is the tendency of some of her own examples and lines of argument. Young argues in favor of special rights for linguistic and cultural minorities, for instance, because cultural assimilation would require "a person to transform his or her sense of identity." Despite this statement, she confines language and cultural rights to "sizeable . . . minorities living in distinct" communities; she appears to deny them to individual "persons who do not identify with majority language or culture."[58] But if the evil to be prevented is the forcible transforming of personal identity, why should only sizeable groups have their identities protected?

The answer has everything to do with the prominence of groups in her theory of citizenship. Young distinguishes groups from "aggregates" and "associations." An aggregate is "any classification of persons according to some attribute," like blue-eyed people. An association is "a collectivity of persons who come together voluntarily," like a bridge club or a political party. A "social group," by contrast, has a "sense of identity" based on an "affinity" that persons feel with one another and that outsiders recognize in the group. Now, an affinity can either be a resemblance or a liking. Do group members merely resemble one another, or just happen to like one another, or do they like one another because they resemble one another? Young comments that a light-skinned person may still "identify as black," but she then adds that certain "objective attributes" are "sometimes" a necessary condition for group membership. These attributes, generally speaking, are a shared "social status," a common history based on that status, and a "self-identification" with the group.[59]

It is the latter quality that lies at the heart of the social group. Like Marx's economic classes, Young's social groups depend on combining objective class or social position with the subjective consciousness of that position. That is, a person must not only belong to an oppressed group, he must be conscious of his oppression and prepared to do something about it. For Young, one might say, it is the difference between being a woman and a feminist. At any rate, it is the subjective factor that distinguishes groups from associations. Associations are formed by individuals—"already formed persons," in Young's telling phrase—who come together voluntarily, who are capable of making and keeping contracts, including the social contract. Tocqueville spoke of the art and science of associations that could lead men to freedom and dignity, not to mention responsible citizenship.[60] Young prefers groups to associations because groups "define one's very identity"; they provide the sense of belonging and of purpose that humanity itself, that nature itself, cannot afford.

"Group affinity," Young writes, "has the character of what Heidegger calls 'throwness': one finds oneself as a member of a group, whose existence and relations one experiences as always already having been."[61]

Social groups impart meaning or "identity" to their members, who are definitely not "already formed men"; their identity depends decisively on "how others identify" them. Yet the "objective attributes" of group membership reside in race, sex, ethnicity, age—subrational characteristics that particularize persons, that invite stereotyping, but that are made the basis of group "culture" and hence of "differentiated" citizenship in this theory. For social groups do have "capacities, values," and even "cognitive and behavioral styles" unique to them, Young avers; that would mean, to use philosophical language, that the subrational parts of the soul reach all the way up to the rational, and shape or control reason itself.[62] "Heterogeneous" citizenship would then be the variety of citizenships corresponding to the willful and passionate "values" of social groups; or more precisely, it would be the attempt to manage or accommodate these largely incommensurable worldviews.

Young tries to avoid this problem by retreating from the "throwness," the givenness of group identity. At one point, she compares the defining quality of group identity to what "being Navajo might" be like. A few sentences later, however, she announces that "from the throwness of group affinity it does not follow that one cannot leave groups and enter new ones. Many women become lesbian after identifying as heterosexual, and anyone who lives long enough becomes old."[63] If group loyalties are fluctuating, evolving, and crosscutting, then one may not have to worry so much about the passionate commitments or, in some cases, fanatical resentments underlying identity politics. But then identity politics and bourgeois interest-group politics would not be so far apart, a state of affairs that would likely lead to an identity crisis for identity politics: It has staked too much on its German philosophical borrowings to be unmasked as just another form of utilitarianism.

At any rate, the goal of respect or recognition marches hand in hand with the goal of greater socioeconomic equality in Young's group theory of citizenship. Greater economic equality implies the redistribution of wealth and power from privileged to oppressed groups, and this is the task not of revolution but of group representation in her scheme. She proposes that "a democratic public, however that is constituted," should provide mechanisms and resources to promote "effective representation and recognition" of its "oppressed or disadvantaged" groups (disadvantaged is now virtually the same as oppressed). Effective representation requires three things: "self-organization" of group members so that they may feel empowered and fully conscious of themselves as oppressed; "voicing" a group's perspective on policy proposals and aiding them in generating new proposals; and "having veto power regarding specific policies that affect a group directly."[64] It is characteristic of Young's argument that she calls for the "democratic public" to provide or foster the "self-organization" of groups; the groups are too diffuse, needy, or spiritless actually to organize themselves and make political or policy claims on their own. Their demand for recognition becomes truly self-confident only after the public or its representatives have validated it by reassuring the (potential) group members that, yes, they are oppressed. In fact, they are so oppressed or oblivious that they cannot or will not demand freedom and equality for themselves, without government's blessing—and without the leadership of vanguard intellectuals like Young.

A new form of group participation in political deliberation, conjoined to a veto power for each group over policies directly affecting it—these then are the specific political reforms she is advancing. "Reproductive rights for women" is one of Young's examples of a policy over which the veto power would extend, though it is unclear exactly at what level, for what reasons, in what manner, and by whom such a veto would be cast. Are the internal politics of the groups, e.g., women, based on majority rule (and of all women, or only those enrolled in feminist organizations?) or on some form of centralized decision-making among the leaders of the existing organizations? Young does not say, but she does emphasize that the purpose of representation for disadvantaged groups (privileged groups do not need it and do not get such a veto) is "to undermine oppression," to weaken or overthrow the advantaged groups and their policies.[65] This political goal could perhaps be achieved through a radical rehabilitation of all citizens or of citizenship itself, however, and it is to this less partisan purpose that most of her arguments are ostensibly directed.

Redeeming American Citizenship?

The new "responsible" citizen, Young explains, will be "concerned not merely with interests but with justice," and this means "acknowledging that each other person's interest and point of view is as good as his or her own," and furthermore that "the needs and interests of everyone must be voiced and be heard by the others, who must acknowledge, respect, and address those needs and interests." Yet Young admits that "persons from one perspective or history can never completely understand and adopt the point of view of those with other group-based perspectives and histories." If no one can finally understand another person's point of view, however, why regard it as "as good as his or her own"? Perhaps the answer is that no one can ever understand his own or his own group's point of view, either, because that view is grounded so firmly in the mysterious fate ("throwness") of race, ethnicity, and gender—bodily or subrational factors, all. Young cautions that she does not think "cultural differences" arise from "natural, unalterable, biological attributes," but instead from "the relationship of bodies to conventional rules and practices." But "bodies" are biological, and hence "cultural differences" turn out to include such items as "body comportment," "gesture," "biological sex difference" (only women get pregnant), and "bodily difference" (including "persons with physical and mental disabilities," thus incidentally tracing mind back to body, again).[66]

If the culture of social groups is rooted in race, ethnicity, gender, and other bodily differences, then culture shares the privateness or the privatizing quality of bodily things. If I prick my finger, no one else actually feels my pain, however much others may sympathize with me. Reason, by contrast, allows human beings to transcend their bodily differences: when I think $2 + 2 = 4$ or "all men are created equal," others (regardless of race, etc.) may think the same thought along with me. Thought is color-blind, because the objects of reason in the highest sense are universals: the idea of man, qua man, for example, is devoid of accidental attributes of color, height, weight, and so forth. Culture is more like the former than the latter, according to Young, except that culture does not have a natural standard of pleasure and pain by which to guide it. Hence social groups based on cultures really do have unique points of view—which cannot be known to be good and thus are regarded as "good" only insofar as they are authentic or truly one's own.

Citizenship based on group cultures must therefore be "heterogeneous" in the precise sense that each group's "interest and point of view" is "as good" as any other's. In Young's words, "a general perspective does not exist . . . from which all experiences and perspectives can be understood and taken into account," and therefore "no one can claim to speak in the general interest, because no one of the groups can speak for another, and certainly no one can speak for them all." The "public" as a particular community sharing a universal or general view of justice does not exist; the "general will" is an illusion, and an oppressive one to boot. No one can even "claim" to speak in the general interest, then. Instead of "self-deceiving self-interest masked as an impartial or general interest," every group will assert plainly its own self-interest and point of view.[67]

Young's theory rests on two enormous non sequiturs. The first is that because any group's point of view is "as good" as any other's, every group should be heard and represented. But this does not follow: If no group's point of view is better than your own, why not insist on your own? To put it differently, if politics is not about the clash of claims over universal justice—which claims might, in principle at least, be adjudicated

by reason—but instead is about the clash of identities backed up by particularistic assertions of group will, then a democratic regime of equality
and easygoing tolerance will hardly be the inevitable or logical outcome.
Heidegger's own politics of group authenticity led him to be a resolute
Nazi. Young herself spares no effort to be inclusive. In fact, her list of
"oppressed social groups" in America comprises "women, blacks, Native
Americans, Chicanos, Puerto Ricans and other Spanish-speaking Americans, Asian Americans, gay men, lesbians, working-class people, poor
people, old people, and mentally and physically disabled people."[68] In
sum, the vast majority of Americans; but one should not forget that group
representation is not extended to the oppressors, to the privileged groups
who "behave as though they have a right to speak and be heard." She
never says that they do have a right to speak and be heard.[69]

Young's second non sequitur is to assume that, because every group has
a unique interest and point of view, justice will result from the full airing
of this diversity. "Group representation is the best means to promote just
outcomes to democratic decision-making processes," she declares. For
justification, she resorts to "Habermas's conception of communicative
ethics." Absent "a Philosopher King who reads transcendent normative
verities," Young explains, "the only ground for a claim that a policy or
decision is just is that it has been arrived at by a public which has truly
promoted free expression of all needs and points of view."[70] Yet the claim
that the "free expression" of needs and values yields justice is itself an
assertion of a transcendent or at least an immanent normative verity. And
besides, what ensures that the result of group representation and free expression is justice as opposed to, say, cacophony and stalemate?

Assume, for the sake of argument, that free expression and representation for all oppressed groups were a necessary condition for justice; would
it be a sufficient condition? Yes, if whatever policy emerges from such a
forum is, by definition, just, which seems to be Young's contention. In
fact, according to her, free expression guarantees not only justice but wisdom: "group representation also maximizes knowledge expressed in discussion, and thus promotes practical wisdom." Members of social groups
know "different things about the structure of social relations" and "have
different ways of understanding the meaning of social events." For example, "many Native Americans argue that their traditional religion and relation to land gives them a unique and important understanding of
environmental problems."[71] Knowledge is not wisdom, alas, and even if
group representation added to social knowledge, it would not necessarily
add to the wise use of knowledge. The effect of the "free expression of all
needs and points of view" would be more communication among groups,
but not better deliberation, which presupposes shared goals and a shared
inclination to act in pursuit of those goals. Young's "communicative

ethic" promotes the "expression" of group needs and values, not action to secure them.

Thus a failed political movement is her example of group representation in action. Jesse Jackson's "Rainbow Coalition" in his 1984 presidential race fell short of "the promise of group representation," but it pointed the way. In "traditional coalitions," Young writes, diverse groups work together for common ends, suppressing their differences, especially in public. Not in a rainbow coalition, however, in which each group "affirms the presence of the others and affirms the specificity of its experience and perspective on social issues." According to the rainbow ideal, blacks, gays, labor activists, peace movement veterans, and feminists will not only work together but learn to like each other by expressing and affirming their differences—though Young notes that each group must maintain "autonomy in relating to its constituency" and all coalition decisions are to be made by group representation.[72]

Heterogeneous citizenship will be the rainbow coalition writ large. Despite the appeals to Habermas and to his complicated vision of the just society as a vast dialogic community, the basic political features of Young's project are straightforward. The philosophical problems involved in extracting justice from the group dynamics of a rainbow coalition may be insurmountable, but they are also irrelevant, for the fact is that the coalition members already agree on the most important political purpose of their association. They have come together in order to "undermine oppression," to wring some social justice from an unjust society. The pot of gold at the end of the rainbow coalition is the redistribution of wealth and power sought by coalition members and dictated by their new understanding of rights. In consideration of that common goal, the constituent groups will endure—and maybe learn to like, or at least profess to like—large quantities of self-expression and group affirmation. The ideological differences among coalition members are narrow to begin with, then.[73]

Yet a rainbow coalition is not merely a redistributionist ploy. Young's theory of citizenship is based not on the working class but on racial, ethnic, and other sorts of social and cultural groups, and it depends for its implementation not on workers' abandoning their chains but on individuals' forging new meaning in their lives through group membership. Young's project thus encourages individuals to think of themselves primarily as members of one or more groups, and it provides material as well as psychological incentives to do so. The internal danger in heterogeneous citizenship is that it may immure citizens in their group, making them not civic participants but only group-citizens, as it were. Encouraging this tendency is the other major political feature of Young's proposal, the veto that each group would wield over its own special policy areas. This is a weapon to be used against the oppressors, against the privileged groups.

By clogging society's wheels, the disadvantaged groups will prevent injustice to themselves and persuade the powerful to respect the oppressed as fellow citizens. But the veto is also a weapon in internal coalition politics, reminding the other members of the rainbow coalition of the "autonomy" that each group wields on behalf of its own membership.

So the most potent political threat in Young's reformed polity would be the threat of inaction. To understand the orientation of this threat, it helps to know that insofar as there are "heterogeneous publics operating according to the principles of group representation in contemporary politics, they exist only in organizations and movements resisting the majority politics." The overall effect of the group-based veto is to subtract from the political, and moral, authority of constitutional majorities. Young's proposal moves the country away from majority rule, counting each citizen-voter as one, and towards a polity in which political authority resides in organized and favored (privileged?) groups, counting each group, regardless of its size, as one, and empowering each with an absolute negative on the actions of society. "Such structures of group representation should not replace structures of regional or party representation but should exist alongside them," Young explains.[74] But the insertion of group recognition and veto power into the traditional structures would quickly change them, and besides, the larger purpose of the reform is to open a fundamental debate on the nature of representation, rights, and good government in America.

Young might respond that she is proposing merely a shift from one form of majority rule, based on abstract or egoistic individuals, to another, based on man as a social being, who finds his or her identity primarily through affinity with one or more groups. A similar thought was expressed in the nineteenth century in these terms: the United States needs to move away from rule by the "numerical majority"—which is tyrannical because it threatens to override the most cherished affinities and disrupt the deepest sources of identity among oppressed minorities—and toward rule by the "concurrent majority," in which each threatened group would enjoy a salutary veto power over legislation directly affecting it. In the nineteenth-century case, the oppressed minorities were the citizens of the slaveholding states, whose cultural identity and political rights, they felt, were threatened by Northern abolitionists, politicians, capitalists, and immigrants. John C. Calhoun grounded his argument against the "numerical majority" on the forthright denunciation of the notion "that all men are created equal": Rights, he insisted, varied with the group or race to which one belonged, and equality belonged not to human beings per se but to the groups or states in which they organized themselves. His proposal for a "concurrent majority" would have given a veto power to each state to defend itself against obnoxious laws, such as

ones restricting the spread of slavery. And like Young, he thought that
the brinkmanship produced by the use or promised use of vetoes would,
paradoxically, lead to a rebirth of civic spirit.[75] Young's objectives are certainly not Calhoun's, but by their patronage of group representation and
the group veto, both critics move away from republican government based
on individual rights and the rule of constitutional majorities. For "the
vital principle of republican government," as James Madison wrote in ref-
utation of Calhoun, is "*lex majoris partis*, the will of the majority," properly qualified by constitutional protections for personal rights; and
anyone who does not admit this, Madison declared, must "either join the
avowed disciples of aristocracy, oligarchy, or monarchy, or look for a
Utopia."[76]

How, finally, would Young implement her plan for a new kind of citizenship? Whether in national politics or in "factories, offices, universities,
churches, and social service agencies," there are "no models" to follow in
establishing principles of group representation, Young comments, though
she adds immediately that some of the experiments in "publicly institutionalized self-organization" among "women, indigenous peoples, workers, peasants, and students" in Sandinista-ruled Nicaragua come close to
the conception she has in mind. Again, the contradiction in terms—
"publicly institutionalized self-organization"—this time presided over by
the Nicaraguan Communists suggests the extent to which implementation
of the new citizenship has to be top-down, to say the least. Young es-
chews, however, all specifics as to "which groups" are to be represented
initially and "by what procedures" that decision might be made, other
than to observe that "a public must be constituted" to make such decisions and that "the principles guiding the composition of such a 'constitutional convention'" must somehow be found through the process of
politics itself. Despite her uncharacteristic reticence, she confirms that the
addition of group representation amounts to a kind of regime change or
refounding, requiring a "constitutional convention" to authorize the
emergence of a new public. And as for the "mechanisms" of group representation itself, they will take many evenings, for citizens must constantly
"meet together in democratic forums" in order to "discuss issues and
formulate group positions and proposals" as well as take part in "democ-
ratized decision-making processes" in "neighborhood or district assemblies" and in the "group assemblies" of oppressed groups.[77]

Young's elaborate scheme of group meetings is dedicated to turning
American constitutionalism into something like, in T. Alexander Aleinikoff's approving words, "a contract under constant renegotiation."[78] Neither individual natural rights nor majority rule under the Constitution
are "privileged" parts of the social contract, in her view, and she admits
that even her program of group representation may have to give way if

"in some utopian future there will be a society without group oppression and disadvantage."[79] In the meantime, however, some form of group representation is needed in order to bind the American public to its groups, and the groups to the public. Lost in the middle is the original American idea of a self-governing people, instituted and operated by the consent of the governed, who are citizens bearing God-given or natural rights. Lost, also, is the love of country—of its Constitution, laws, statesmen, history, and promise—that once bound citizens together and that was so zealously cultivated by the Founders, who knew that citizens would have to be prepared to fight and, if necessary, to die for America. Young says nothing about national defense or the need for "heterogeneous" citizens to defend their country.

Young's proposal tends to replace these ideas with the concept of a nation of groups, even as today's cosmopolitan critics of citizenship urge that national sovereignty be reconsidered in light of what groups of nations might do for world peace and justice. Either sort of proposal threatens the unity of a self-governing people like the Americans, and seems to promise, in order to keep watch over fractious and unnatural groups, only a further bleak centralization of administrative power. This is why, to say the least, none of Young's arguments for "heterogeneous" citizenship is persuasive enough to justify abandoning American citizenship as the Founders conceived it. Especially given the tendency of group representation to blur the meaning of rights and enhance the role of power, it is impossible that her style of multicultural citizenship would be compatible, over the long run, with limited government and the rule of law.

Far better to reflect on how Abraham Lincoln sought to fulfill the promise of American citizenship amid the Republic's gravest crisis, when millions of Americans set out deliberately to renounce their citizenship and tear the Union asunder. Two years before the crisis came, he described the promise of American citizenship in words that may serve as our conclusion. Anticipating, in a way, the claims of our citizens today who do not yet feel a part of the American nation, Lincoln spoke of the many Americans who were not blood descendants of the Founders, but who nevertheless had something infinitely more important in common with the revolutionaries of 1776:

> If they look back through this history to trace their connection with those days by blood, they find they have none, they cannot carry themselves back into that glorious epoch and make themselves feel that they are part of us, but when they look through that old Declaration of Independence they find that those old men say that "We hold these truths to be self-evident, that all men are created equal," and then they feel that that moral sentiment taught in that day evidences their relation to those men, that it is the father of all

moral principle in them, and that they have a right to claim it as though they were blood of the blood, and flesh of the flesh, of the men who wrote that Declaration—and so they are. That is the electric cord in that Declaration that links the hearts of patriotic and liberty-loving men together, that will link those patriotic hearts as long as the love of freedom exists in the minds of men throughout the world.[80]

Notes

1. W. B. Allen, ed., *George Washington: A Collection* (Indianapolis: Liberty Classics, 1988), 548.

2. George Washington, "General Orders," April 18, 1783, in Allen, *George Washington: A Collection*, 237; "Letter to the Volunteer Association of Ireland," December 2, 1783, in *Writings of George Washington*, ed. John C. Fitzpatrick, vol. 27 (Washington, D.C.: Government Printing Office, 1931–44), 254. Cf. Matthew Spalding, "From Pluribus to Unum: Immigration and the Founding Fathers," *Policy Review*, Winter 1994, 35–41.

3. On the peculiar, and continuing, effects of black slavery on the character of U.S. citizenship, see Judith N. Shklar, *American Citizenship: The Quest for Inclusion* (Cambridge: Harvard University Press, 1991). For a historical summary, see James H. Kettner, *The Development of American Citizenship, 1608–1870* (Chapel Hill: University of North Carolina Press, 1978).

4. For further details, see Reed Ueda, "Naturalization and Citizenship," in *Harvard Encyclopedia of American Ethnic Groups*, ed. Stephen Thernstrom (Cambridge: Harvard University Press, 1980), 734–48.

5. Rogers M. Smith, *Civic Ideals: Conflicting Visions of Citizenship in U.S. History* (New Haven: Yale University Press, 1997), 36–37. See also Shklar, *American Citizenship*, 7–8, 13–14.

6. For an intelligent overview, see Will Kymlicka and Wayne Norman, "Return of the Citizen: A Survey of Recent Work on Citizenship Theory," *Ethics* 104 (January 1994): 352–81.

7. Robert W. Johannsen, ed., *The Lincoln–Douglas Debates* (New York: Oxford University Press, 1965), 196. For the grounds and limitations of Douglas's argument, see Harry V. Jaffa, *Crisis of the House Divided: An Interpretation of the Lincoln–Douglas Debates* (Chicago: University of Chicago Press, 1982).

8. Willmoore Kendall, "Equality and the American Political Tradition," in *Willmoore Kendall Contra Mundum*, ed. Nellie D. Kendall (New Rochelle, N.Y.: Arlington House, 1971); reprinted in William F. Buckley, Jr., and Charles R. Kesler, eds., *Keeping the Tablets: Modern American Conservative Thought* (New York: Harper & Row, 1988), 71–83, at 71.

9. See Edmund Burke, *Reflections on the Revolution in France*, in *The Writings and Speeches of Edmund Burke* (Boston: Little Brown, 1901), vol. 3, 259: "A state without the means of some change is without the means of its conservation." Cf. 274–75 and 455–57. Consider also Friedrich A. Hayek, *The Constitution of Liberty* (Chicago: University of Chicago Press, 1960), 54–70.

10. Madison, in *The Federalist Papers*, ed. Clinton Rossiter (New York: Mentor, 1961), no. 42, 266.

11. Madison, *The Federalist Papers*, No. 54, 337.

12. This is not Kant's own position exactly, because he distinguished between moral and legal duty. Pure or categorical morality made it one's duty never to break the established law, even if it is very imperfect, according to Kant. Nonetheless, he distinguished sharply between the mere "political moralist" and the admirable "moral politician," whose goal is to make politics bend its knee before right. See Immanuel Kant, "To Perpetual Peace: A Philosophical Sketch," Appendix I, in *Kant's Political Writings*, ed. Hans Reiss (Cambridge: Cambridge University Press, 1970), 116–25; and Kant, "The Metaphysics of Morals," in *Kant's Political Writings*, 143–47.

13. Johannsen, *The Lincoln–Douglas Debates*, 304. Lincoln is quoting from his speech on the Dred Scott decision, originally delivered in 1857.

14. Frederick Douglass argued that it was in the slaves' own interest for the Constitution to be ratified, even with its compromises over slavery, because the alternative was a sundering of the Union and thus a much greater chance for slavery to expand and perpetuate itself across the South and the rest of the continent. "My argument against the dissolution of the American Union is this," he wrote. "It would place the slave system more exclusively under the control of the slaveholding states, and withdraw it from the power in the Northern states which is opposed to slavery." Frederick Douglass, "The Constitution of the United States: Is It Pro-Slavery or Anti-Slavery?" in *The Life and Writings of Frederick Douglass*, ed. Philip S. Foner, vol. 2 (New York: International Publishers, 1950), 478.

15. Cf. Aristotle, *The Politics*, trans. Carnes Lord (Chicago: University of Chicago Press, 1984), 1327b23–33.

16. Fustel de Coulanges, *The Ancient City*, trans. W. Small (Garden City, N.Y.: Doubleday, 1956); originally published in 1864.

17. Aristotle, *The Politics*, 1253a30–31.

18. Aristotle, *The Politics*, 1228b12–13, 1229a27–33. Cf. Aristotle, *Topics* 105a5–8, 115b32–35.

19. Aristotle, *The Politics*, 1275a2–23. For good commentaries, see Harry V. Jaffa, "Aristotle," in *History of Political Philosophy*, ed. Leo Strauss and Joseph Cropsey, 2nd ed. (Chicago: Rand McNally, 1972), 94–116; Harvey C. Mansfield Jr., *Responsible Citizenship, Ancient and Modern* (Eugene: University of Oregon Books, 1994), 4–12; and Mary P. Nichols, *Citizens and Statesmen: A Study of Aristotle's Politics* (Lanham, Md.: Rowman & Littlefield, 1992), 55–61.

20. Aristotle, *The Politics*, 1275a2–1275b20, 1284a3–17, 1284b25–34, 1288a17–29.

21. Aristotle, *The Politics*, 1276b16–1277b32, 1287a1–1287b35.

22. See Mansfield, *Responsible Citizenship*, 6.

23. Aristotle, *The Politics*, 1275b21–33.

24. Allen, *George Washington: A Collection*, 271.

25. The following paragraphs are adapted from Charles R. Kesler, "Civility and Citizenship in the American Founding," in *Civility and Citizenship in Lib-*

eral Democratic Societies, ed. Edward C. Banfield (New York: Paragon House, 1992), 65–68.

26. Thomas Jefferson, letter to Roger Weightman, June 24, 1826, in *Thomas Jefferson: Writings*, ed. Merrill D. Peterson (New York: Library of America, 1984), 1517.

27. For exhaustive proof of the universalism of the Founders' basic principles, see Thomas G. West, *Vindicating the Founders: Race, Sex, Class, and Justice in the Origins of America* (Lanham, Md.: Rowman & Littlefield, 1997).

28. Religious disestablishment was primarily the work of state governments, not the federal government, which under the First Amendment was clearly forbidden to establish a national church, but not empowered to abolish the established churches then existing in some states. Virginia's disestablishment of Anglicanism in 1786 led the way; and by 1833 the argument for separation of church and state had swept away the last of the state churches.

29. Thus, as William B. Allen contends, the American Founders' account of sovereignty "replaces the nation-state with the state-nation . . . Nationality no longer operates to secure the relevant distinctions, which consist primarily in determinations of the extent to which rights are guaranteed . . . The existence of the state serves to create de facto that class of human beings whose nominal rights are actually enforceable in contrast to those whose rights are subject to abuse . . . Modern sovereignty requires the death of nationality or community membership, not as vital memory, but as a primary and active basis of civic association." Allen, "The Truth About Citizenship: An Outline," *Cardozo Journal of International and Comparative Law* 4 (Summer 1996), 355–72, at 368–69.

30. West, *Vindicating the Founders*, 157. Emphasis added by West.

31. Philip B. Kurland and Ralph Lerner, eds., *The Founders' Constitution*, vol. 1 (Chicago: University of Chicago Press, 1987), 11.

32. West, *Vindicating the Founders*, 156.

33. Max Farrand, ed., *Records of the Federal Convention*, vol. 2 (New Haven: Yale University Press, 1966), 238. Quoted in West, *Vindicating the Founders*, 157. In a sense, immigration and naturalization became the model for citizenship. As Reed Ueda comments, "Since naturalization had been central to the process of forming colonial societies, the colonists began to see political allegiance as reflecting the essential character of naturalization itself and to hold that allegiance was volitional and contractual." Ueda, "Naturalization and Citizenship," 736.

34. On the subject of tacit consent, see John Locke, *Two Treatises of Government*, ed. Peter Laslett (New York: Mentor, 1965), II, secs. 104–12, 116–22.

35. Samuel Eliot Morison, ed., *Sources and Documents Illustrating the American Revolution* (New York: Oxford University Press, 1923), 164. Cf. Vattel, *The Law of Nations, Or The Principles of Natural Law*, trans. Charles G. Fenwick (Washington, D.C.: Carnegie Endowment, 1916), 37–38, 88–91, 140–41, 151, 154–55.

36. Vattel, *The Law of Nations*, 91–93; and Smith, *Civic Ideals*, 525 f42.

37. Letter to John Augustine Washington, June 15, 1783, in Allen, *George Washington: A Collection*, 256.

38. Allen, *George Washington: A Collection*, 515.

39. See Noah M. J. Pickus, "'Hearken Not to the Unnatural Voice': Publius and the Artifice of Attachment," in *Diversity and Citizenship: Rediscovering American Nationhood*, ed. Gary Jeffrey Jacobsohn and Susan Dunn (Lanham, Md.: Rowman & Littlefield, 1996), 63–84; and Charles R. Kesler, "Federalist 10 and American Republicanism," in *Saving the Revolution: The Federalist Papers and the American Founding*, ed. Charles R. Kesler, 13–39.

40. See *The Federalist Papers*, No. 49, 314–17; and No. 37, 226–27.

41. *The Federalist Papers*, No. 37, 230–31 and No. 49, 317; cf. No. 78, 467–68.

42. *The Federalist Papers*, No. 78, 466–68; cf. No. 51, 321.

43. Benjamin Franklin, "Information to Those Who Would Remove to America," in *Benjamin Franklin: Writings*, ed. J. A. Leo Lemay (New York: Library of America, 1987), 975–83, at 978–82.

44. Franklin, in *Benjamin Franklin: Writings*, 982.

45. Smith, *Civic Ideals*, 159–60.

46. In his famous discussion of slavery's injustice in *Notes on the State of Virginia*, Query 18, Jefferson hopes eventually for "a total emancipation . . . with the consent of the masters, rather than by their extirpation." He admits that in the event of a violent "revolution," however, "The Almighty has no attribute which can take side with us in such a contest." Remarkably, Jefferson refers to slavery as a condition in which "one half the citizens . . . trample on the rights of the other," thus acknowledging, at least rhetorically, that black slaves were or ought to be equal citizens. Peterson, *Thomas Jefferson: Writings*, 288–89.

47. Peterson, *Thomas Jefferson: Writings*, 210–12.

48. The first U.S. naturalization law (1790) set the residency requirement at two years, which was raised to five years (1795) and then fourteen years (1798). Jefferson's proposal for immediate naturalization was not passed, but the Democratic Republicans did reset the requirement to five years (1801), where it has remained since. See Ueda, "Naturalization and Citizenship," 737.

49. Smith, *Civic Ideals*, 153–70, 190–92; West, *Vindicating the Founders*, 154.

50. Alexander Hamilton, "The Examination," nos. 7–9 (1802), in *Papers of Alexander Hamilton*, ed. Harold C. Syrett et al., vol. 25 (New York: Columbia University Press, 1961–79), 491–501. Quoted in West, *Vindicating the Founders*, 154–55.

51. The British naturalization laws of 1740 and 1761, which permitted foreigners in the colonies to become British subjects without special appeals to King or Parliament, had contained religious tests in addition to residency requirements. The 1740 law, in fact, prohibited the naturalization of Catholics. The effect of the U.S. naturalization act of 1790 and its successors was to replace religious tests with a test of "good character" as a prerequisite for U.S. citizenship; and, of course, to replace allegiance to the Crown with allegiance to the Constitution. See Ueda, "Naturalization and Citizenship," 735, 737–38.

52. Much scholarly work has recently been done on the republican virtues, as it were, immanent in liberalism. See, e.g., Stephen Macedo, *Liberal Virtues: Citizenship, Virtue, and Community* (Oxford: Oxford University Press, 1990); and William Galston, *Liberal Purposes: Goods, Virtues, and Duties in the Liberal State* (Cambridge: Cambridge University Press, 1991).

53. See Charles R. Kesler, "Education and Politics: Lessons from the American Founding," *The University of Chicago Legal Forum* (1991): 101–22.

54. Iris Marion Young, "Polity and Group Difference: A Critique of the Ideal of Universal Citizenship," *Ethics* 99 (January 1989): 250–74, at 267. Cf. Herbert Marcuse, "Repressive Tolerance," in Robert Paul Wolff, Barrington Moore Jr. and Herbert Marcuse, *A Critique of Pure Tolerance* (Boston: Beacon Press, 1965), 81–117.

55. Young, "Polity and Group Difference," 250–51.

56. Young, "Polity and Group Difference," 269.

57. Young, "Polity and Group Difference," 269.

58. Young, "Polity and Group Difference," 272. Will Kymlicka distinguishes, in his more moderate version of differentiated citizenship, between "multicultural" or "polyethnic rights," intended to help citizens express their particularity and cultural pride but without hindering their integration into society, and "self-government rights," belonging to distinct cultures or peoples occupying a given homeland or territory, who wish to maintain, like the Quebecois, their separate cultural and even political identity. Kymlicka, *Multicultural Citizenship: A Liberal Theory of Minority Rights* (Oxford: Oxford University Press, 1995).

59. Young, "Polity and Group Difference," 259–60.

60. See Alexis de Tocqueville, *Democracy in America*, trans. George Lawrence (Garden City, N.Y.: Doubleday, 1969), 189–95, 506–24.

61. Young, "Polity and Group Difference," 259–60. On "thrownness" (*Geworfenheit*), see Martin Heidegger, *Being and Time*, trans. John Macquarrie and Edward Robinson (New York: Harper & Row, 1962), secs. 29 and 38.

62. Young, "Polity and Group Difference," 260, 268–69.

63. Young, "Polity and Group Difference," 260.

64. Young, "Polity and Group Difference," 261–62.

65. Young, "Polity and Group Difference," 262.

66. Young, "Polity and Group Difference," 258, 262, 270–71.

67. Young, "Polity and Group Difference," 262–63.

68. Young, "Polity and Group Difference," 261. "In short, everyone but healthy, relatively well-off, relatively young, heterosexual white males," comment Kymlicka and Norman in "Return of the Citizen," 374 n26.

69. Young, "Polity and Group Difference," 262.

70. Young, "Polity and Group Difference," 263. Young does criticize Habermas for retaining "an appeal to a universal or impartial point of view from which claims in a public should be addressed," as opposed to her emphasis on "the expression of the concrete needs of all individuals in their particularity." Cf. Seyla Benhabib, *Critique, Norm, and Utopia* (New York: Columbia University Press, 1986), for a similar critique.

71. Young, "Polity and Group Difference," 264, 267.

72. Young, "Polity and Group Difference," 264–65.

73. The "test of whether a claim on the public is just," Young writes, ". . . is best made when persons making it must confront the opinion of others who have explicitly different, though not necessarily conflicting, experiences, priorities, and needs." "Polity and Group Difference," 263.

74. Young, "Polity and Group Difference," 265.

75. See Ross M. Lence, ed., *Union and Liberty: The Political Philosophy of John C. Calhoun* (Indianapolis: Liberty Fund, 1992), 3–78, 369–400, 565–70.

76. James Madison, "Majority Governments," in *The Mind of the Founder: Sources of the Political Thought of James Madison*, ed. Marvin Meyers (Indianapolis: Bobbs-Merrill, 1973), 520–30, at 528, 530.

77. Young, "Polity and Group Difference," 265–66.

78. T. Alexander Aleinikoff, "A Multicultural Nationalism?" *The American Prospect*, January-February 1998, 80–86, at 84.

79. Young, "Polity and Group Difference," 261.

80. Abraham Lincoln, speech at Chicago, July 10, 1858, in *Collected Works of Abraham Lincoln*, ed. Roy T. Basler, vol. 2 (New Brunswick, N.J.: Rutgers University Press, 1953), 499.

Citizenship in Theory and Practice: A Response to Charles Kesler

Kwame Anthony Appiah

Charles Kesler's chapter provides a very helpful framing, I think, of some of the deepest issues that face us in addressing questions of immigration policy. Our actual debates about these matters are bound to be framed as debates about what it means to be an American, and these questions are bound to be framed through interpretations of American history, beginning, of course, with the language and texts of the Founders. Inspired by a brief conversation with Joseph Carens,[1] I would point out, however, that there is, as a matter of philosophical method, a different way in which we could proceed. We could ask not what the Founders thought and meant, but what the right principles are for thinking about citizenship in general, and immigration and naturalization in particular. It would then be an interesting historical question how much of the truth the Founders grasped. In thinking about that question we should have to begin by exploring the ethical justification of the division of the world into a system of states. This question is surely quite a challenging one for liberalism, since the system of states means that all individuals in the world are obliged, whether they like it or not, to accept the political arrangements of their birthplace—however repugnant those arrangements are to their principles or ambitions—unless they can persuade somebody else to let them in.[2] Kesler observes that liberal principles require us to allow those who do not care for our social contract to leave, but that is an empty right if there is nowhere to go. And for many people in the world today, there is no escape from oppressive government or from economies without

---

This essay was written in response to a draft of Charles R. Kesler's chapter, presented at the Duke University Workshop on Citizenship and Naturalization, October 30–November 1, 1997.

prospects because states with liberal regimes and rich economies will not take them.

Kesler also argues that, because the moral process of creating a people must be grounded in consent, every society has the right to exclude whomever it wishes from immigrating: He endorses the preamble to the Massachusetts constitution which sees the "whole people" covenanting with "each citizen, and each citizen with the whole people." But this seems to me not so obvious. Societies are reproduced largely not by immigration but by the raising of children. Children cannot covenant, because covenanting involves making informed choices and infants have neither the reason nor the information to choose. Even if they did, on the theory of the Massachusetts constitution, they would generally have no options among which to choose since, if every society has the right to exclude whomever it wishes, there is no reason to suppose that there must be somewhere for them to go. As a result it is a pious fiction that the people of the United States—the current body of citizens—is the product of individual consent. With the exception of American Indians and African Americans, most Americans have ancestors who chose America and many have ancestors who chose to be American. (People whose ancestors came before the Declaration of Independence cannot be said to have done even that.) But that would be morally relevant only if my ancestors' choices were binding on me. The fact that I am free, on the theory of the Massachusetts constitution, to leave reflects the extent to which we liberals (and like Kesler I am using that term in a sense that includes not just Barney Frank but Bill Clinton and Newt Gingrich) do not think that is so.

Once you begin to think about children and birthright citizenship, it seems to me you have to give up the idea that real consent, of the sort that liberals have imagined—that is, free choice among real options—is really what underlies the citizenship of most citizens anywhere, even in the liberal democracies, today.

I offer this line of thought as an example of the sort of places to which one might be led by thinking about immigration without the constraint of having to fit our interpretation to the history of American law, ideology, and political rhetoric. And, inspired as I say by Carens, I ask us to think about why we should care about what George Washington or Thomas Jefferson or Abraham Lincoln thought about these matters. If they were right, then we can agree with them; if they are wrong, we must reject them. What matters, surely, is what is right. If that is so, then the question Kesler asks as to "whether those original principles are so disfigured by racism, ethnocentrism, and other ills as to be unworthy" will not much trouble us, since we will be grounding our principles elsewhere. I think there is something to be said for a more abstract approach since, unlike him, I do not think we can get away from the fact that, while some of the Founders' principles are not so marred, others of them are. Like all of us, the Founders were not entirely consistent: They did not always agree with themselves let alone with each other, and consent to the founding documents was given in a complex series of staged processes by many people for many different sorts of reasons.

One answer, of course, to the question of why we should care about the Founders is the one I gave at the start: This is how the debate will be carried on. But another answer, one given by Michael Oakeshott many years ago, is that effective citizenship requires that we all have "a knowledge as profound as we can make it, of our tradition of political behaviour."[3] Oakeshott isn't just saying (as I did) that we need this for the instrumental reason that this is how people actually do argue; rather, he is saying it because he thinks it is the only way to argue about such matters, that only within a tradition of thought and practice is there any political argument to be had. I don't think I agree with Oakeshott's way of defending this claim. But even if I did, I should say that "our" tradition of political behavior includes a great deal of abstract philosophical argument—from John Locke to John Rawls—and therefore that level of argument is important, even if the public debates of our fellow citizens will largely be framed at a less abstract level.

With so much about one methodological preliminary, I should like to return to Kesler's historically inspired framing of the issues. Fundamentally he has asked us to view the question of what we should require of those who become citizens by immigration as properly answered by distinguishing between two aspects of the cultural understanding of every human being. On the one hand there is political or civic understanding, that is, a civic culture, what we here call our civil religion. It is agreed on all—or, at least, almost all—sides that there is a core of political values, including adherence to the Constitution and its principles, that must be assented to by every naturalizing immigrant. As Lawrence Fuchs pointed out,[4] it is, in practice, even more important to require this of birthright citizens. The stability of liberal institutions depends on a practical assent to our constitutional arrangements.

On the other hand, there is a body of culture, of which religion in this country is the official paradigm, about which we say that it is up to each citizen to make his or her own choices. We do not have religious tests for public office as a matter of deep constitutional principle; but we do not have them for immigrants either. This is because we are committed to liberal principles, and religious freedom is historically central to liberalism.

With this framing we can ask the central questions about naturalization: How much of immigrant culture should be treated, like religion in this model, as assimilable without alteration? How much of it, like political culture, must be altered where it does not fit with what "Americanness" requires?

The liberal instinct, I think, is to insist that we should require of citizens in the realm of culture only what must be required in order to preserve the republic. I think it follows that we cannot impose a national culture on birthright citizens more substantial than a knowledge of the language of government and of the political culture—which includes, in my judgment, not just acceptance of the Constitution but some understanding and acceptance of liberal principles. In the case of birthright citizens this does not mean that we can expel those who refuse this understanding: We cannot kick out the Aryan nation or those who endorse the republic of New Africa. But it does mean that it is a reasonable political project—one that properly shapes public education—to raise as many citizens as we can with a faith in the American political creed.

Notice, however, that since immigrants are being invited into a contract, we could ask more of them than that. Once we agree that we are free to keep out some people who want to come in—and that is part of what we accept in accepting a system of nation-states—then we are free to think about the basis on which we will let them in. Because birthright citizens do not have a real choice and because, as citizens willy-nilly, they have the same right as the rest of us to determine what the culture is, we cannot impose on them what we can impose on immigrants.

That is how things stand, I think, as a matter of abstract principle. Of course, there are moral constraints on what we can ask. We cannot ask them to give up their rights, including freedom of conscience; we cannot set up a system of immigration that is racist, because racism is wrong; we cannot, as a matter of morality, refuse entry to those whose return would lead to their persecution or death. But we certainly can ask them to take on more than the political culture, if we want to, as a matter of abstract principle.

The question, however, is not whether we may do this, but whether we should. And here I confess I am on the side of asking less rather than more. Those who want to ask more are usually motivated by the thought that unassimilated immigrants will lead us down the path to balkanization, to the disuniting of America. But there is no reason at all to think that most, even many, immigrants need to be coerced into accepting Americanization. My colleague Diana Eck in her project on new American religions is finding that the religions of East and South Asia that have taken up full residence here have followed the pattern set by Catholicism and Judaism and become in their political theology quite Protestant, accepting not only the separation of church and state (which is the view of the vast majority of American Muslims, Buddhists, Jains, and so on) but also moving towards views that stress the individual conscience. My view is that there is no real need to require anything of immigrants in the cultural quarter because there is no real danger of balkanization. Even about those immigrants who hold un-Protestant understandings of religion, I am inclined to say that, if we have a reason to let them in, they pose no greater threat to the republic than do the isolationism and eccentricity of the Amish.

Language here is the exception not because of the cultural inassimilability of those who speak languages other than English, but because it is a precondition of proper participation in the civic culture. But, here again, if we have reason to allow in immigrants (for example, as spouses or parents of citizens), then the few who do not learn English do not pose much of a threat to the stability of the republic.

It tells us something about this country that, when I spoke at the conference, I said "us" Americans without hesitation even though I was then stuck in a nine-month backlog between the naturalization examination and my swearing-in as a citizen. That delay deprived me of the opportunity of voting in my first American local elections, which I had been hoping to do despite (or perhaps, in part, because of) the cynicism that my expression of this desire elicited among so many of my (now) fellow citizens. As I swore the naturalization oath in Faneuil Hall, with John Quincy Adams and Frederick Douglass both looking on, I found myself moved, as so many new Americans have found themselves moved, by this moment of formal commitment and incorporation.

Not everyone around me that day was willing to admit to emotion. One of my neighbors had lived in the United States all his adult life, having emigrated from Portugal; he had a native-born American wife and American children. He admitted to nothing more than practical motivations—he wanted, for example, a passport with which to travel to reconcile himself with his elderly father—and complained a good deal that the length of the proceedings was delaying our lunch. Another was an elderly Dominican, who understood none of the questions he was asked by the INS official; finally, the official sought (and found just a few seats away) someone who could speak to him in "his language" so that she could confirm that he had, indeed, not been married or divorced in the interval since his examination. And a third was a Cambodian who asked me how to write his name, since the instructions required both that you should use your normal signature and that you should sign each of the names on the form separately in cursive roman script. His own normal signature did not, as he showed me, meet these specifications, so he signed the document in an artificial signature, designed to meet all the conditions save that the signature should be normal.

This experience reinforced in me a conviction that I felt often at our conference; namely, that in thinking about immigration and naturalization we should always bear in mind that it is a process engaged in by particular human beings with their particular circumstances, purposes, and needs. Theories of naturalization that require too much of these particular persons will only invite them to feign feelings and beliefs that they do not have. What Locke, that great liberal, said apropos of religious conviction goes as well for patriotic sentiment and belief: you cannot coerce the "voluntary and secret choice of the mind."

The image stays with me of that Cambodian, reading a form that told him that his naturalization document would be invalid if he did not sign it in the prescribed manner—even though, as a result, what he wrote could not be, in any reasonable understanding, his normal signature. This is not, of course, a substantial imposition, even if it is a thoughtless and unreasonable one. But those who want to ratchet up the demands for naturalization in the name of an ideal image of American citizenship ought, I think, to be asked always to bear the human effects of their demands in mind. They ought also to ask themselves how it is that the republic has survived so long with native-born citizens who often could not meet the demands they would impose.

I speak English of a sort; I am committed to the liberal principles that I see in what is best in American tradition at the founding and since; and I know something of the documents that embody that tradition and something of the history that has been its life. That—along with a life free from felony, drug abuse, alcoholism, and prostitution—is most of what was asked of me as I sought to become a citizen. I do not see that the stability of the republic requires from me and other immigrants much more than this, but I know there are others who want me to be filled up with stories of Washington and Lincoln, the plot of *Moby Dick*, a taste for Longfellow or Hawthorne or Dickinson, and a whole lot else.

My view is that (assuming the moral acceptability of the system of nation-states) we *could* ask such things of immigrants who are not political asylees (to whom we have a duty that makes the imposition of such conditions morally intolerable) or spouses of citizens (whom we ought to admit because of the right of citizens to a family life). But I confess I do not think America should ask more. If asked why, I would say that the fundamental liberal vision—the fundamental American vision—is of humans as free men and women constructing a common life; and in making up your own life, the options you appropriate in the sphere of culture beyond the civic are so central that that vision suggests we should leave them up to you.[5]

Notes

1. This conversation occurred on the opening night of our conference, and it helped me a great deal both in my response to much of what was said in those few days and in my thinking since.

2. Some very interesting work on this question can be found in Robert McKim and Jeff McMahan, eds., *The Morality of Nationalism* (New York: Oxford University Press, 1997).

3. Michael Oakeshott, "Political Education," in *Rationalism in Politics and Other Essays* (Indianapolis: Liberty Fund, 1991), 61.

4. In his opening remarks at our conference.

5. It is important to insist that a concern for autonomy is not inconsistent with valuing sociality and relationship. An autonomous self is a human self; and we are, as Aristotle long ago insisted, creatures of the *polis*, social beings. We are social in many ways and for many reasons. Sociality is, first, a human end—something valued for itself. Then, there is the sociality of mutual dependence. And, finally, we are social because many other things we value—literature and the arts, education, money, food, and housing—depend essentially on society for their production. This is instrumental sociality. To have autonomy as a value is not, therefore, to refuse to acknowledge the dependence of the good for each of us on relationships with others. See my "Preliminary Thoughts on Liberal Education," *New Political Science* 39 (Winter/Spring 1997): 41–62.

2

"Am I an American or Not?"[1] Reflections on Citizenship, Americanization, and Race

Juan F. Perea

In this chapter I focus on the roles that race and racism have played in our conception of American citizenship and in the distribution of opportunities to acquire American citizenship. Racism in American history poses formidable challenges to traditional conceptions of the meaning of American citizenship and nationality. One challenge posed by the persistence of racism throughout our history lies in whether statements of liberal, egalitarian founding principles of American citizenship are accurate and complete descriptions. A theoretical challenge posed by racism is the extent to which our theory of American citizenship should be derived from history or should exist in an abstract realm of principle somewhat independent of the experience of different American peoples. As Lawrence Levine has written:

> To teach a history that excludes large areas of American culture and ignores the experiences of significant segments of the American people is to teach a history that fails to touch us, that fails to explain America to us or to anyone else.[2]

Charles Kesler's chapter argues for a traditional, aspirational view of American citizenship. Kesler argues that the meaning of American citi-

My thanks to participants in the Duke University Workshop on Citizenship and Naturalization for their helpful comments on an earlier draft of this paper. I owe special thanks to Noah Pickus, conference organizer, and Michael Olivas for their insightful comments. Quotations from other authors in this volume are taken from drafts presented at the Duke Workshop.

49

zenship should be founded on abstract principles articulated in the founding documents and in the words of the Framers during the founding era. He finds American citizenship "grounded in the natural rights of mankind, pledged to liberty of conscience, commanded to distribute its privileges and immunities to all." Later, Kesler quotes George Washington's promise of haven for "the oppressed and persecuted of all nations and religions," and concludes that the United States lived up to Washington's promise, adopting an unprecedentedly liberal immigration policy "and generously extending—to some sooner, to others later, but eventually to all new Americans—the privileges of citizenship on an equal basis with the original inhabitants." Kesler then describes, summarily, many instances in which the government has not lived up to its promises to immigrants or to nonimmigrant slaves and women.

There is much that is appealing in Kesler's view. The vision of American citizenship that he advances is reassuring, even inspiring. Over time, as I understand his views, we have gotten better as a nation at being inclusive and at accomplishing the difficult task of living up to those founding ideals. If this is the (or a) true story of American citizenship, then we can accept that the Framers were essentially right in the principles upon which they founded citizenship, that the country is dedicated to the welfare of all its citizens and immigrants, and that deviations from the Framers' principles represent regrettable but temporary, individual deviations from an ongoing narrative of increasing inclusion and respect for human dignity for all, regardless of race.

However, I believe that Kesler's aspirational view of American citizenship is neither accurate nor complete. Conceding that there is truth in and historical support for his views on the founding principles, I think his views do not take adequate account of the profound role that racism and racial difference have made in the allocation of opportunities for citizenship and in the treatment of nonwhite citizens of the United States, themes that also enjoy much historical support, as I shall describe later. I disagree with this limited view of the role of race in the allocation and meaning of citizenship. Rather, I assert that race has been, and continues to be, fundamental in our conception of American citizenship. I agree with Rogers Smith that, side by side with the liberal traditions of which Kesler writes, lie much less frequently acknowledged "illiberal, undemocratic traditions of ascriptive Americanism," traditions seeking to "maintain white supremacy, to preserve old gender roles, to uphold Protestantism in public life," and in other ways "to resist many egalitarian demands in liberal and democratic ideologies."[3]

A second challenge posed by American racism is the extent to which our theory of American citizenship should be derived from history. Kesler responds to this challenge by suggesting that we should detach political theory from history: "One difficulty with so readily turning history into theory—identifying historical practice with organic political principle—is that it underestimates how difficult it is to live up to the precepts of liberal republicanism." The course of racism in this country suggests either (and perhaps both) that it is difficult to live up to liberal republican principles or, as I have suggested, that these principles, not taking account of racism and a commitment to the maintenance of white supremacy, are not the full set of operative principles.

Profound difficulties also arise when political theory becomes too detached from historical experience. Kesler's views make it easy to marginalize the experiences of many nonwhite Americans as isolated instances of deviation from the "true principles" of commitment to egalitarian ideals and inclusion. Kesler's views ignore the enormous amount of social struggle that has been necessary for the achievement of greater equality for blacks, other nonwhites, and women. The Civil War, political struggles over the Reconstruction amendments, post-Reconstruction retrenchment and segregation, and the civil rights struggles of the 1940s–1960s belie the degree of national commitment to egalitarian ideals. Improvements in equality have been hard and slowly won, demonstrating how contested all egalitarian ideals have been in this country.

Another flaw in Kesler's view is that ultimately it fails to provide a persuasive explanation for a substantial portion of both American history and current events. As I describe below, for the major part of our history, race-based criteria have defined access to naturalized citizenship and to immigration. If demonstrable racism has been present as part of our traditions from the founding, and if this racism has played itself out fairly consistently until the present, then it is simply not persuasive to view racism as individual deviations from true national aspirations. The better, more persuasive explanation is to attempt to see the racism on its own terms, as an important and constitutive, rather than isolated, element in the formation of our national identity. Another, related difficulty concerns the value of a statement of principles that can be shown not to correspond well with historical experience. While such statements contribute to a celebratory tradition regarding American citizenship, the celebration tends to obscure a more balanced and realistic appraisal of American citizenship and ways that we need to continue to work to improve it.

A final challenge, illustrating the problem posed by consideration of the role that history should play in our conception of American citizenship, is whether the concept of Americanization itself can be divorced from its deployment in American history. In other words, can the term "Americanization" be reclaimed and made ours, in the words of the late Barbara Jordan, presumably with different meaning than it had during its period of ignominy during the 1920s? Or is the better view that the rightly condemned excesses of the Americanization movement are so inherently a part of the term's meaning that any renewed Americanization program would be likely to repeat the errors of the first?

By studying certain examples of the Americanization and citizenship of peoples of color, I conclude that Americanization and American citizenship can have a differential and highly contingent value dependent on one's race. Whites can be most secure in their Americanization: It appears to be the least contingent and the least apt to fluctuate in value and social meaning.[4] However, even extraordinary efforts to Americanize on the part of peoples of color, and even the achievement of American citizenship, can be extremely contingent and of little protective value when opposed by the will of the majority. Accordingly, a very significant racial component is built into American citizenship, American identity, and Americanization itself.

The Views of the Framers

There is substantial historical evidence, briefly summarized here, that the political community imagined by the Framers was intended to be limited to white, English-speaking persons.[5] Benjamin Franklin, in his *Observations on the Increase of Mankind* (1751), lamented the presence of Germans and African slaves who would render impure or darken the "lovely white and Red" complexion of the English in America. Regarding the Germans, Franklin asked:

> Why should the Palatine Boors be suffered to swarm into our settlements and, by herding together, establish their language and manners, to the exclusion of ours? Why should Pennsylvania, founded by the English, become a colony of the aliens, who will shortly be so numerous as to Germanize us instead of our Anglifying them, and will never adopt our language or customs anymore than they can acquire our complexion?[6]

Regarding African slaves, Franklin wrote, "all Africa is black or Tawney. Why increase the sons of Africa, by planting then in America, when we have so fair an opportunity, by excluding all blacks and Tawneys, of increasing the White and Red?"[7]

These excerpts show Franklin's design for a white and English-speaking America. America was deemed to belong to the English, from a very early period of our history. From Franklin's writing about the Germans, we can see that, from the beginning, one of the problems of the English colonies prior to the Revolution was the cultural, linguistic, and racial tension caused by the reaction of the dominant English population to persons who looked and sounded different from them. Therefore, in Franklin's view, those who could be made more like the English would be so shaped: The Germans had to be anglified. Those who could not be anglified (in Franklin's view, blacks) must be excluded.

Franklin was not alone in his wish for a white, English-speaking America. Thomas Jefferson and other Framers sought the same thing: a homogeneous, white, English-speaking America. Jefferson believed that blacks were intellectually and in other ways inferior to whites and that blacks "could never be incorporated into white society on equal terms."[8] Accordingly, Jefferson also proposed expelling Africans. The "African was to be removed beyond the reach of mixture," either to Santo Domingo or to Africa as the last resort.[9]

Jefferson was more accepting and admiring of the many Indians populating the new states. Although he dealt with them quite paternalistically, his view was that Indians were ultimately assimilable, able to adopt the forms of English society and the English language. They could therefore assimilate by adopting white ways. However, this was not to be a choice. Indians would either adopt the ways of the white colonists or face forcible removal from their lands and possibly extermination.[10]

Regarding language, Jefferson contemplated covering "the whole Northern, if not the southern continent, with a people speaking the same language."[11] To deal with the predominance of French speakers in newly acquired Louisiana, Jefferson proposed resettlement, at government expense, of 30,000 English-speaking Americans to "make the majority American, [and] make it an American instead of a French state."[12] In Jefferson's view, then, "American" meant English-speaking, adapted to English culture, and predominantly white, a nation from which blacks must be excluded.

The view of America as a white nation still ran strong when whites first encountered Mexicans. Senator John Calhoun opposed, on racial grounds, the U.S. annexation of Mexican lands during and after the war with Mexico:

> I know further, sir, that we have never dreamt of incorporating into our Union any but the Caucasian race—the free white race. To incorporate Mexico would be the very first instance of the kind of incorporating an Indian race; . . . I protest against such a union as that! *Ours, sir, is the Government of a white race.*[13]

Ironically, despite Calhoun's protest, the ideology of Manifest Destiny and white Anglo-Saxon supremacy had served as justification for the war against Mexico and for the subsequent annexation of approximately half of formerly Mexican territory.[14]

As another example, Stephen Douglas, during his famous debates with Abraham Lincoln, stated his view of the intent and purposes underlying American government:

> For one, I am opposed to negro citizenship in any form. I believe that this government was made on the white basis. I believe it was made by white men for the benefit of white men and their posterity forever, and I am in favor of confining the citizenship to white men—men of European birth and European descent, instead of conferring it upon Negroes and Indians, and other inferior races.[15]

While these examples are few, they are representative. They demonstrate that throughout our pre-twentieth-century history American leaders expressed the view that this country should be a white, English-speaking country.[16] This view was also implemented in our earliest naturalization statutes. The first condition for naturalized citizenship under both the naturalization laws of 1790 and 1795 was that an aspiring American be a "free, white person." This statute excluded all blacks, whether free or enslaved, and all Indians from naturalized citizenship. Although different points of view existed at the time regarding slavery and freedom, and regarding the status and possibilities for citizenship of different American peoples, it remains significant that the compromise struck in the legislation permitted only whites to naturalize. Early in our history, then, membership in the polity had strict racial and gender components: Only white males could become full members.

Naturalization and Race

In 1790, and again in 1795, only "free white persons" could become naturalized American citizens, which excluded all blacks and Indians from membership in the body politic.[17] Whiteness persisted as a condition for naturalized citizenship for eighty years, until 1870. In 1870, the naturalization laws were extended to aliens of African nativity and to persons of African descent.[18] This alteration in the naturalization laws conformed to the enactment of the Fourteenth Amendment, which reversed the *Dred Scott* decision and granted citizenship to blacks (and others) born in the United States. So as of 1870, whites and blacks were fully eligible, at least in a formal sense, for U.S. citizenship.

In 1882, the federal Chinese exclusion act suspended the immigration of Chinese laborers to the United States for ten years.[19] This act also prohibited the naturalization of Chinese persons currently resident within United States. In 1924, Congress enacted the race-based national origins quotas, which curtailed immigration severely and which attempted to replicate the demographic composition of immigrants from the late nineteenth century, most of whom were from northern European countries.[20] Also in 1924, all Indians born within the territorial limits of the United States were finally made citizens of the United States by a congressional act.[21] This act naturalized 125,000 native-born Indians. In 1943, out of deference to our Chinese ally in World War II, Congress made Chinese immigrants eligible for naturalization.[22] Finally, in 1952, the Immigration and Nationality act abolished all racial restrictions on naturalization.[23] However, the restrictive national origins quotas of 1924 remained in effect until 1965.[24] It is only since 1965, in our immigration laws, and since 1952, in our naturalization laws, that the United States can claim to be granting admission and citizenship without racial qualifications. Race neutrality in our immigration laws is a very recent event in our much longer immigration history. We have been race-conscious and racially restrictive for a much longer time than we have acted with race neutrality.

"Am I an American or Not?"

The challenge that racism poses to the liberal, egalitarian principles that represent the best of the ideology of the Founders is well demonstrated through historical example. As the brief survey of the slow, and relatively recent, abandonment of race and national origin-based exclusions in our naturalization laws shows, race has played an overt, important role in constructing the citizenry. Further historical examples will show that Americanization and its culmination, full citizenship, appear to have a contingent value, largely dependent on race, that is not widely recognized.[25] These examples provide an important counterpoint to the idea that we should not derive organic principle or political theory from history. The counterpoint is to demonstrate the limited usefulness, in explanatory and predictive power, of theory or principle divorced from history and practice. To demonstrate this point, I will discuss the Americanization of the eighteenth-century Cherokee and the citizenship of twentieth-century Japanese Americans, Mexican Americans, and the recently contested birthright citizenship of U.S.–born children of illegal immigrants.

The Cherokee

The case of the Cherokee provides a fascinating, if little known, example of attempted assimilation and adoption of American ways of life (that is, Americanization) that went for nought. Originally considered heathens like all their American Indian brethren, under the influence of Christian missionaries during the late eighteenth and early nineteenth centuries, the

Cherokee assimilated to English American society to a remarkable degree.[26]

Prior to their removal to Indian territory, the Cherokee Americanized and prospered. They learned English and attended schools for this purpose.[27] The Cherokee learned to own land as individuals and to cultivate the land and livestock as their white neighbors did. Many Cherokee became prosperous landowners and slaveholders. They accumulated property and wealth in exactly the same way that Southern whites did.[28] They also adopted the religious beliefs of the white missionaries who worked with them, becoming Methodists and Baptists.[29] The Cherokee also became expert in understanding and using the American legal system and adopted a constitutional, bicameral form of government.[30]

Reviewing this history, it is clear that the Cherokee made remarkable and successful efforts to conform to the English culture that encroached on their lands and their sovereignty. What more could any people do than adopt the cultural and legal norms of the majority society and attempt to resolve their disputes using those forms? In the words of one scholar,

> [The Cherokee] were the test case for a major re-examination of the "Indian question." They were the prime example of how far a tribe of heathen hunters could progress under benevolent guidance within one generation. Their nation contained more mission churches, more schools, more farms, more Christians than any other. They had the most stable and republican form of government. They were the most prosperous and economically self-sufficient. If one needed proof of the potential of the Indian to become a white American in everything but the color of his skin, the Cherokees provided it. For the people of Georgia, the Cherokees were a test case precisely because they were so successful.[31]

Despite the success of the Cherokee Americanization, it did not prevent their removal when confronted with the desire of white Georgians for their land. The desires of whites for Indian lands, coupled with the "alleged racial inferiority of the Indian," proved much more powerful than even highly successful assimilation by the Cherokee nation.[32] President Andrew Jackson, who sided with white Georgians in their desire to remove the Cherokee and to possess their desirable lands, was principally responsible for the removal of the Cherokee to Indian territory west of the Mississippi.[33] Although the situation of the Cherokee may be viewed as unusual because of the limited sovereignty granted to Indian tribes, this does not change the basic proposition that even the successful Americanization of the Cherokee, their concerted attempt to conform to American culture, was insufficient to appease majoritarian sentiment against them and desire for their lands.

Japanese Americans and World War II

In the many years that elapsed between Cherokee removal and World War II, there were significant changes in the American Constitution, most particularly the adoption of the Fourteenth Amendment, which guaranteed birthright citizenship and equal protection of the laws. While Japanese immigrants remained ineligible for naturalized citizenship, the U.S.-born sons and daughters of Japanese immigrants were United States citizens, by operation of the Fourteenth Amendment. But this fact alone did not settle whether they would be treated like citizens. The mass imprisonment of Japanese American citizens and Japanese aliens in concentration camps within the United States was and remains unprecedented and is now widely condemned. Approximately 70,000 of 120,000 prisoners were American citizens, yet their citizenship meant little or nothing when confronted with majoritarian desire for their exclusion from the West Coast.[34]

All of the plaintiffs in these wartime cases challenging the curfew and exclusion orders would be considered well-assimilated, Americanization success stories.[35] All were United States citizens by birth. All spoke English. Min Yasui and Mitsuye Endo were raised as Methodists. Gordon Hirabayashi was a Quaker. Min Yasui was a second lieutenant in the army infantry reserve, though after Pearl Harbor, he was told he was unacceptable for service because of his race. Fred Korematsu was a welder who attempted to volunteer for service in the navy in June 1941. Because of medical problems, he was classified 4–F and was unable to serve. Mitsuye Endo was a twenty-two-year-old clerical worker for the state of California.

Gordon Hirabayashi was twenty-four years old at the time of his incarceration. A senior at the University of Washington, he was a student officer of the YMCA and joined the university Quaker meeting. Hirabayashi dropped out of school when the Civilian Exclusion Order was issued on March 29, 1942, figuring he would not be around very long. After months of complying with curfew orders, eventually he resented the demand it placed on his life. In his words:

> I expected like every citizen to obey the law, and I did. There were twelve of us living in the YMCA dorm, and they all became my volunteer timekeepers—"Hey, it's five minutes to eight, Gordy"—and I'd dash back from the library or the coffee shop. One of the times I stopped and said, "Why the hell am I running back? *Am I an American or not?* Why am I running back and nobody else is?"[36]

Hirabayashi's loyalty, assimilation, and citizenship, however, just as that of approximately seventy thousand other Japanese Americans, were no impediment to his incarceration and to the ultimate conclusion that his imprisonment was constitutional.[37] It is by now well established that the reason for the incarceration of Japanese Americans and Japanese aliens was racism. General J. L. Dewitt, who issued and enforced the orders, testified that

> I don't want any [persons of Japanese ancestry] here. They are a dangerous element. There is no way to determine their loyalty. . . . It makes no difference whether he is an American citizen, he is still a Japanese. American citizenship does not necessarily determine loyalty. . . . we must worry about the Japanese all the time until he is wiped off the map.[38]

The discriminatory treatment of Japanese Americans because of their race becomes very clear by comparing their treatment with that of German and Italian citizens and aliens who might have posed similar threats of sabotage during World War II. Only German and Italian *aliens* were burdened by curfew and exclusion orders, and those excluded were permitted to return home promptly, unlike the Japanese. It is also clear that the degree of threat presented by Japanese citizens and aliens was knowingly and grossly exaggerated; there was never any significant military threat posed by persons of Japanese ancestry. The Justice Department's lawyers, in their briefs and representations to the Supreme Court, suppressed evidence that showed that responsible military authorities, including members of the FBI and the Office of Naval Intelligence, felt that evacuation and detention of all persons of Japanese ancestry were unnecessary and that individualized determinations of loyalty were both possible and preferable to mass, race-based incarceration.[39]

Mexican Americans and Forced Repatriation

The treatment of Mexican immigrants and citizens during the forced repatriations of the Depression era and the end of the Bracero program provides a third example of the differential value of citizenship by race. Beginning early in the twentieth century, Mexican laborers have been used as a kind of disposable labor force, pressed into service when needed, then expelled when the temporary need ends.[40] Under pressure from agricultural employers in the Southwest, Congress allowed the admission of Mexicans as temporary workers during the 1920s.[41] During the Depression, however, the enormous economic slowdown eliminated the demand for Mexican workers, who then held jobs desired by unemployed American workers. Responding to majoritarian demand for their expulsion, many lawful resident alien Mexicans were repatriated to Mexico, along with their U.S.-born citizen children. The repatriation yielded crises for Mexican American families: the parents could leave their U.S. citizen children behind as they were forced to leave, or they could take their Americanized, English-speaking, U.S. citizen children to Mexico, with absolutely no assurance that the children could return.[42] Indeed, to return, the children faced daunting requirements of documentary proof of citizenship, so that most of the "repatriated" young Mexican American citizens had no hope of ever returning to the United States.[43] Thousands of American citizens were thus "repatriated" to Mexico, or rather, forcibly removed from the United States. Here is one account of the hardships and the violation of constitutional and human rights that occurred during this episode:

> As in the days of slavery, when families were split asunder by selling certain members "downriver," Mexican families suffered the same fate. Wives often refused to return to Mexico with their husbands because their children were American born and were entitled to remain in the United States. The situation became truly heart wrenching when older children refused to join their parents on the trek south. Younger children who had no choice but to accompany their parents suffered wholesale violations of their citizenship rights. This accounts for the fact that *approximately 60 percent of those summarily expelled were children who had been born in the United States and were legally American citizens.*[44]

A similar expulsion of American citizens of Mexican descent occurred during the prosecution of "Operation Wetback," a massive crackdown on illegal immigration and drive for deportation of the 1950s. During the mass deportations, approximately 3.7 million Mexican immigrants were deported, including an unknown number of American citizens.[45] According to one scholar of the period, "There were widespread reports of abuses by the Border Patrol and charges that legal residents and in some cases American citizens had been deported, harassed and/or beaten."[46]

Denying Birthright Citizenship for Children of Undocumented Immigrants

It is tempting to believe that the repeal of racial and national origin qualifications for naturalization in 1952, the repeal of national origins quotas in 1965,[47] and the legislative achievements of the civil rights movement have successfully eliminated the worst discrimination in our immigration, naturalization, and domestic law. One could argue, therefore, that since our laws now call for equal treatment, the differential treatment of citizens by race that I identified earlier is less of a problem, or perhaps no problem at all. After all, there has been demonstrable progress in civil rights for blacks and women since this time. One could also interpret these developments as a demonstration that Kesler's version of the found-

ing principles is correct: In fact, slow, steady progress toward that difficult goal of equality can be shown.

However, more recent developments tell another story. During the
1990s we are witnessing a resurgence of nativism, anti-immigrant sentiment in many respects like the nativism of the 1920s.[48] Interestingly, far
from celebrating the relative race neutrality in our laws after 1965, some
current advocates of immigration restriction *blame* these same laws for
what they perceive as a threatening and disunifying degree of racial and
ethnic diversity in the country. Immigration restrictionists complain bit-
terly that the national origins quotas were abandoned in a deceptive way
that deliberately understated the amount of immigration from Latin
America and Asia over the past thirty years. As Peter Brimelow has written in *Alien Nation*, "The current wave of immigration—and therefore
America's shifting ethnic balance—is wholly and entirely the result of
government policy. Specifically, it is the result of the Immigration Act of
1965, and the further legislation of 1986 and 1990."[49] Brimelow laments
the increasing number of people of color in the United States and argues
for a return to its white racial roots: "The American nation has always
had a specific ethnic core. And that core has been white."[50] Brimelow's
argument for a return to race-conscious immigration policies designed to
restore white supremacy confirms the importance of race as a current
variable in immigration debates and in the conception of American nationality. While there are many less objectionable, valid arguments for
immigration restriction, and while Brimelow's may represent an extreme
position, the popularity of his book suggests that he represents a significant current of thought among those opposed to immigration.

In tandem with Brimelow's restrictionist arguments, for several years
now there have been unprecedented proposals to amend the Fourteenth
Amendment to deny birthright citizenship to U.S.-born children of undocumented immigrants. The first sentence of that amendment provides
that "All persons born . . . in the United States, and subject to the jurisdiction thereof, are citizens of the United States."[51] It is currently well accepted that U.S.-born children of undocumented immigrants are U.S.
citizens because of the Fourteenth Amendment.[52] Seeking to alter the nature of birthright citizenship in the United States, California's Governor
Pete Wilson has proposed, and Representative Elton Gallegly has sponsored, a constitutional amendment that would repeal the first sentence of
the Fourteenth Amendment and replace it with the following language:
"All persons born in the United States . . . of mothers who are citizens or
legal residents of the United States . . . are citizens of the United States."[53]
If adopted, this proposed amendment would deny birthright citizenship
to the children of undocumented immigrants. Legislation has also been
proposed, more recently, to attempt to accomplish the same objective by

defining the jurisdictional language of Section 1 of the Fourteenth Amendment to exclude the children of undocumented immigrants in the United States.[54]

These current proposals to amend the Fourteenth Amendment demonstrate the differential value of citizenship, dependent on race, in a dramatic way. According to 1996 estimates, these are the top five countries of origin of unlawful migrants: Mexico (by far the largest source at 2,700,000); El Salvador (335,000); Guatemala (165,000); Canada (120,000); and Haiti (105,000).[55] Proposals to deny citizenship to U.S.-born children of undocumented immigrants will target principally Mexican American and other Latino citizen children because of the disproportionately larger number of undocumented immigrants from Mexico and other Central American countries.

But it seems there is a racial dimension to the problem as well. Why is there such concern about an increase in the Latino citizen population of the United States, except for implicit concern about the racial and linguistic composition of the population? There appears to be no commensurate concern about whites illegally here (although this may, in part, be explained by their much smaller numbers). Dorothy Roberts has written eloquently about these proposals that seek to curtail birthright citizenship for some:

> Laws restricting the birth of citizens attempt concretely to control the demographics of the country. They are designed to reduce the actual numbers of disfavored groups in the population, but their broader impact is mainly metaphysical. They send a powerful message about who is worthy to add their children to the future community of citizens. Denying dark-skinned immigrants the right to give birth to citizens perpetuates the racist ideal of a white American identity.[56]

The attempt to amend the Fourteenth Amendment can thus be understood as an attempt to limit both the number and the rate of increase in the proportion of Latino citizens of the United States. It is an attempt to manipulate the future racial composition of the citizenry by changing the definition and understanding of birthright citizenship. By reducing the otherwise larger number of Latino U.S. citizens, this amendment also seeks to limit the political influence and participation of Latino people in U.S. politics. The proposed amendment implies that undocumented Latinos, and other illegal immigrants, are less valuable contributors to the American citizenry than others. Once again, the citizenship of people of color, this time the birthright citizenship of Mexicans and other Latinos, is being treated as less valuable than the citizenship of others.

Even though the proposed amendment appears unlikely to succeed for now, the current distaste for undocumented immigrants and for the demographic changes occurring in the United States provides a political climate in which such an amendment could succeed in the future. Commentators have recognized the damage to equality that this amendment would reap.[57] Some commentators have also recognized that if birthright citizenship becomes contingent on a notion of communitarian consent—which is the flawed conceptual underpinning of the proposed amendment—then we have renewed our embrace of the *Dred Scott* decision and its consensual logic, based on the Framers' intent to exclude American blacks from citizenship.[58]

The early experience of the Cherokee demonstrates that even consummate assimilation does not guarantee acceptance by a hostile majority. As in the case of Japanese Americans during World War II, the treatment of Mexican American citizens during the mass repatriation of the 1930s and Operation Wetback demonstrates that U.S. citizenship had very little value for these groups when confronted with majoritarian will for their expulsion. Rather than protect Japanese American and Mexican American citizens and rather than act deliberately to ascertain loyalty or possible citizenship, respectively, government authorities relied on group determinations based on race and ancestry and ignored the citizenship of many of those imprisoned or forced to leave the United States. So in extreme circumstances, when constitutional principles are tested and the perceived need for national unity is great, we can observe a majoritarian tendency to act against minority citizens, regardless of Americanization and regardless of citizenship.

The proposed amendment to the Constitution in particular wreaks havoc, I think, with the cogency of Kesler's promise and principles of American citizenship. For how, after the important changes to our immigration and naturalization laws of the 1950s and 1960s, can we find consistency between principles of equal citizenship and liberal egalitarianism and the move to exclude from citizenship a group of people defined largely by national origin and nonwhite race? It seems very difficult, and not persuasive, to minimize the importance of a proposed constitutional amendment, together with our long history of race-based exclusion from citizenship, as mere stray deviations from otherwise sound principles. The better view—better because it explains why an amendment denying birthright citizenship would even be proposed today—is to recognize the important, constitutive roles of race, racism, and maintenance of white supremacy as parts of American ideology and nationality.

The Proposed Revival of Americanization

If I am right that the value of citizenship varies by race, then I necessarily raise a question about the relation of race to Americanization, the process through which the country attempts to assimilate immigrants and make them citizens. I have argued earlier that assimilation, in the cases of the Cherokee and Japanese Americans, was of little avail when their civil rights interfered with the will of a majority of Americans. So I would argue that, like citizenship, Americanization has less value, in general, for people of color than for white immigrants. Indeed, some commentators have remarked on the extent to which Americanization has depended on adopting our existing racial hierarchies.[59]

The Commission on Immigration Reform has reiterated "its call for the Americanization of new immigrants, that is, the cultivation of a shared commitment to the American values of liberty, democracy and equal opportunity."[60] The commission envisions the core of American nationality as adherence to these principles: "Lawfully admitted newcomers of any ancestral nationality—without regard to race, ethnicity, or religion—truly become Americans when they give allegiance to these principles and values."[61] The commission's 1997 report states several recommendations: for orienting and educating immigrants about our civic culture; for the acquisition of English; for testing the English-language competence of aspiring immigrants; and for federal and state support for these aspects of Americanization.[62] The commission recognizes that immigration represents a *mutual and reciprocal* process and that "Americanization cannot be forced."[63] The commission report states:

> Immigration presents mutual obligations. Immigrants must accept the obligations we impose—to obey our laws, to pay taxes, to respect other cultures and ethnic groups. At the same time, citizens incur obligations to provide an environment in which newcomers can become fully participating members of our society.[64]

The commission also recommends education in our history and civic culture for all students, "immigrants and natives alike."[65] The commission advocates a strong role for federal, state, and local governments and private institutions in the education of immigrants and aspiring citizens, regarding our civic culture, our democratic institutions, and English-language instruction.

The commission has altered its view of Americanization from the traditional view of one-way adaptation by immigrants to majoritarian norms to a reciprocal and more mutually respectful process. I believe this change is crucial, for Americans must learn to appreciate their new citizens and aspiring citizens and to treat them with less resentment, racism, and distrust. A reconceived Americanization, based on widespread education in the content and ideals of our civic culture, begins to counteract the massive anti-immigrant rhetoric that has swept the country in recent years, fomenting distrust and animosity towards legal and illegal immigrants alike.[66]

The commission has written that Americanization involves "a shared commitment to the American values of liberty, democracy, and equal opportunity." These are core American values, and I believe this is the most important meaning of Americanization and U.S. nationality: Joining the nation must mean agreeing to abide by its enduring values and constitutional, democratic structures for political expression. In my view, the phrase "commitment to the American values of liberty, democracy, and equal opportunity" expresses well the essence of the civic culture that we ask aspiring immigrants to join.

Interestingly, the commission's current expression of the substance of our civic culture does not seem very different from much earlier understandings of American nationalism, including Kesler's exposition of the founding principles. As Philip Gleason has written, American nationalism was always based on ideology:

> A sense of distinctive peoplehood could be founded only on ideas . . . because the great majority of Americans shared language, literature, religion, and other cultural traditions with the nation against which they had successfully rebelled. . . . The United States defined itself as a nation by commitment to the principles of liberty, equality, and government on the basis of consent, and the nationality of its people derived from their identification with those principles.[67]

However, the commission's current sense of equality as an essential component of our civic culture and ideology seems more well founded than ascribing that principle to the nation's Founders. Prior to the Fourteenth Amendment, "equality" was tautological and race-based: Only propertied white men considered themselves and each other equal. There was no notion of equality in the Constitution until 1868, with the adoption of the Equal Protection Clause of the Fourteenth Amendment. Even that equality-granting language was understood by its drafters to apply only to a formal legal equality—that is, equality in access to civil rights—and not to "social equality"—that is, full equality of stature and respect and full access to our public and private institutions. It was this very limited understanding of equality that made the separate-but-equal doctrine consistent with the equal protection clause.[68]

It is not until much later, the period between the 1940s and the 1960s, that a commitment to equality in its present-day sense of full equal treatment can be considered part of American ideology and constitutive of American nationality.[69] As a result of antidiscrimination efforts during and after World War II and the civil rights movement of the 1950s and

1960s, some national commitment to equality in all the spheres of life seems unquestionably to be part of our civic culture. However much we may debate the proper means of accomplishing equality, and the degree of its present accomplishment, equality as a constitutional and social goal seems firmly established today.

I think Americanization must be reframed, as the commission has, as a reciprocal and mutual process of accommodation, rather than a one-way process of assimilation by immigrants. Immigrants, aspiring Americans, have a relationship with current American citizens and with the country they wish to join. This relationship implies a mutuality of responsibility and obligation. As long as existing Americans do not fulfill the obligations of their civic culture, as long as we fail to honor the principles of liberty, democracy, and perhaps most importantly, equality, then we make Americanization an impossible dream. I suggest that, historically, problems of failed Americanization or assimilation are problems caused by the fear and racism of American citizens who feel little if any duty or obligation to ensure the success of aspiring immigrants, especially if those immigrants look different from them.

Existing Americans, therefore, are truly in need of Americanization. Americans must be educated about their civic culture, which includes those crucial ideals of equality, liberty, and democracy. Americans must accept the responsibility of making full membership possible to people of all races. Americans must accept that the American identity of the future, as well as the American identity of our past, has been a multiracial, not solely a white, identity. They must bury, not resurrect, the Framers' conception of America as an all-white nation.[70]

The government should educate the public in a significant way about the importance of immigrants and the value of immigrants in the future development of our society. If Congress concludes that immigration is beneficial, then our citizens should understand why immigration is deemed necessary and important. Immigrants should be seen for what they are: the building blocks of the American future, rather than unwelcome interlopers interfering in the achievement of prosperity for existing Americans. In fact, immigrants have always made prosperity possible.

Beyond Americanizing the Americanizers, immigrants must have opportunities to learn important skills that will assist them in this country. Those skills include access to education in English, access to education about our form of government, and actual participation in our government.

According to the commission's report, "The nation is strengthened when those who live in it communicate effectively with each other in English, even as many persons retain or acquire the ability to communicate in other languages."[71] This conclusion seems fairly uncontroversial and argues for expanding access to English-language classes for immigrants. No conscious immigrant can fail to recognize the utility and necessity of acquiring English to take advantage of social, employment, and educational opportunities in the United States.

Here again, a reconceived concept of Americanization as a mutual and reciprocal set of obligations is helpful. Immigrants should and will learn English. The economic and social incentives to do so are overwhelming. Indeed, recent evidence suggests that recent immigrants, especially Latinos, are acquiring English at least as fast, if not faster than past generations of immigrants.[72] But Americans should learn to respect the languages of immigrants. Americans should recognize that the United States has been a multilingual country from its beginning, when German, Dutch, French, and Indian languages could be heard in addition to English, until the present.[73] The Articles of Confederation were ordered published by the Continental Congress in French and German, in addition to English.[74] Indeed, several states were officially bilingual in different languages during the nineteenth century and, in the case of New Mexico, until 1952.[75]

Our history cautions against restriction of the use of other languages as a way of supporting the use of English. Nativism has often sought expression through the restriction of foreign languages. The nativism of the World War I–era led to numerous state laws prohibiting the teaching and use of German.[76] Today the Official English movement seeks legislation that would prohibit the federal government from acting in any language other than English, except in exceptional circumstances.[77] The suppression sought by the Official English movement is so strong that it sought to enjoin a federal naturalization ceremony conducted in Spanish for the benefit of all the newly naturalized citizens whose primary language was Spanish.[78]

Both the old and new foreign-language suppression movements sought and seek, respectively, to consolidate American identity and unity through coerced use of only English. This intent to suppress the use of non-English languages should not be confused with a genuine desire to facilitate the acquisition and use of English. One facilitates language acquisition by providing meaningful opportunities to learn, not by suppressing the use of languages with which a speaker is comfortable.

The commission's report recommends, apparently, more rigorous testing of the English-language competence of applicants for naturalization to be conducted by a standardized testing service.[79] The risk with such a proposal is that such tests might be used to deny fair access to citizenship in an ostensibly neutral way. One can ask why more rigorous requirements are deemed necessary now, at a time when immigrants are acquiring English quickly and when, as the commission report concedes, the demand for English-language instruction far exceeds the available resources.

Legal history sheds some light on the past use of language and literacy tests to exclude immigrants. In the late nineteenth century, the first goal of proponents of immigration restriction was a literacy test that, its proponents assumed, would exclude a large proportion of persons seeking admission to the United States.[80] Once such a literacy test was passed, in 1917, it failed as an exclusionary device because immigrants, chiefly from Southern Europe, were far more literate than restrictionists had anticipated.[81] Shortly thereafter, in 1924, the overtly restrictive numerical quotas based on national origins were passed. The initial creation of an English literacy requirement for naturalization is also instructive. During the height of public fears over communism and the threat to American institutions posed by foreign immigrants, this requirement was enacted by Congress, virtually without debate, in the Subversive Activities Control Act of 1950. Its intent was to exclude aliens from citizenship and voting.[82]

Any approach that makes naturalization more difficult will exclude some aspiring Americans from citizenship. In light of the past use of language restrictions to exclude aliens from citizenship, the reasons why more rigor is necessary now should be examined critically. The better approach, also recommended by the commission, is to expand the availability of English-language instruction. We need not fear the political participation of citizens whose primary language is not English. As the Supreme Court wrote in upholding provisions of the Voting Rights Act which nullified New York's literacy requirement for voting:

> Congress might well have concluded that as a means of furthering the intelligent exercise of the franchise, an ability to read or understand Spanish is as effective as ability to read English for those to whom Spanish-language newspapers and Spanish-language radio and television programs are available to inform them of election issues and governmental affairs.[83]

The commission's report also recommends a renewed and important role for the private sector in providing educational opportunities for adult immigrants:

> In recognition of the benefits they receive from immigration, the Commission urges leaders from businesses and corporations to participate in skills training, English instruction, and civics education programs for immigrants. Religious schools and institutions, charities, foundations, community organizations, public and private schools, colleges and universities also can contribute resources, facilities, and expertise.[84]

The problem with the commission's appeal to the private sector is that it recalls the private Americanization efforts of the 1920s, which often resulted in discriminatory excesses against immigrants. Some private groups can and will play a constructive role in helping immigrants adapt to U.S. society. For example, the Catholic Church and other social service groups were very helpful during the legalization programs for undocumented persons during the 1980s. However, there is also risk of reintroducing the oppressive Americanization exemplified by the Ford Motor Company's Americanization rituals of the early twentieth century, in which Americanization conveyed "a unified notion of what it meant to be American and more than a hint of nativism. It was something the native middle class did to immigrants, a coercive process by which elites pressed WASP values on immigrant workers, a form of social control."[85]

Delegating the teaching of English and crucial elements of American culture to some institutions risks discrimination and condescension towards aspiring immigrants. Under current law, for example, employers can and do legally fire employees for speaking languages other than English in the workplace.[86] Some employers engage in this practice because they and their customers are intolerant of Spanish (and Spanish speakers) and of other languages. While such an employer might be delighted to support English-language instruction, what attitude toward Spanish speakers and others is this employer going to convey in such classes? The danger in this proposal is that the prejudices of private entities will be expressed and inflicted upon aspiring immigrants, as has happened historically.

The commission's renewed emphasis on Americanization, its attempt to "take the word back" and reclaim it with a different meaning than it came to have in the 1920s, raises the crucial issue of whether Americanization can be divorced from its history such that the term can have a different meaning today than it had during the time of its greatest excesses. I do not believe it is possible to uncouple this term from the history of its implementation. So the risk posed by renewed Americanization is that there will be nothing new about it. Despite the commission's apparently more balanced approach, the risk is that "Americanization" will mean the same coerced, one-way Anglocentric assimilation that it meant in the past. For these reasons, I believe it is a mistake to resurrect "Americanization." There is much less harm in simply offering to immigrants, without fanfare or "Americanization," instruction in the English language and in American ways of government and then letting them contribute to America as they will.

The problems of a renewed Americanization mirror the problems with Kesler's promises of American citizenship. The attempt to detach principle from historical experience fails, ultimately, because it fails to account for the divergent experiences of many Americans who, because of racial differences from white Americans, do not participate in the promise of American citizenship on equal terms. The principles fail "to explain America to us or to anyone else," in the words of Lawrence Levine.[87] Worse, insistence on their exclusive validity as principles of citizenship leads to the marginalization of a parallel tradition of inegalitarianism. Excessive celebration of the aspirational principles of citizenship may lead us to forget the lived experience of many Americans. Aspiration must always be tempered by an appreciation of history and the divergent experiences of different peoples, even under ostensibly similar principles. After all, for approximately one hundred years, the separate-but-equal regime was accepted as fulfilling the Constitution's command of equal protection. But "equality" clearly meant something better for whites than for blacks during this era.

The attempt to detach Americanization from much of our historical understanding of it is bound to fail and to be unsatisfying for the same reasons. John Miller's chapter in this volume presents a one-sided and incomplete view of the Americanization movement. Miller celebrates what he calls the "original spirit" of Americanization, embodied by Frances Kellor and other hardworking Americanizers motivated by a positive desire to help new immigrants. There is no doubt that some Americanizers approached their task with good will and with the wish to include new immigrants fully in American life. Other Americanizers acted out of the more oppressive desire to achieve as much Anglo-conformity as could be achieved among predominantly Southeastern European immigrants. There is also no doubt, however, that the Americanization movement hardened, in large part because of World War I, into a harsh nativist movement. As historian John Higham has written, "The struggle with Germany . . . called forth the most strenuous nationalism and the most pervasive nativism that the United States had ever known."[88] Among the excesses of the Americanization movement were laws prohibiting the use and teaching of foreign languages, particularly German, and persecution of Americans who spoke languages other than English. Many Americans fled the United States or abandoned non-English languages to escape persecution by "superpatriots."[89]

The problem posed by any renewed attempt to reclaim the term "Americanization" is whether it is possible to detach the term from its full historical meaning, both good and bad. Can the United States adhere to some "original spirit" of Americanization, itself contested and of uncertain content, or will reintroduction of the term inevitably open the door to the multiple motivations and nativism characteristic of much of the movement? I believe that, during this time of resurgent nativism, calls for renewed Americanization will look a lot like the excesses of the 1920s version of Americanization.[90]

Miller celebrates what he calls the "original spirit" of Americanization and congratulates the commission on reintroducing this term as the way we introduce immigrants to American society. Just as with Charles Kesler, however, Miller's determination to celebrate Americanization in the abstract provides only a justification for the status quo and for repetition of a justly criticized movement. If one looks only at the positive side of Americanization (like the positive side of the founding principles), one is forced to ignore or marginalize an enormous amount of history and lived experience. To continue to ignore or minimize the real implications of that history and experience seems to me a grave error.

Celebrating the aspirational side of the founding principles and American history and ignoring or minimizing racism is insufficient, for it leads to the complacent position that aspiration, and not actuality, is good enough. The grant of citizenship alone is not enough. Incorporating in full the meaning of race and racism in our history counsels unending vigilance in the service of real equality and equal treatment for all.

Notes

1. Gordon Hirabayashi, quoted in Peter Irons, *Justice at War* (New York: Oxford University Press, 1983), 90.

2. Lawrence W. Levine, *The Opening of the American Mind* (Boston: Beacon Press, 1996), 169.

3. Rogers M. Smith, *Civic Ideals: Conflicting Visions of Citizenship in U.S. History* (New Haven: Yale University Press, 1997), 36–37.

4. Even some groups considered white, however, face differential value and contingency in the value of their citizenship. I am thinking of American Jews and the marked increase in antisemitism of recent years. Nor do I want to minimize the harshness of the Americanization movement as directed at German immigrants and citizens during the era during and after World War I. See generally John Higham, *Strangers in the Land* (New Brunswick, N.J.: Rutgers University Press, 1988), 260.

5. I rely here on the concept of the "imagined community" articulated by Benedict Anderson in *Imagined Communities: Reflections on the Origins and Spread of Nationalism*, 2nd ed. (New York: Verso, 1991).

6. Benjamin Franklin, "Observations Concerning the Increase of Mankind, Peopling of Countries, Etc.," in *Benjamin Franklin's Autobiography and Selected Writings*, ed. Larzer Ziff (New York: Holt, Rinehart, and Winston, 1967), 216, 224.

7. Franklin, "Observations," 224–25.

8. Winthrop D. Jordan, *White Over Black* (New York: Penguin Books, 1969), 436.

9. Thomas Jefferson, "Notes on the State of Virginia, Query XIV" (1844), reprinted in *Thomas Jefferson: Writings*, ed. Merrill D. Peterson (New York: Library of America, 1984). See also Juan F. Perea, *"Los Olvidados:* On the Making of Invisible People," *New York University Law Review* 70 (1995): 965, 972–75 (describing in more detail the Framers' plan for a white America). See generally Ronald Takaki, *Iron Cages: Race and Culture in Nineteenth-Century America* (New York: Knopf, 1979), 49–50 (describing Jefferson's thoughts about dealing with America's African population).

10. See Takaki, *Iron Cages,* 58–63.

11. Thomas Jefferson, "Letter to James Monroe" (Nov. 24, 1801), in *Thomas Jefferson: Writings.*

12. Thomas Jefferson, "Letter to John Dickenson" (Jan. 13, 1807), in *Thomas Jefferson: Writings,* 1169–70.

13. Cong. Globe, 30th Cong., 1st Sess., 98 (1848) (remarks of Sen. Calhoun), excerpted in *Foreigners in Their Native Land: Historical Roots of the Mexican Americans,* ed. David J. Weber (Albuquerque: University of New Mexico Press, 1973), 135.

14. For a superbly documented account of Manifest Destiny and the racial ideology at its core, see Reginald Horsman, *Race and Manifest Destiny: The Origins of American Racial Anglo–Saxonism* (Cambridge: Harvard University Press, 1981).

15. Harold Holzer, ed., *The Lincoln-Douglas Debates* (New York: HarperCollins, 1993), 54–55 (quoted excerpt from the first joint debate at Ottawa, 21 August 1858); see also 151–52, 224.

16. For a superbly researched accounting of the multiple traditions contributing to American nationality, including white supremacist and racist traditions, see Smith, *Civic Ideals.*

17. T. Alexander Aleinikoff and David Martin, *Immigration: Process and Policy,* 2nd ed. (St. Paul, Minn.: West Publishing Co., 1991), 949.

18. Aleinikoff and Martin, *Immigration: Process and Policy,* 945 (n3).

19. Aleinikoff and Martin, *Immigration: Process and Policy,* 3–5.

20. Aleinikoff and Martin, *Immigration: Process and Policy,* 52. See also Robert A. Divine, *American Immigration Policy, 1924–1952* (New Haven: Yale University Press, 1957), 10–18.

21. Felix S. Cohen, *Handbook of Federal Indian Law* (Albuquerque: University of New Mexico Press, 1942), 82. Prior to 1924, many Indians were made citizens by treaty.

22. Aleinikoff and Martin, *Immigration: Process and Policy,* 945 (n3).

23. Aleinikoff and Martin, *Immigration: Process and Policy,* 952.

24. Aleinikoff and Martin, *Immigration: Process and Policy,* 57.

25. For another account of similar examples, see Michael A. Olivas, "The Chronicles, My Grandfather's Stories, and Immigration Law: The Slave Traders' Chronicle as Racial History," *St. Louis University Law Journal* 34 (1990): 425, 430–39 (discussing America's decimation of the Cherokee nation, the history of Chinese exclusion, and discrimination against Mexicans and Mexican Americans through the Bracero program and "Operation Wetback").

26. All of the facts following in the text come from William G. McLoughlin, *Cherokees and Missionaries 1789–1839* (Norman, Okla.: University of Oklahoma Press, 1995).

27. McLoughlin, *Cherokees and Missionaries*, 124–26, 131, 184.

28. McLoughlin, *Cherokees and Missionaries*, 127–28.

29. McLoughlin, *Cherokees and Missionaries*, 148–49, 150–79.

30. McLoughlin, *Cherokees and Missionaries*, 124–25, 231–32.

31. McLoughlin, *Cherokees and Missionaries*, 245.

32. McLoughlin, *Cherokees and Missionaries*, 245.

33. McLoughlin, *Cherokees and Missionaries*, 265.

34. The wartime evacuation and exclusion of persons of Japanese ancestry was entirely consistent with the decades of prejudice and the movement for Japanese exclusion prior to the 1920s, aptly described in Roger Daniels, *The Politics of Prejudice* (Berkeley: University of California Press, 1977).

35. See *Hirabayashi v. United States*, 320 U.S. 81 (1943); *Korematsu v. United States*, 323 U.S. 214 (1944); *Yasui v. United States*, 320 U.S. 115 (1943); and *Ex Parte Mitsuye Endo*, 323 U.S. 283 (1944).

36. Irons, *Justice at War*, 90.

37. Only Mitsuye Endo was released pursuant to a petition of habeas corpus.

38. *Korematsu v. United States*, 323 U.S. 236 n.2 (Murphy, J., dissenting) (quoting testimony of General Dewitt).

39. See Irons, *Justice at War*, 186–218; and Philip Tajitsu Nash, "Moving for Redress and Justice for All: An Oral History of the Japanese American Detention Camps" (book review), *Yale Law Journal* 94 (1985): 743. Harrop A. Freeman summarized the following evidence, all known by the army and much of which was available to the Supreme Court and the public prior to the court's decisions:

> Although an army intelligence officer has made a report finding 75 per cent of the Japanese on the west coast loyal and advocating individual examinations; although the advisability of individual hearings was recognized in the Tolan reports; although individual hearings were accorded aliens other than Japanese and the vast group of Italian aliens and Italian citizens was cleared of disloyalty by October, 1942, and German aliens were permitted to return to the west coast by July; although the English experience of 73,353 hearings in six months resulting in 569 persons interned, 6,782 restricted, and 64,254 freed completely was well known, and although the army was able to test loyalty individually when it inducted evacuees into the army, it was unable to stop long enough in March, 1942, to permit of individual hearings to test the loyalty of American citizens. *That greater consideration should be accorded aliens than citizens is a bitter pill for any citizen to swallow.* (Harrop A. Freeman, "Genesis, Exodus, and Leviticus: Genealogy, Evacuation and Law," *Cornell Law Quarterly* 28 [1943]: 414, 455–56, reprinted in *The Mass Internment of Japanese Americans and the Quest for Legal Redress*, ed. Charles McClain (New York: Garland, 1994), 90–134.)

40. See generally Gilbert Paul Carrasco, "Latinos in the United States: Invitation and Exile," in *Immigrants Out! The New Nativism and the Anti-Immigrant*

Impulse in the United States, ed. Juan F. Perea (New York: New York University Press, 1997), 190–204.

41. Carrasco, "Latinos in the United States," 193.

42. Carrasco, "Latinos in the United States," 193–94; see also Abraham Hoffman, *Unwanted Mexican Americans in the Great Depression: Repatriation Pressures 1929–1939* (Tucson: University of Arizona Press, 1979), 94–96, 149–51.

43. Hoffman, *Unwanted Mexican Americans*, 95.

44. Francisco E. Balderrama and Raymond Rodriguez, *Decade of Betrayal: Mexican Repatriation in the 1930s* (Albuquerque: University of New Mexico Press, 1995), 216.

45. Carrasco, "Latinos in the United States," 197–98.

46. Kitty Calavita, *Inside the State: The Bracero Program, Immigration and the I.N.S.* (New York: Routledge, 1992), 54; and Fuchs, *American Kaleidoscope*, 124 ("Roundups also led to violations of the civil rights of Mexican-Americans. Thousands of Mexican-American citizens as well as resident aliens were arrested and detained, and some even were deported illegally").

47. Aleinikoff and Martin, *Immigration: Process and Policy*, 56–58.

48. See Joe R. Feagin, "Old Poison in New Bottles: The Deep Roots of Modern Nativism," in *Immigrants Out!*, 13–43.

49. Peter Brimelow, *Alien Nation* (New York: Random House, 1995), 75.

50. Brimelow, *Alien Nation*, 10.

51. United States Constitution, Amendment XIV, Section 1.

52. Christopher L. Eisgruber, "Birthright Citizenship and the Constitution," *New York Law Review* 72 (1997): 54–55.

53. See Note, "The Birthright Citizenship Amendment: A Threat to Equality," *Harvard Law Review* 107 (1994): 1026–27, quoting H.J. Res. 129, 103rd Cong., 1st Sess. (1993). See also H.J. Res. 117, 103rd Cong., 1st Sess. (1993) (similar in substance).

54. See H.R. 1363, 104th Cong., 1st Sess. (introduced March 30, 1995).

55. U.S. Commission on Immigration Reform, Executive Summary, "Becoming an American: Immigration and Immigrant Policy" (Washington, D.C.: Government Printing Office, 1997), 34.

56. Dorothy E. Roberts, "Who May Give Birth to Citizens? Reproduction, Eugenics, and Immigration," in *Immigrants Out!*, 205.

57. Eisgruber, "Birthright Citizenship and the Constitution," 54, 88–90; and Note, "The Birthright Citizenship Amendment," 1026, 1027–28, 1038–43.

58. For the conceptual heart of current moves to amend the Fourteenth Amendment, see Peter H. Schuck and Rogers Smith, *Citizenship Without Consent: Illegal Aliens in the American Polity* (New Haven: Yale University Press, 1985). For apt criticisms of their argument from mutual consent, see Gerald L. Neuman, "Back to Dred Scott?" *San Diego Law Review* 24 (1987): 485; and Joseph H. Carens, "Who Belongs? Theoretical and Legal Questions About Birthright Citizenship in the United States," *University of Toronto Law Journal* 37 (1987): 413.

59. Toni Morrison, "On the Backs of Blacks," in *Arguing Immigration: The Debate Over the Changing Face of America*, ed. Nicolaus Mills (New York:

Simon & Schuster, 1994); and James R. Barrett, "Americanization from the Bottom Up: Immigration and the Remaking of the Working Class in the United States, 1880–1930," in *Discovering America: Essays on the Search for an Identity*, ed. David Thelen and Frederick E. Hoxie (Urbana, Ill.: University of Illinois Press, 1994), 162, 172.

60. U.S. Commission on Immigration Reform, "Becoming an American," 6–7.

61. U.S. Commission on Immigration Reform, "Becoming an American," 5.

62. U.S. Commission on Immigration Reform, "Becoming an American," 8–12.

63. U.S. Commission on Immigration Reform, "Becoming an American," 6–7.

64. U.S. Commission on Immigration Reform, "Becoming an American," 7.

65. U.S. Commission on Immigration Reform, "Becoming an American," 10–11.

66. See, for example, Brimelow, *Alien Nation*.

67. Philip Gleason, "American Identity and Americanization," in *Concepts of Ethnicity*, ed. William Peterson, Michael Novak, and Philip Gleason (Cambridge: Harvard University Press, 1982), 59.

68. *Plessy v. Ferguson*, 163 U.S. 537 (1896).

69. Michael Kammen, *Spheres of Liberty* (Madison: University of Wisconsin Press, 1986), 161–62 (arguing that the correlation between liberty and equality arises prominently in the United States only in the twentieth century). See also Michael Omi and Howard Winant, *Racial Formation in the United States*, 2nd ed. (New York: Routledge, 1994).

70. See Brimelow, *Alien Nation*, the best–selling book which argues for restricting immigration because current immigration is changing the racial and ethnic character of the United States.

71. U.S. Commission on Immigration Reform, "Becoming an American," 5.

72. See James Crawford, *Hold Your Tongue: Bilingualism and the Politics of "English Only"* (Reading, Mass.: Addison Wesley, 1992), 126–29 ("There is no evidence that linguistic assimilation is slowing down. To the contrary, the process appears to be speeding up. This phenomenon is best documented in the case of Hispanic immigrants, whose anglicization rate has increased by 4 to 5 percent per decade over the past half century").

73. See Juan F. Perea, "Demography and Distrust: An Essay on American Languages, Cultural Pluralism, and Official English," *Minnesota Law Review* 77 (1992): 269–373 (reviewing the legal history of American multilingualism and placing the Official English movement in historical context).

74. Perea, "Demography and Distrust," 286.

75. Perea, "Demography and Distrust," 309–28.

76. See Higham, *Strangers in the Land*, 260.

77. See, for example, H.R. Rep. No. 728, 104th Cong., 2nd Sess. 1996, 1996 WL 443733 (Bilingual Voting Requirements Repeal Act of 1996). See also statement of Juan F. Perea concerning S. 356, the Language of Government Act of 1995, before the United States Senate Committee on Governmental Affairs (7 March 1996), 1996 WL 107203 (Testimony opposing proposed legislation). In response to Miller's comments about my description of the Official English movement and its

legislative results, it is worth noting that every instance of legislated multilingualism he mentions is currently under attack. The legislation cited above, if passed, would eliminate multilingual ballots. Bilingual education is currently under attack in California.

78. Mark Shaffer, "Controversial ceremony in Spanish brings tears to eyes of 76 new citizens," *Arizona Republic*, 3 July 1993.

79. U.S. Commission on Immigration Reform, "Becoming an American," 11–13, 15.

80. See Perea, "Demography and Distrust," 269, 333; Divine, *American Immigration Policy*, 5.

81. Perea, "Demography and Distrust," 335.

82. Perea, "Demography and Distrust," 337–40.

83. *Katzenbach v. Morgan*, 384 U.S. 641 (1966).

84. U.S. Commission on Immigration Reform, "Becoming an American," 12.

85. Barrett, "Americanization from the Bottom Up," 162–63.

86. See, for example, *Garcia v. Spun Steak Co.*, 998 F.2d 1480 (9th Cir. 1993), cert. denied, 512 U.S. 1228 (1994); *Garcia v. Gloor*, 618 F.2d 264 (5th Cir. 1980), cert. denied, 449 U.S. 1113 (1981). On the prevalence of national origin discrimination generally, see Juan F. Perea, "Ethnicity and Prejudice: Reevaluating 'National Origin' Discrimination Under Title VII," *William and Mary Law Review* 35 (1994): 805. In response to Miller's assertion that the EEOC sues private companies that have English-only work rules, I know of no instance in which the EEOC is prosecuting such a lawsuit. Although the EEOC has promulgated guidelines that describe English-only work rules as invalid national origin discrimination, the courts have been fairly uniform in rejecting the EEOC's guidelines and in not enforcing them against employers. See Perea, "Ethnicity and Prejudice."

87. Levine, *Opening of the American Mind*, 169.

88. Higham, *Strangers in the Land*, 332.

89. See Frederick C. Leubke, "Legal Restrictions on Foreign Languages in the Great Plains States 1917–1923," in *Languages in Conflict; Linguistic Acculturation on the Great Plains*, ed. Paul Schach (Lincoln, Nebr.: University of Nebraska Press, 1980), 1, 9; and Juan F. Perea, "Ethnicity and the Constitution," *William and Mary Law Review* 36 (1995): 571, 588–90.

90. For a detailed examination and comparison of today's nativism with the nativism of the 1920s, see Perea, *Immigrants Out!*

Reviving Americanization:
A Response to Juan Perea

John J. Miller

> And if a stranger sojourn with thee in your land, ye shall not vex
> him. But the stranger that dwelleth with you shall be unto you as one
> born among you, and thou shalt love him as thyself; for ye were
> strangers in the land of Egypt. . . .
>
> —Leviticus 19:33–34[1]

Just as the Bible encourages the people of Israel to welcome foreigners,
Juan Perea urges today's native-born Americans not to look askance at the
strangers in their land. Indeed, he suggests, the problem of assimilation is
not that newcomers aren't willing to adapt to the American way of life,
but that the folks already here won't help them do it. Specifically, he
charges, the fatal flaw of Americanization has been its unwillingness to
include nonwhites. The situation has deteriorated to the point, he writes,
that Americans are "truly in need of Americanization." He puts a little
more flesh on these bones several pages later: "A reconceived concept of
Americanization as a mutual and reciprocal set of obligations is helpful."

These passages sound like an echo—an echo that reaches back more
than eighty years to when Frances Kellor was a prominent leader of the
Americanization movement: "We shall never have an Americanized foreign-born population until we have an Americanized native-born population—nationalized and giving definitely of its thought, time, and strength
to making a better America for everybody," she said in 1916.[2] "From the
moment [the immigrant] arrives in America he needs the creative aggres-

---

This essay was written in response to a draft of Juan Perea's chapter, presented
at the Duke University Workshop on Citizenship and Naturalization, October
30–November 1, 1997.

sive attention of American institutions," she wrote in her book *Straight America*.³

Juan Perea shares more in common with the early twentieth-century Americanization movement than he may realize. The original Americanizers had many motives, but one of the primary driving forces behind what they did grew out of profound belief that foreign nationals could become patriotic Americans, so long as they received a bit of help along the way. And the Americanizers worked tirelessly to provide help for many years. By 1910 or so, writes Edward George Hartmann in his history of the Americanization movement, "practically every chamber of commerce or similar organization of every municipality of significance containing an alien population had a special immigration committee taking a vigorous and active part on behalf of the Americanization of the immigrant."⁴ The Americanizers offered classes on everything from English to hygiene to citizenship—what it meant and how to get it. They published thousands of documents on American history and government. They sponsored enormous parades. On National Americanization Day held on July 4, 1915, about 150 cities across the country participated. In Pittsburgh, an audience of 10,000 immigrants listened to 1,000 children sing patriotic songs and form a giant American flag. In Indianapolis, recently naturalized citizens gave speeches in eleven languages on the duties of American citizenship. At bottom, there can be no doubt that the Americanization movement embodied a spirit of welcoming liberal nationalism. For many years it undercut nativism's political power and created the environment in which millions of immigrants could pass through Ellis Island and become Americans.

There was no hard and fast rule saying that native-born Americans at the turn of the twentieth century had to accept strange and exotic newcomers from southern and eastern Europe just because they were white. They were deemed racially inferior by Prescott Hall and Madison Grant. According to Alabama Congressman Thomas Abercrombie, "The color of thousands of them [i.e., Slavs, Magyars, Jews, etc.] differs materially from that of the Anglo–Saxon."⁵ For years the uplifting, optimistic spirit of Americanization, however, triumphed in a way that we all should celebrate.

Perea's paper is bleak throughout, with its meditations on the Cherokee and Japanese internment, as well as its dutiful references to the illiberal views of Franklin and Jefferson—two figures, we must never forget, who were great liberals in their day. It also lacks an appreciation for a founding myth that all Americans of all backgrounds can believe and support. The stories of Chinese exclusion and Mexican deportation programs are regrettable, to be sure. They cannot and should not be forgotten. But they are not the only stories we have, and the paper unfortunately ignores the

United States' remarkable and unmatched record for generosity toward the foreign-born. Here's a story about Americanization that begins tragically but ends happily. When President William McKinley fell in 1901 to the bullet of anarchist Leon Czolgosz—an American by birth but of apparent foreign extraction—people looked to naturalization, not restriction, as an answer to their so-called immigrant problem. After McKinley's death, the Sons of the American Revolution rushed to print a small leaflet entitled *A Welcome to Immigrants and Some Good Advice*. It urged immigrants to become citizens as soon as possible. An event that might have sparked nativist paranoia did not, thanks in large part to the welcoming tradition of Americanization, which was at that point coming into fruition.[6]

Nobody can deny that Americanization fell on hard times, beginning in World War I, and was ultimately coopted by the very nativists who were its enemies for so long. But we can make a distinction between the idea of Americanization promoted by Frances Kellor and her colleagues, and the demeaned version of it that erupted some time later. We must remember that for a long time Americanization had a good run. And there's no reason why it cannot have another one now. As the late Barbara Jordan said of the word "Americanization" in 1995, "it is our word, and we are taking it back."[7]

Those who would have us believe that the Americanization movement was unremittingly bad from its inception are terribly misguided. They ignore Americanization's countless success stories. One of the best comes from *The American Kaleidoscope* by Lawrence H. Fuchs. He writes of Salvatore DeMeo, an Italian immigrant whose belongings Fuchs discovered in an old Corona cigar box. DeMeo worked at one of the mills in Waltham, Massachusetts, as a day laborer. Judging from his passport, he had earned enough money to travel back and forth between the United States and Italy several times. After his last trip, however, he settled down and took courses in the English language and American citizenship for three years, receiving hundreds of hours of instruction. DeMeo kept a sixty-seven page manual on American history and government—a typical product of the Americanization movement. In this well-worn booklet, DeMeo learned that being 100-percent American did not depend on where his grandfather came from but on obeying the laws of the United States. "All residents of America should become citizens of America. . . . America needs all the wisdom of all the people who live under her flag," he read. Underlined was the statement that a naturalized citizen should vote at every opportunity, "not just when he feels like it." He should learn about the candidates and "vote for what I believe in my own heart is right, and for the best man, no matter what his race or creed or ancestry." Fuchs found one more item in the cigar box: DeMeo's naturalization papers. We may never be able to tell from this little time capsule whether or not DeMeo became a patriotic flag-waver. But we do know that he led a productive life, worked very hard to learn about his new home, and eventually became an American citizen. And that would have been enough to make any Americanizer proud.[8]

What lessons can the old Americanization movement teach us today? Most important, Americans must have some common understanding of what it means to be an American and why being an American is special. That is exactly what the Americanization movement did as it mobilized massive amounts of private and public resources to help immigrants become Americans. A consensus formed around the spirit of Americanization and the need for native-born Americans to reach out and help their newest neighbors adjust to life in the United States. They felt a sense of responsibility. Many people thought that, if the case for assimilation were made compassionately and logically, immigrants would do what they must to win full membership in U.S. society. "Americanization is a process of education, of winning the mind and heart through instruction and enlightenment," said P. P. Claxton, the commissioner of education. He also stressed its voluntary nature. "It must depend . . . on the attractive power and the sweet reasonableness of the thing itself," he said.[9]

The U.S. Commission on Immigration Reform deserves high praise for trying to recapture the original spirit of Americanization, especially in its choice of the word "Americanization"—a tremendously useful word that nicely describes a necessary project today. The commission's report is far from perfect, but its aggressive attempt to create an environment in which immigrants can become Americans and Americans can embrace immigration is worthwhile. Far from being a "scary proposal," as Perea calls it in his original paper, the report has an inspiring faith in the decency and goodwill of ordinary Americans—a plurality of whom, according to a recent PBS poll, would like to see the flow of legal immigration remain at its current level.[10] It's tempting to nitpick at some of Perea's plainly absurd claims, such as when he speaks of "new foreign-language suppression movements" and the "coerced use of only English" at a time when millions of Hispanic children are enrolled in bilingual education programs that intentionally delay the teaching of English for many years, when federal voting laws require local political jurisdictions to print foreign-language ballots, and when the Equal Employment Opportunity Commission sues private companies that have English work rules.

Indeed, the greatest threat to American unity today comes not from the exclusionary right, but from a left that seems never to meet a group right it refuses to embrace. Americanization succeeds in fending off the particularist claims of both a nativist right that says immigrants cannot assimilate and a multicultural left that says they should not bother. Properly understood, Americanization is pro-immigrant, pro-assimilation, and grows directly out of the strongest and best traditions of our nation of immigrants.

Notes

1. This is also the epigraph to John Higham, *Strangers in the Land: Patterns of American Nativism 1860–1925* (New York: Atheneum, 1963).

2. Frances A. Kellor, "Americanization as Opportunity," *Journal of the Association of College Alumnae* (September 1916): 9, as cited in William Joseph Maxwell, "Frances Kellor in the Progressive Era: A Case Study in the Professionalization of Reform" (Ph.D. dissertation, Teachers College, Columbia University, 1968), 214.

3. Frances Kellor, *Straight America: A Call to National Service* (New York: Macmillan, 1916), 70.

4. Edward George Hartmann, *The Movement to Americanize the Immigrant* (New York: Columbia University Press, 1948), 92.

5. Quoted in Higham, *Strangers in the Land*, 168.

6. Hartmann, *Movement to Americanize*, 33; and Higham, *Strangers in the Land*, 111, 237.

7. Barbara Jordan, "The Americanization Ideal," *New York Times*, 11 September 1995, A15.

8. Lawrence H. Fuchs, *The American Kaleidoscope: Race, Ethnicity, and the Civic Culture* (Hanover, N.H.: Wesleyan University Press, 1990), 66.

9. P. P. Claxton, "Americanization," in *Immigration and Americanization: Selected Readings*, ed. Philip Davis (Boston: Ginn, 1920), 621–22.

10. Susan Page, "Poll: Fear of Immigrants Eases," *USA Today*, 13 October 1997, A1.

Part II

Nationalism and Citizenship

3

Nationalism, Cosmopolitanism, and the United States

David A. Hollinger

"Citizens of the world" rightly pride themselves on being able to see beyond the parochialism and prejudices of tribe or nation, but they have always had a hard time finding institutional structures and political constituencies to advance their cause. Even today, when economic and technological interdependence render the ideal of world citizenship more compelling than ever, the claims of tribe and nation are reasserted with an intensity that keeps *Weltburgertum* on the idealistic margins of political discourse. And for reasons demanding some respect. The claims of tribe and nation are not always products of hate. These claims are sometimes advanced as instrumental reactions to the inequalities of the global capitalist economy and to the cultural hegemony of the North Atlantic West. The human need for solidarities smaller than the species, moreover, is primal. The drive for belonging is more than an atavism to be renounced by all mature selves, and it is not easily detached from politics. The challenge is to draw "the circle of the we" in scale and specific shape that take realistic account of the legitimate demands, in our historical circumstances, of the ethnos as well as of the species.[1]

It is in relation to this challenge that the merits of national projects, including that of the United States, need to be critically assessed. Yet few discussants of nationalism, until recently, have confronted this challenge directly. Instead, we have seen an endless succession of warnings about the dangers of nationalism that dodge the question of just what affiliations can be realistically encouraged as instruments of transnational ends, and an equally endless succession of assertions of the value of group solidarity

For critical suggestions that have influenced the shape and character of this essay, I wish to thank Linda Bosniak.

that only nod at transgroup endeavors or suspect such endeavors of covertly advancing the interests of certain, particular groups. It has proven easier to laud cosmopolitanism against tribalists or to defend bounded communities against rootlessness than to bring these two perpetually satisfying but divergent discursive practices together in a single analysis of politically effective solidarities.[2] When someone suggests that elements of cosmopolitanism can be incorporated into nationalism, the risk-free response for a theorist is to mock this idea as conceptually confused, or naïve, or both.

The discussion of national projects has been encumbered, moreover, by a widespread assumption that nationalism is always essentially the same. The diversity of theories of nationalism derives, it would seem, not so much from the diversity of nationalism's manifestations and potentialities as from the failure of this or that theorist to see the essence of nationalism clearly. Thus it is said that Ernest Gellner or Anthony Smith got it right, or wrong, or that Benedict Anderson understands nationalism better than Liah Greenfeld does, or that nationalism and liberalism have defining features that render them the oil and water of modernity. By debating what nationalism ostensibly *is*, energies are deflected from the analysis of what kinds of nationalism have actually existed and what kinds are now defensible in what contexts.

What has been most often missing among theorists is a determination to build simultaneously on two simple insights that most of today's students of nationalism, however much they disagree among themselves, would probably accept if they were asked. The first is that even the least blood-intensive and least chauvinistic of national solidarities threaten to inhibit transnational projects that might serve the interests of a wider human population. The second insight is that the primal human need for belonging is poorly satisfied by solidarities that might be large enough to act effectively on challenges that are global in scope.

Fortunately, these two ideas are increasingly combined under the sign of "liberal nationalism." In the mid-1990s, prominent contributions to this movement have been made by Ernest B. Haas, Will Kymlicka, Michael Lind, Robert McKim, Jeff McMahan, David Miller, and Yael Tamir.[3] This movement is often credited with reconciling liberalism's emphasis on individual rights with nationalism's emphasis on group membership, or is accused of ignoring what are said to be structural incompatibilities of the two.[4] The movement has also directed attention to the contingency of the process by which groups are formed, perpetuated, and redefined. But the movement has been especially helpful in dealing with two concerns of many liberals.

The first is a voluntarist concern that individuals should not be bound by obligations to which they have not actually consented. Although national citizenship entailing obligations often does have a voluntary component, birth and other circumstances obviously limit choice of nationality. The second is a distributionist concern that the benefits of human community will be distributed unfairly if members of an in-group favor their own kind over the rest of humanity. Insofar as loyalty to a nation entails the favoring of one's conationals over others, national solidarity obviously diminishes one's responsiveness to the needs of the "others." At the base of these two concerns are commitments to freedom, in the first instance, and equality, in the second, that yield the dilemmas cogently invoked by Samuel Scheffler:

> We are swayed by the sophisticated, cosmopolitan rhetoric of global integration, and we are genuinely moved by the scenes of starvation and disease in faraway lands, but, at the same time, we resist those ideals of global justice that might broaden the scope of our own responsibility and threaten our standard of living. We recoil in horror from the bloody ethnic conflicts of which television has made us all spectators, but we celebrate diversity and difference and are suspicious of the idea of a common culture. We decry the fragmentation of our societies, but we seek above all else to protect and promote the interests of those who are dearest to us. We insist on our status as autonomous agents and on the centrality of freedom to choose, but increasingly we see ourselves as victims and blame others for our misfortunes, as if to indicate how little we see our own choices as counting for in a world of complex interdependencies, massive institutional structures, and breathtaking new technologies.[5]

Liberal nationalists, working in the context of the tensions identified by Scheffler, are inclined to accept group loyalties as inevitable, but to distinguish sharply between groups on the basis of liberal values, and to seek ways for people to act on group loyalties with minimal damage to people outside the group.[6] Working from the insight that goals for the species as a whole are difficult to set and even more difficult to endow with effective tools, theorists of liberal nationalism seek to clarify the means by which the instinct for belonging can be recognized while taking the least destructive of its possible forms. Not everyone is positioned to claim as their own a civic nation with democratic-egalitarian principles, but those who are so positioned can do much worse than to treat their own civic nation as a starting point for human solidarity, as an instrument for transnational goals that can mediate between the ethnos and the species. It is in this liberal nationalist frame that I want to address "the circle of the we" in relation to the national solidarity of the United States.

The case of the United States demands special attention for a number of reasons. The United States is the largest and arguably the most successful nationalist undertaking in modern history, yet it has been given short shrift in nearly all of the major treatises and anthologies on nationalism.[7] The United States has carried out its national project along lines that have been more "liberal" for a longer period of time than has been the case with most other major national projects, yet even theorists of liberal nationalism, with few exceptions, allude only in passing to the case of the United States while fashioning what they take to be a universal model.[8] More scrutiny needs to be given to the reforms of Progressivism, the New Deal, and the Great Society. All were nationalist and liberal in ways that put useful, but rarely invoked, empirical pressure on the common complaint that "liberal nationalism" is a contradiction in terms. The United States displays, moreover, an unusually large number of different ethnic groups and an exceptionally high degree of cross-group marriage and reproduction. Hence the nationalism of the United States is more thoroughly "civic" than that of many other civic nations rightly distinguished from "ethnic" nations. Although these considerations render the case of the United States worth scrutiny in the context of liberal nationalist theory, two additional considerations led me to focus on this case. This nation is the one with which I, as a specialist in U.S. history, am the most familiar; whatever contribution I may be able to make is here. I am also a citizen of the United States, and thus feel a strong interest in clarifying the character of its nationalism in relation to liberal political ends.

Why Affirm National Solidarity Now?

What is to be gained by affirming national solidarity in the United States at this time? Instead of encouraging any kind of nationalism, should not American liberals be supporting transnational causes and the interests of diasporic minorities within the United States? Given the ease with which the affirmation of the national "we" has historically gotten out of control, fostering a conformist, "100 percent Americanism," perhaps the national community has more than enough momentum already?

Reasonable as these skeptical questions are, they are not without good answers. Any society that cannot see its diverse members as somehow "in it together" is going to have trouble acting on those parts of the liberal political agenda that seek the more equitable distribution of a nation's resources. This is the primary justification for viewing sympathetically a sense of solidarity as "Americans." The United States has the lowest taxation rate in the industrialized world, yet it is awash with efforts to reduce yet further the obligations that wealthy and even comfortably middle-class Americans have for the basic health and well-being of the rest of the population. The halting efforts in the direction of social democracy taken by the United States during the Progressive Era, the New Deal, and the

Great Society were predicated on a strong national "we," as were the triumphs of the civil rights movement. In more recent years, a relatively weak sense of national community has surely been a major factor in preventing the United States from developing a system of national health care comparable to those of most industrialized nations. This weak sense of mutual obligation also facilitates the decay of the public school system, and its replacement by a series of radically unequal private and public systems designed to serve the interests of Americans of very different stations. The ideal of national solidarity is best understood, then, as directed more against the "separatism of the rich" than against the separatism of diasporic ethnoracial communities.[9]

The ethnoracial groups, whose expressions of cultural particularity are sometimes said to portend the "balkanization of America" actually serve, in today's multiculturalist milieu, to diminish the danger that American nationalism will again take on the Anglo–Protestant tribalism that has often deformed it in the past, especially in the 1920s. The ideal of national solidarity in the United States today is decidedly not ethnoracial in foundation. This ideal thus contrasts vividly with the ideals of nationalist movements of varying intensity and success that have recently been launched or renewed by Basques, Croats, Flemings, Kurds, Macedonians, Quebecois, Scots, Serbs, Sikhs, Slovakians, Tamils, and Ukrainians. The far-right politicians and white-supremacist militias who replay and extend the Anglo–Protestant chauvinism of Madison Grant are at the margins of American politics. The potential value of national solidarity is too great to be downplayed for fear that it will be taken over by Pat Buchanan.

The ethnoracial diversity of the United States also enables its civic nation to mediate more effectively than many civic nations can between the species and the varieties of humankind. The national community of the United States is a "we" that stands midway between communities of descent, on the one hand, and humanity as a whole on the other. In an era of "ethnic cleansing," political communities that cross ethnoracial barriers without pretending to be universal are vital grist for the liberal nationalist mill. Other civic nations with ethnically diverse populations—India, Kenya, Indonesia, and Canada are obvious examples—also perform this mediating function, but the United States is a conspicuous case. Its population derives from a number of different European countries, as well as from Africa, Asia, and Latin America, and it thus displays a greater range of descent-communities than do most of the established, major nation-states of Europe, Asia, and Latin America to which the United States is accustomed to comparing itself, including Argentina, China, France, Germany, Italy, Japan, Mexico, Spain, Sweden, and the United Kingdom. One need not fall into the trap of a mystical "American exceptionalism" to recognize empirically warranted differences between the United States

and certain other, specific nations and to appreciate the value of any solidarity that diminishes the constraints that often follow from ascribed
status according to descent.

The multitude of descent-communities within the United States makes
it more realistic to speak of multiple identities, of which one's identity as
"an American" can be strong without eclipsing other identities. Multiple
identities are a more important part of the history of the United States
than is often recognized. The number and intensity of religious identities
even within Christianity is a prime example. Multiple identities and affiliations are now more widely accepted within American society than ever
before. This acceptance is marked by the recent turn away from the rigid
varieties of "identity politics" that stress single, ascribed, and enduring
identities at the expense of multiple, chosen, and changeable identities.
This striking change in the doctrinal weather has helped to create an at-
mosphere in which American national solidarity can be more vigorously
explored. For that reason, this new appreciation for multiple identities
and voluntary affiliation invites a brief overview here. It is a climate in
which the hope of injecting a "cosmopolitan" element into "nationalism"
flourishes.

In the year 1995 alone, a flurry of books and articles distributed widely
through the disciplines used the prefix "post" to try to get around the
dead ends of the "identity" discourse of multiculturalism. A "post-identity" outlook, according to the editors of *After Identity*, an anthology of
legal academic writings, is a "desire to develop methodologies for thinking affirmatively about cultural identity without freezing differences
among social groups."[10] In the same year these words about "post-identity" were used to introduce this manifesto of law professors, Michael
Dyson, a professor of communications well known for his study of the
career and legacy of Malcolm X, sketched what he described as a "post-
multiculturalism" designed to respect "the integrity of particularity"
while seeking "race-transcending grounds of common embrace." Dyson's hope was to "move beyond pluralism" in order to achieve "a concrete interpretation of what diversity really means."[11] It was in 1995, too,
that I published a book entitled *Postethnic America: Beyond Multiculturalism*, in which I called attention to the historical particularity of the ethnoracial pentagon and to the deleterious effects of its use for the purposes
of cultural reform.

One of the most arresting items in the extensive but doctrinally concentrated outpouring of 1995 is Ross Posnock's essay, "Before and After
Identity," published in *Raritan*. This piece is a wide-ranging review of
what Posnock calls the "post-identity" turn. At the center of this turn,
argues Posnock, is a rehabilitation of "cosmopolitanism," understood not
as the repudiation of ethnicity but as the loosening of "its parochial grip"

and the recovery of ethnicity's connection to "the universalist tenor of the civil rights movement." Posnock describes "the new cosmopolitanism" as not just "another group identity," but as a trans- and multi-ethnic stance "wary of appeals to authenticity as regressive and insistent upon the fact that contemporary collective identities often overlap." Among the leading exemplars of this cosmopolitanism Posnock identified is a group of black intellectuals currently at Harvard: Kwame Anthony Appiah, Orlando Patterson, Randall Kennedy, Cornel West, and Henry Louis Gates Jr.[12]

Although the overused prefix "post" is not foregrounded in Todd Gitlin's *The Twilight of Common Dreams*, or in Jennifer Hochschild's *Facing up to the American Dream*, or in Michael Lind's *The Next American Nation*, or in Walter Benn Michaels's *Our America: Nativism, Modernism, and Pluralism*, these four antiphonal, widely discussed, additional books of 1995 contribute massively to the impression that this particular year was, if not a turning point, at least a chronological moment at which criticism of the confusion of color with culture and community reached an intensity and discursive range not seen in American academia for a quarter-century.[13] And the trend is intensifying well beyond academia. In 1996 a Cuban American physician wrote a powerful memoir for the *New York Times Magazine* complaining of the ascription to him of membership in a given "community" regardless of his own chosen affiliations,[14] and a group of grassroots community organizers brought out a book entitled *Beyond Identity Politics*.[15] In 1997 the radical magazine *Mother Jones* published a special issue putting identity politics behind it, and even treating the apparent demise of affirmative action as an opportunity to create new alliances across color lines.[16]

If Not Nations, What?

If the mid-1990s recognition of the dead ends of identity politics has led some defenders of the interests of minorities to look again to the American nation as a source of support, the appeal of the American national community has been simultaneously enhanced by something else: global politics in the wake of the collapse of Soviet-led communism. Nationalism, after having been treated for decades as a holdover from the past, or as something more "imagined" or "invented" than was class or ethnicity, suddenly came to be accepted as a basic reality. "Being national is the condition of our times," Geoff Eley and Ronald Grigor Suny declared in 1996.[17] Anyone who wants to see racism diminished at any place on the globe has reason to attend carefully to civic nation-states more responsive to ethnoracial diversity than the national solidarities in the Balkans and elsewhere producing headlines about "ethnic cleansing." In an utterance characteristic of the new openness to liberal varieties of nationalism, Eley and Suny declared that nationalism need not, "like racism," lead to "a politics of blood," but "could potentially lead" to the "acceptance, even celebration, of difference."[18]

If nations are going to dominate the world for at least a while longer, it becomes a matter of some importance to distinguish critically among various, specific national projects rather than to dismiss them all as equally problematic. This is so even if we cling to the long-term hope that prophets of *Weltburgertum* are not eternally to be mocked by events. But drawing those distinctions depends on a clear set of terms.

Adequately assessing a nationalism for the United States that might be defended requires attention, above all, to *cosmopolitanism*. The common equation of cosmopolitanism with world-citizenship perpetuates the either-or sense of affiliation for which Germany has been a strong vehicle, and makes cosmopolitanism seem very close to universalism.[19] One's obligations, it then seems, are either to the species or to the ethnos. What gets lost in the conflation of cosmopolitanism with universalism is the perspective on multiple identities and a culturally diverse national solidarity that Posnock attributed to a group of Harvard intellectuals when he called them, as quoted above, "cosmopolitans." In contrast to the classical notion of "rootless cosmopolitanism" so congruent with the idea of world-citizenship, the new term "rooted cosmopolitanism" has come into vogue as a way of indicating a commitment to diversity and to historical particularity at the same time.[20] One of the individuals mentioned by Posnock, the philosopher Kwame Anthony Appiah, has indeed begun to call himself a "cosmopolitan patriot," thus purposively mixing two ostensibly antithetical personae.[21] In another juxtaposition of terms generally held to be in tension with one another, the legal scholar T. Alexander Aleinikoff has recently called for a "multicultural nationalism," which is Aleinikoff's contemporary rendering of what Randolph Bourne meant by "cosmopolitanism" in 1916.[22] Yet Bourne's "cosmopolitanism" has often been taken to be a form of "pluralism," another word that can carry somewhat different meanings for different speakers. It may be helpful here to indicate how "cosmopolitanism," "universalism," and "pluralism" can be used to flag, rather than to obscure, distinctions vital to the discussion of the national project of the United States.

The word "cosmopolitanism" can serve us best if we use it to denote a push for solidarities less all-inclusive than the species-wide "we" for which the word "universalism" works very well. We can distinguish between a universalist will to find common ground and a cosmopolitan will to engage human diversity. In this view, cosmopolitanism shares with all varieties of universalism a suspicion of enclosures, but cosmopolitanism is marked by an additional element not essential to universalism itself:

recognition, acceptance, and eager exploration of diversity. Cosmopolitanism urges each individual and collective unit to absorb as much varied experience as it can, while retaining its capacity to advance its aims effectively. For cosmopolitans, the diversity of humankind is a fact; for universalists, it is a potential problem. A national solidarity can be informed by a strong cosmopolitan drive without pretending to be universalist. This is the basic outlook that Aleinikoff calls "multicultural nationalism" and that Appiah calls "cosmopolitan patriotism." This injecting of a cosmopolitan element into nationalism stops well short of a nation-denying, monolithic "world-citizenship," although cosmopolitan nationalism is compatible with the enthusiastic development and support of given transnational and even species-wide solidarities, including those directed at human rights and global warming.

Necessary as it is to distinguish "cosmopolitanism" from "universalism," it is equally important to distinguish cosmopolitanism's perspective on diversity from one that can be helpfully denoted by the word "pluralism." If we instead treat the two as synonyms, we obscure a distinction that has turned out to be a deep one within the ranks of people committed to the celebration of cultural diversity. Some of these celebrants of diversity are most concerned to protect and perpetuate the cultures of established communities of descent, while others are more inclined to encourage the voluntary formation of new communities of wider scope. "Pluralism" works well as a label for the orientation of the first of these, and "cosmopolitanism" works equally well as a label for the orientation of the second. Pluralism, in this view, is more conservative in style: It is oriented to the preexisting group and is likely to ascribe to each individual an identity with one ethnoracially defined community. Cosmopolitanism and pluralism have often been united in the common cause of promoting tolerance and diversity, but cosmopolitanism is more liberal in style: It is oriented to the individual, and expects individuals to be simultaneously and important affiliated on a voluntary basis with a number of groups (including civic and religious communities, as well as communities of descent). The particularistic emphases that came to be called "identity politics" flowed from the pluralist impulse within the multiculturalist movement, while the frustration with this politics by celebrants of diversity flowed from the cosmopolitan impulse within the same movement.

Yet "cosmopolitanism" continues to carry certain connotations for many contemporaries that render the term problematic. Cosmopolitanism seems to be an outlook appropriate only for jet-set intellectuals like Salman Rushdie and Martha Nussbaum, or is associated with eighteenth-century Paris and Konigsburg, or has been taken over by Helen Gurley Brown's "Cosmo Girl," or is simply too tied to universalism to convey the texture that many of today's self-styled cosmopolitans seek to express.

It was to break free of these difficulties of vocabulary that I developed the concept of "postethnic." It seems not to have worked. "The term *postethnic*," I explained in introducing my 1995 book, *Postethnic America*, "marks an effort to articulate and develop cosmopolitan instincts" while working within the recent era's "greater appreciation for a variety of kinds of *ethnic* connectedness." The postethnic builds upon, rather than repudiates, a recognition of the value of the ethnos, I declared. I then went on to argue for "the renewal and critical revision of those communities of descent whose progeny choose to devote their energies to these communities even after experiencing opportunities for affiliation with other kinds of people."[23] Although these ideas still strike me as sound, and appear to be more and more widely shared as the decade of the 1990s approaches its end, the term "postethnic" is rarely used to refer to this cluster of ideas. I probably should have followed my publisher's advice and entitled my book *A Cosmopolitan Manifesto*. It is sometimes better to struggle to redefine an old word than to develop and popularize a new one.[24]

The kind of nationalism indicated by "cosmopolitan" and "postethnic" as I have used these words here is a nationalism that can get along with a much thinner, less sharply defined national culture than is characteristic of most nationalisms. The very concept of "national culture" frightens some liberals, who prefer to think of national solidarity in terms of loyalty to a set of procedures and institutions.[25] Yet the constitutional order of the United States is not simply a list of abstract liberal values. It is more than an instrument of cosmopolitanism. Rather, the constitutional order of the United States is a finite historical entity with a record of specific tragedies, successes, failures, contradictions, and provincial conceits that are lost to view if we look upon it as merely a set of ideals and rules for political conduct. Millions of people, moreover, do have an "ethnic" feeling for the United States as a community to which they truly "belong."

Although efforts to clarify the basic principles of the nation are not to be disparaged, the most effective mode for presentation of a national culture for a cosmopolitan, postethnic solidarity is narrative. A national narrative true to the history of democratic institutions in the United States provides ample opportunity to address the differences as well as the similarities of Americans at different times. Part of "the story" to be told, moreover, is how the boundaries of the national solidarity came into being, how and when they were challenged and sometimes changed, and by whom. How has the United States drawn and redrawn its social borders to accommodate, repel, or subjugate this or that group? How has racism and the struggle against it proceeded in a sequence of distinctive settings? Answers to these vital questions are among the proudest products of recent scholarship. These answers can help constitute the story the nation tells about itself, and can thus partake of the "national culture" without precluding the telling of other empirically warranted stories about subnational and transnational solidarities, including communities of descent.

The United States now finds itself in a position to develop and act upon a cultural self-image as *a national solidarity committed, but often failing, to incorporate individuals from a great variety of communities of descent, on equal but not homogeneous terms, into a society with democratic aspirations inherited largely from England.*[26] There is much more to the history of the United States than this, but it is a defensible focus for a national narrative. It is defensible because the statement is true, and because it can serve to reinforce the national solidarity of the United States on liberal and cosmopolitan terms without denying the parts of American history that are not liberal and not cosmopolitan.

This conception of the national story affords ample room to display two truths now vouchsafed to historians, but often resisted by much of the public: the great extent to which the flourishing of the United States has depended on the exploitation of nonwhites, and the relative weakness, during most of the national history, of egalitarian ideals. This conception also recognizes the incontrovertible but often circumvented fact that the democratic aspirations of the republic derived primarily, although not exclusively, from England—the specific European country from which virtually all American political leaders of the Revolutionary generation directly descended. The formulation underscored above also acknowledges the individualistic focus of the American polity; individuals, not groups, are incorporated into the nation. Finally, this formulation expresses the vital idea that people can be politically equal without being culturally identical.

Historians can be expected to disagree among themselves on exactly how the narrative of the nation should be constructed; yet agreement on what the story should be primarily about may not be so elusive. The sense of that basic story sketched above may enable more scholars to tell more truths to more people about more of the nation's character than can other, comparable, one-sentence charters for the national narrative. Historians should have no client but the truth, but one truth about the world in which they practice is that it confronts them with choices about how and where to disseminate the knowledge they gain. The national culture of the United States will always include a semiofficial national narrative, no matter what historians do or do not do in relation to it. If professional historians do not try to influence that narrative, and hence the national culture of which it is so vital a part, others will control that narrative and that culture even more fully than they now do.[27]

One reason I believe historians and other scholars should try to influence the national narrative and the national culture of the United States is that men and women of learning are well equipped to remind the American public that their nation, however much it is to be cherished, is but one of many imperfect instruments of transnational goals. Loyalty to it need not be incompatible with loyalties to larger segments of humankind. Scholars are not immune from chauvinism, but they can bring to discussions of the nation a global perspective that nationalists desperately need if they are to draw "the circle of the we" as widely as their capabilities enable them to do. Plutarch tells us that Socrates declared himself to be "not an Athenian or a Greek, but a citizen of the world." Being both is a more promising ideal for our own time. Acting upon that ideal may not be easy, but the alternatives we see around us make the effort worthwhile.

Notes

1. This chapter builds upon my several previous engagements with this challenge, especially David A. Hollinger, "How Wide the Circle of the We? American Intellectuals and the Problem of the Ethnos Since World War II," *American Historical Review* 98 (1993): 317–37; David A. Hollinger, *Postethnic America: Beyond Multiculturalism* (New York: Basic Books, 1995); David A. Hollinger, "National Solidarity at the End of the Twentieth Century: Reflections on the United States and Liberal Nationalism," *Journal of American History* 84 (1997): 559–69; and David A. Hollinger, "National Culture and Communities of Descent," *Reviews in American History* 26 (1998): 312–28.

2. Just how deeply satisfying these two activities can be, and how difficult it is to withdraw from one in order to take full account of the other, is revealed in the exchanges between Martha Nussbaum and her critics in a symposium organized around Nussbaum's vindication of world citizenship. See Martha Nussbaum et al., *For Love of Country: Debating the Limits of Patriotism* (Boston: Beacon Press, 1996).

3. Ernest B. Haas, *Nationalism, Liberalism, and Progress* (Ithaca: Cornell University Press, 1997); Will Kymlicka, *Multicultural Citizenship: A Liberal Theory of Group Rights* (New York: Oxford University Press, 1995); Michael Lind, *The Next American Nation* (New York: Free Press, 1995); Robert McKim and Jeff McMahan, eds., *The Morality of Nationalism* (New York: Oxford University Press, 1997); David Miller, *On Nationality* (New York: Oxford University Press, 1995); and Yael Tamir, *Liberal Nationalism* (Princeton: Princeton University Press, 1993). Other contributors to the movement include Anthony Appiah, Kenneth Cmiel, Liah Greenfeld, Russell Hardin, Jennifer Hochschild, Michael Ignatieff, Neil MacCormick, Avashai Margalit, Martin Marty, Joseph Raz, Richard Rorty, Samuel Scheffler, Roman Szporluk, and Bernard Yack. These writers display many variations on liberal nationalism and often disagree among themselves

on many points. Although Julia Kristeva defines herself against nationalism, the specific notion of the French nation she defends in her *Nations Without Nationalism*, trans. Leon S. Roudiez (New York: Columbia University Press, 1993), is similar in vital respects to the ideal of civic nationality espoused by many self-styled liberal nationalists, in whose company she might well be counted.

4. For examples of these themes in critical assessments of liberal nationalism, see the special issue, "Philosophical Perspectives on National Identity," ed. Omar Dahbour, *Philosophical Forum* 28 (Fall 1996–Winter 1997), and "Symposium on David Miller's *On Nationality*," *Nations and Nationalism* 2 (1996): 407–51. See also Sanford Levinson, "Is Liberal Nationalism an Oxymoron?" *Ethics* 105 (1995): 626–45, and Andrew Vincent, "Liberal Nationalism: An Irresponsible Compound?" *Political Studies* 45 (1997): 275–95.

5. Samuel Scheffler, *Families, Nations, and Strangers* (Lawrence: University of Kansas Department of Philosophy, 1995), 19.

6. See especially Scheffler, *Families, Nations, and Strangers*; Jonathan Glover, "Nations, Identity, and Conflict," in McKim and McMahan, *Morality of Nationalism*, 11–30; Thomas Hurka, "The Justification of National Partiality," in McKim and McMahan, *Morality of Nationalism*, 139–57; and Stephen Nathanson, "Nationalism and the Limits of Global Humanism," in McKim and McMahan, *Morality of Nationalism*, 176–87.

7. This is true, for example, of three of the most important collections of the 1990s: Homi Bhabha, ed., *Nation and Narration* (New York: Routledge, 1990); John Hutchinson and Anthony D. Smith, eds., *Nationalism* (New York: Oxford University Press, 1994); and Geoff Eley and Ronald Grigor Suny, eds., *Becoming National: A Reader* (New York: Oxford University Press, 1996). Even Benedict Anderson provides only episodic treatment of the United States while discussing "creole nationalism" in his influential book, *Imagined Communities: Reflections on the Origins and Spread of Nationalism* (New York: Verso, 1991). The United States is mentioned only in a single footnote in Ernest Gellner, *Nations and Nationalism* (Ithaca: Cornell University Press, 1983).

8. This is true even of the excellent essays collected in McKim and McMahan, *Morality of Nationalism*. One adamantly Americocentric defense of liberal nationalism is Lind, *Next American Nation*, written not by a political theorist but by a journalist. The treatment of the United States in one of the most rigorous of the works contributed to the debate by a philosopher—Kymlicka's *Multicultural Citizenship*—is weakened by its author's apparent belief that a model for dealing with cultural diversity can be defended in one liberal society only if it can also be defended in all liberal societies.

9. Here, I draw on formulations I offered in David A. Hollinger, "Postethnic Nationality and the Separatism of the Rich," *Public Historian* 19 (1997): 23–28.

10. Dan Danielsen and Karen Engle, eds., *After Identity: A Reader in Law and Culture* (New York: Routledge, 1995), xv.

11. Michael Dyson, "Contesting Racial Amnesia: From Identity Politics to Post-Multiculturalism," in *Higher Education Under Fire: Politics, Economics, and the Crisis of the Humanities*, ed. Michael Berube and Cary Nelson (New York: Routledge, 1995), 336–44, esp. 343.

12. Ross Posnock, "Before and After Identity," *Raritan* 15 (Summer 1995): 101–02.

13. Todd Gitlin, *The Twilight of Common Dreams* (New York: Holt, 1995); Jennifer Hochschild, *Facing Up to the American Dream* (Princeton: Princeton University Press, 1995); Michael Lind, *Next American Nation*; and Walter Benn Michaels, *Our America: Nativism, Modernism, and Pluralism* (Berkeley: University of California Press, 1995).

14. Rafael Campo, "'Give Back to Your Community,' She Said," *New York Times Magazine*, 1 September 1996, 42–45. For a more angry account of being subjected to ascribed categories, see Jim Chen, "Unloving," *Iowa Law Review* 80 (1994): 145–75, which also includes a more elaborate theoretical and constitutional argument against the use of ethnic and racial classifications by universities. In relation to Campo's personal testimony, however, see especially Chen's narrative (147–49) of how he was treated by administrators and by an Asian American student organization during a recruitment visit to the law school at UC Berkeley.

15. John Anner, ed., *Beyond Identity Politics: Emerging Social Justice Movements in Communities of Color* (Boston: South End Press, 1996).

16. *Mother Jones*, October 1997. See especially the editorial introduction to that issue, "The Race Course," and Michael Lind's article "Changing Colors," 3, 39–43, 75.

17. Eley and Suny, "Introduction," in *Becoming National*, 32.

18. Ibid.

19. Friedrich Meinecke, *Cosmopolitanism and Nation-State*, trans. Robert B. Kimber (Princeton: Princeton University Press, 1970).

20. Mitchell Cohen, "Rooted Cosmopolitanism," *Dissent*, Fall 1992, 487–93; Bruce Ackerman, "Rooted Cosmopolitanism," *Ethics* 114 (1994): 516–35.

21. Kwame Anthony Appiah, "Cosmopolitan Patriots," *Critical Inquiry* 23 (Spring 1997).

22. T. Alexander Aleinikoff, "A Multicultural Nationalism?" *American Prospect* (January–February 1998): 80–86. Aleinikoff builds upon Randolph Bourne, "Trans-national America," originally published in *Atlantic Monthly* in 1916 and reprinted in *The American Intellectual Tradition: A Sourcebook*, ed. David A. Hollinger and Charles Capper, 3rd ed. (New York: Oxford University Press, 1997), 171–80.

23. Hollinger, *Postethnic America*, 4–5, 118. As I explain in that book, the term "postethnic" first came to my attention in the writings of Werner Sollors, whose influence on my own thinking I am always glad for another opportunity to acknowledge.

24. For an important collection critically exploring the political potential of the cosmopolitan ideal today, see Pheng Cheah and Bruce Robbins, eds., *Cosmopolitics: Thinking and Feeling Beyond the Nation* (Minneapolis: University of Minnesota Press, 1998), especially the essay by Amanda Anderson, "Cosmopolitanism, Universalism, and the Divided Legacies of Modernity."

25. The most eloquent critique of the concept of national culture written by someone whose views are otherwise similar to my own is Kwame Anthony Appiah. See his "Against National Culture," in *Text and Nation: Cross-Disciplinary*

Essays on Cultural and National Identities, ed. Laura Garcia-Moreno and Peter C. Pfeiffer (Columbia: University of South Carolina Press, 1996), 175–90, and "Cosmopolitan Patriots."

26. I draw here on a formulation of a "charter" for a national narrative I first offered in "National Culture and Communities of Descent," 325–26.

27. For helpful accounts of recent disputes over the National History Standards, the Enola Gay exhibit at the Smithsonian Institution, and other efforts to construct a semiofficial national narrative, see Gary Nash, Ross Dunn, and Charlotte Crabtree, *History on Trial: Culture Wars and the Teaching of the Past* (New York: Knopf, 1997), and Edward T. Linenthal and Tom Engelhardt, eds., *History Wars: The Enola Gay and Other Battles for the American Past* (New York: Holt, 1996).

A National Solidarity? A Response to David Hollinger

Linda S. Bosniak

David Hollinger's paper is an extremely thoughtful reflection on the intellectual anatomy of culture wars in recent American thought, and makes an important contribution to the debates over American national identity as well. There is a great deal to say in response, but given my limited space, I am going to focus on what I take to be his ultimate normative point, which is that we ought not to be afraid to treat the American nation as a fundamental and vital source of social solidarity—and that, indeed, we ought to actively foster and celebrate American national solidarity.

Hollinger doesn't actually use the word "citizenship" in his paper, but his argument on behalf of national solidarity in the United States clearly embodies a particular vision of citizenship. As I see it, this vision has two principal features. First, as against the multiculturalists and postnationalists, he argues that the nation-state must still be regarded as the preeminent site of citizenship. That is not to say we don't maintain other important commitments and affiliations, but the solidarity we maintain at the level of the nation—the solidarity of national citizenship—ought to be regarded as primary.

Second, as against traditional liberal thinkers, Hollinger argues for what we might call a "thicker," more substantial sense of national citizenship identity. Where liberals tend to regard the civic nation of the United States as a kind of neutral container in which people's various subnational solidarities and cultures can flourish, Hollinger views the American nation as itself both an object of community solidarity and as a source of culture.

This essay was written in response to a draft of David Hollinger's chapter, presented at the Duke University Workshop on Citizenship and Naturalization, October 30–November 1, 1997.

I would like to make three comments on his vision of national solidarity, each of which I can only touch on. The first concerns the marriage he proposes between liberalism and nationalism, the second addresses the plausibility of his vision of national solidarity, and the third its desirability.

First, on liberal nationalism: Hollinger is one of a growing group of scholars who have recently begun to urge a rehabilitation of nationalism in liberal terms.[1] This literature represents an important effort to resolve the endless debates in academic circles between liberals and communitarians by attempting to accommodate the kinds of commitments embraced by both camps.[2] But liberal nationalisms are not all alike, and I have two observations about Hollinger's approach in particular.

The first is simply to note that Hollinger is not addressing what is probably regarded as the thorniest question that the liberal nationalist project has to face: that is the question of whether it is possible to combine the liberal commitment to ethical universalism with the particularist claims associated with the nation. The tension between universalism and particularism that is inherent in the liberal nationalist project is what prompted Sanford Levinson to ask in a recent essay whether liberal nationalism should be regarded as an "oxymoron."[3] Hollinger sidesteps this question by focusing on the tensions between universalism and particularism as they are played out *within* the nation-state. In other words, he begins by presuming the nation to be the relevant normative universe, and then asks what kind of nation we are going to have—one with universalist values or one with particularist values? This is why he uses the term "cosmopolitanism" the way he does. By cosmopolitanism, he does not mean what he elsewhere calls "species-wide solidarity,"[4] which is what many political philosophers mean by the term; rather he means liberal nationalism, as contrasted with particularist forms of nationalism. The point is simply that he does not begin the discussion at the beginning by asking the fundamental liberal question of why we should embrace nationalism at all. He assumes nationalism and simply asks what kind.

My other observation about Hollinger's liberal nationalism is that there is a certain ambiguity about the role that liberalism ends up playing in the young marriage. As I said earlier, Hollinger views American cultural liberalism not merely as a neutral enabling environment for the diversity of cultural commitments that Americans maintain, but as itself a form of culture—the predominant national culture, whose defining ethos is openness to diversity. In this formulation, liberalism is no longer being treated in purely procedural terms; it is being treated as a substantive cultural value in itself.

The problem with this approach is that liberalism-as-procedure and liberalism-as-substance are sometimes going to be at odds with one another. Take the question of what an applicant for citizenship should be required to know of American politics and culture in order to naturalize. On the one hand, Hollinger's staunch commitments to pluralism and diversity and liberal tolerance would suggest that imposing any but the most minimal requirements would be inconsistent with core American cultural values. (In fact, he makes a point of noting that France, another nation-state committed to civic-national principles, is "more totalizing in its cultural demands than is the contemporary United States in its response to immigrants.") The problem, though, is that a purely laissez-faire approach might end up undermining the country's liberal culture in the long run, since many new citizens might not share the knowledge and convictions that provide this culture's foundation. One might therefore argue that, to ensure that this country's distinctively liberal national culture is embraced and fostered, a mastery of at least some core American values and principles is essential. But of course, imposing such a requirement presents the prospect of endorsing a distinctly illiberal policy in the name of liberalism. These are paradoxes that we need to address.

My second broad comment concerns the plausibility of developing the kind of American national solidarity that Hollinger advocates. Clearly, "the story" he tells of how this country "now finds itself in a position to develop and act upon a cultural self-image as a national solidarity" is a very hopeful one. But I wonder how realistic this story is, either for today or for the foreseeable future. Because even conceding that he is right that this country is now culturally positioned to move beyond both racism and the most divisive forms of identity politics, race and culture are by no means all that divides Americans. The vast economic disparities among Americans may be far more fundamentally divisive. I don't think there is much reason to believe that the poorest members of the nation will have much sustained investment in a culture of national solidarity, especially since so little solidarity has been shown to them.[5] And these inequalities are only exacerbated by the process of global economic integration to which he refers. Jobs have been lost, wages are down, wealth has become even more concentrated—and, as Robert Reich and others have argued, the country's elites have more or less seceded from public national life.[6] Under these circumstances, Hollinger's aspiration of developing a culture of national solidarity seems rather remote; and that is true, as I said, even if the culture wars were indeed to subside.

It is also worth mentioning that many recent immigrants in this country continue to maintain primary solidarities with their home countries even after they have lived here for many years, thereby disrupting the usual expectation that solidarity and territoriality go together.[7] This trend (which is also a product of globalization) suggests that many new Americans are interested not so much in developing an affirmative American national solidarity as in the opportunity to pursue their separate national solidarities once here.

For all of these reasons, I think Hollinger's hopeful story could actually be characterized as a potential tragedy. Here is the tragic version: Although the United States is finally positioned on the cultural front to develop a truly tolerant civic nationalism, the process of globalization has worked to exacerbate a variety of other schisms that divide its citizens, thereby undermining the prospects for the development of a robust American national solidarity any time soon.

Of course, this story is tragic only if the ideal of national solidarity is, in fact, desirable. But ought we aspire to it? Certainly, the content of the national culture Hollinger describes that would ground an American national solidarity is very attractive. But I wonder why we don't just leave it at that: Why isn't it enough to advocate, or defend, a culture of diversity and tolerance for difference, without then putting that culture in the service of some broader project of national solidarity? For me, the notion of American national solidarity (especially when it is treated as the primary solidarity) is troubling—not so much for cultural reasons, but on political and normative grounds. I personally see no reason we should categorically privilege the interests of nationals over outsiders, as any model of national solidarity does. And I worry, as a practical matter, that the concept of national solidarity will be deployed to justify a restrictive immigration policy (again, not for cultural reasons but on economic and political grounds) and that it will easily translate into exclusionary policies directed toward noncitizens who live among us, especially the undocumented.

I am not suggesting, as an alternative, that we adopt a "species-wide" notion of solidarity—the kind of liberal cosmopolitan vision that Martha Nussbaum recently defended in her essay on "world citizenship."[8] If anything, I find more compelling a stance that maintains solidarity with the powerless and marginalized across the world.[9] But I am most of all committed to a political and cultural position that repudiates any overarching, authoritative form of solidarity, and that ensures the space for disparate visions of solidarities and citizenship identities—including, but not subordinated to, national solidarities and national citizenship identities.

Notes

1. See, for example, Yael Tamir, *Liberal Nationalism* (Princeton: Princeton University Press, 1993); Michael Lind, *The Next American Nation* (New York: Free Press, 1995); Will Kymlicka, *Multicultural Citizenship: A Liberal Theory of Minority Rights* (Oxford: Clarendon Press, 1995); and David Miller, *On Nationality* (Oxford: Clarendon Press, 1995). David Hollinger has set out his liberal national-

ist views more fully in *Postethnic America: Beyond Multiculturalism* (New York: Basic Books, 1995).

2. For a useful introduction to the debate between liberalism and communitarianism, see Will Kymlicka, *Contemporary Political Philosophy: An Introduction* (Oxford: Oxford University Press, 1990), esp. 50–94, 199–237.

3. Sanford Levinson, "Is Liberal Nationalism An Oxymoron? An Essay For Judith Shklar," *Ethics* 105 (April 1995): 626–45. See also Judith Lichtenberg, "How Liberal Can Nationalism Be?" *Philosophical Forum* 28 (Fall–Winter 1996–1997): 53–72.

4. See Hollinger, *Postethnic America*, especially chapter 3.

5. For a useful recent summary of the data on the unequal distribution of wealth in this country, see Edward N. Wolff, *Top Heavy: A Study of the Increasing Inequality of Wealth in America* (New York: Twentieth Century Fund Press, 1995).

6. See Robert B. Reich, *The Work of Nations* (New York: Vintage Books, 1991), especially chapters 20–25.

7. See, for example, Linda Basch, Nina Glick Schiller, and Cristina Szanton Blanc, *Nations Unbound: Transnational Projects, Postcolonial Predicaments and Deterritorialized Nation-States* (Basel, Switzerland: Gordon & Breach Publishers, 1994); Alejandro Portes, "Global Villagers: The Rise of Transnational Communities," *The American Prospect* (March–April 1996): 74; and Robert Smith, "Assimilation, Political Community and Transnational Migration," in *The City and the World* (New York: Council on Foreign Relations Press, 1997).

8. Martha C. Nussbaum, "Patriotism and Cosmopolitanism," in *For Love of Country: Debating the Limits of Patriotism*, ed. Martha C. Nussbaum (Boston: Beacon Press, 1996).

9. I have elsewhere discussed some of the challenges associated with developing such a stance. See Linda S. Bosniak, "Opposing Prop. 187: Undocumented Immigrants and the National Imagination," *Connecticut Law Review* 28 (Spring 1996), esp. 555–619, 596–617.

4

To Make Natural: Creating Citizens for the Twenty-First Century

Noah M. J. Pickus

Applications for U.S. citizenship have nearly quadrupled in recent years.[1] This increase has raised concern in Congress and in many regions of the country over the integrity of the naturalization process and the value of American citizenship. Representative Lamar Smith (R-Tex.), chairman of the House Immigration Subcommittee, for example, has charged that Vice President Al Gore pressured the Immigration and Naturalization Service (INS) to lower its standards for naturalization, enabling more new citizens to participate in the 1996 elections and cheapening the meaning of citizenship in the process. "This is the first time . . . to my knowledge that politics has ever been mixed with this sort of sacrosanct procedure that we call naturalization or becoming a citizen," he asserted.[2] Others have criticized recent welfare legislation that stripped legal immigrants of benefits, suggesting that it contributes to the devaluation of citizenship by inducing newcomers to naturalize for purely material reasons. Still others have criticized this legislation as threatening democracy by excluding a class of national residents from possessing precious rights.[3]

These concerns over the naturalization process mark a significant departure from those years in which few paid attention to the creation of new citizens. Until Doris Meissner became commissioner of the INS in 1992 and immediately began to emphasize citizenship, the "N" in INS was woefully neglected.[4] The INS was far more concerned with keeping immigrants out than with welcoming those already here. For their part, immigrant advocates more often pressed Congress and the courts to accord greater rights to noncitizens than they encouraged immigrants to naturalize or to consider citizenship as a fundamental transformation in their sense of self and membership.

Yet if naturalization was once largely ignored, all that has now changed.

The INS is currently undertaking a historic revision of the naturalization examination. The Commission on Immigration Reform has just issued its recommendations on the naturalization, Americanization, and integration of legal immigrants. America has not seen such a widespread reconsideration of its immigration *and* citizenship policy since the 1910s and 1920s. In that period, the first Americanization movement coincided with the Dillingham Commission's recommendation that Congress reduce the overall level of immigration.

The current controversies raise critical questions about immigration and naturalization and about the meaning of nationhood in an increasingly multicultural and transnational age. What do we mean by citizenship and how, if at all, should citizenship matter? What conceptions of citizenship has our naturalization policy embodied? What ought to be the purpose of the naturalization process? In particular, what standards should guide the INS's review of its naturalization examination?[5]

In this chapter I argue that the naturalization process does not adequately incorporate newcomers, strengthen citizenship, or foster self-government. On the eve of the twenty-first century, as multiculturalism and globalization strain the bonds of nationhood, we need a process that generates a sense of mutual commitment among all Americans, naturalized and native-born alike. To develop this position and to survey contending positions, I begin in section I by describing the fundamental challenges to the traditional civic conception of citizenship in the United States and sketching my own view of what "constitutional citizenship" should look like in the twenty-first century. Section II analyzes two perspectives on citizenship—one rooted in culture, the other in rights. Rather than reforming the naturalization process, the cultural position emphasizes restricting the entry of immigrants, while the latter view stresses the protection of immigrants' rights. Section III then examines the history and current status of the naturalization process. Section IV assesses objections, based on a participatory view of citizenship, to making the naturalization process more substantive and symbolic and outlines the role of naturalization in the incorporation of newcomers.[6]

I. Citizenship and Identity in the Twenty-First Century

Before exploring the purposes of the naturalization process and how well our current process serves those purposes, we must first assess what we mean by citizenship. In particular, we need to consider how the traditional conception of citizenship in the United States is faring in light of significant challenges to its primacy. Since the nineteenth century, most Western polities have defined political identity as individual citizenship in a single nation-state. The nation represents a people whose shared identity serves as the basis for the legitimate authority of the state. In the United States, Americans have traditionally defined what it means to belong as allegiance to a set of political principles.[7]

As we enter the twenty-first century, the nature and legitimacy of the nation is being challenged internally by multiculturalism and alienation and externally by the globalization of markets and the movement of people.[8] Some forms of multiculturalism contest the notion that political community should recognize individual but not group identity. This view suggests that members of minority groups must possess special group representation rights (such as racially drawn voting districts) to ensure that their perspectives are heard, as well as special group cultural rights (such as bilingual and bicultural education) so that political participation does not require cultural assimilation. Such group rights are often defended today by political theorists not merely as temporary aids to level the playing field, but as fundamental requirements of justice.[9] Multiculturalism can challenge the link between the nation and the state because it depends on the state to protect rights and provide benefits, but slights the notion of a common national identity.[10]

A fragile sense of public commitment also threatens a national sense of shared identity. Government seems increasingly remote from individual citizens who doubt its capacity to operate efficiently and equitably. Our legal and political culture's emphasis on rights obscures the importance of obligations and responsibilities. The market economy has helped undermine stable local community, intact families, and an earlier ethos of deferred gratification. Americans often act as if they were "alienated residents" who have lost confidence in the political arena.[11] While these trends weaken any sense of common national identity, their effect on the state is more ambiguous. In some cases, these trends precipitate calls for greater state action to reverse the decline. In other cases, the decline in public commitment leads some to claim that the size of the state contributes to our discontent and therefore its reach should be limited.

The flow across borders of capital, labor, culture, ideas, and even government raises questions about the nation as the singular site of political identity and allegiance. Multinational corporations, David Hollinger notes, can increase profits without attention to the economic and social welfare of their originating nation, since their interests and employees are increasingly scattered across the world. Like the multiculturalists, markets need the state to preserve order, but they have little use for the nation.[12] Moreover, when individuals from different nations develop identities as members of a multinational firm or of a global profession, these new identities may displace traditional national affiliations.[13]

Immigration poses a special challenge to traditional conceptions of citizenship because, in altering membership, it profoundly affects national identity. Traditional models of migration assume migrants settle in one place and take on a new, singular political identity. But a more closely interconnected world means that the link between countries often remains continuous and can even be strengthened by migration.[14] "At a time when so much of the American public is disengaged from civic life," muses Alejandro Portes, "what does it mean to have so many citizens who are, in a very real sense, neither here nor there?"[15] As with multiculturalists and markets, new models of migration create new forms of social membership and political participation. These forms could expand the reach of democratic governance and a shared sense of belonging; on the other hand, they might erode the legitimacy of the nation while strengthening the authority of the state at the expense of democratic processes. In recent years, the bureaucracy and judiciary have gained authority from the increasing role of international accords protecting the rights of migrants. An important question is how much of what is gained in the protection of persons comes at the expense of democratic decision-making.[16]

Constitutional Citizenship

The traditional conception of citizenship is thus increasingly at odds with the reality of modern life. Yet, I will argue, new notions of membership are inadequate guides to a future that preserves democratic principles, self-governance, and rights. We will best serve these multiple purposes by conceiving of membership in the United States as consisting of three components: ideology, emotional attachment, and interpretation. I call this view of membership "constitutional citizenship" because I derive it from the Founders' debates over the requirements for creating citizens of a new constitutional order.[17]

Many distinguished commentators, including Alexis de Tocqueville, Gunnar Myrdal, and Samuel Huntington, argue that American identity has been defined by consent to a set of shared political values. They reject the equation of American citizenship with any cultural heritage. "American symbols and ceremonies are culturally anonymous," writes Michael Walzer, "invented rather than inherited, voluntaristic in style, narrowly political in content."[18] Such a notion reflects a fundamental change from the British conception of membership as "natural, personal, and perpetual."[19] In doing so, it has allowed immigrants from various nations to naturalize and fosters the notion of America as a universal nation.

This ideational and consensual view of U.S. citizenship suffers from a number of deficiencies. For one, Americans disagree deeply over the meaning of such political principles as liberty and equality. For another, citizenship has long been the subject of a contest among ideals of membership, not simply a conflict between one set of ideas and the recalcitrant institutions of the state.[20] Consensual citizenship has itself also posed problems for an ideational vision of citizenship. It permitted the polity, for instance, to deny citizenship to American Indians and blacks by defining Indians as belonging to tributary states and blacks as not part of the original social contract that ratified the Constitution. To establish blacks' claim to citizenship, Congress enshrined birthright citizenship in the Constitution by ratifying the Fourteenth Amendment.

Thus, our citizenship laws mix ascriptive and consensually based criteria, a combination that has contributed to concerns over the meaning of membership today, especially with regard to the children of illegal aliens. It has also produced an asymmetry between naturalized citizens, who have actively consented to the polity, and native-born citizens who have done so tacitly, thus making it harder to claim the contemporaneous allegiances of those born and raised within the polity's borders.[21]

Creating citizens who share common values is a difficult task, even in the relatively bounded community of the nation-state. Citizens' commitments to different levels of community—such as family, religion, and ethnic group—make for overlapping and sometimes conflicting allegiances. While denying that government could make citizens virtuous, many of the Founders wanted to create a citizen whose values and thoughts coincided with the political principles undergirding free government. They considered political, legal, and educational institutions, as well as language and literature, essential to the formation of constitutional citizens.[22]

The first step in this process entailed creating a world in which individuals recognized each other as participants in a common project, as fellow citizens. New citizens would have to regard the Constitution's authority as rooted in their collective status as a people, however much the existence of that people was precisely what the Constitution and *The Federalist Papers* sought to invent. This was artifice, subterfuge if you like, but it was what the Framers deemed necessary.[23]

A shared national identity that is capable of binding citizens requires more than just a commitment to abstract and general principles. It requires some felt sense of communal obligation, some feeling of responsibility derived in part from a perception of shared history and fate. National identity includes a reverential element, an emotional attachment to the polity. "The mind," George Fletcher argues, "becomes more receptive to facts and analytic arguments as the spirit becomes attached to the object of study. As physical education requires more than reading and analysis, the teaching of loyalty requires more than intellectual persuasion."[24]

The noise you hear in the background is the sound of patriotic Americans cheering these comments about reverence, loyalty, and emotional attachment. Yet even they should be made nervous by my invocation of national culture. Our commitment to the principles of liberal democracy can be lost under the weight of a cultural definition of identity. Indeed, cultural definitions of identity have often undermined America's capacity to make any claims to be a truly universal nation. Racial restrictions on who could become a citizen, for instance, characterized American laws from 1790 until 1952.[25]

That danger is one reason why political ideology and emotional attachment must both be supplemented by an interpretive conception of citizenship, by an emphasis on deliberating over the nature and purpose of a people's commitments. More fundamentally, though, a single, unchanging conception of belonging does not fit the requirements of citizenship in a constitutional order. James Madison's initial argument against a bill of rights suggests why neither ideology nor emotional attachment are sufficient grounds for citizenship. He worried that the Anti-Federalist emphasis on habitual allegiance to specific textual provisions would diminish citizens' capacity to reason together about the proper relation between rights and powers. As a result, their grasp of the reasoning behind the principles they revered would wane. This development, he feared, would make active support for the Constitution less likely.[26]

A polity that claims to represent "We the People" must be continually embraced by the people to maintain its legitimacy. For a constitution to maintain a vital degree of allegiance, its authority depends not simply on its having been approved once, at its initial ratification, but on its ratification by subsequent generations. Citizens need to explore and repudiate alternative systems of rule if they are to make solid commitments to a polity. If the present order is all that a citizen knows, how can he be said to have chosen it over an alternative system? Citizens who lack real choices may also lack real commitment. Since little appears to be at stake in vigorously supporting the polity, citizens will never have to devote themselves to it. Reasoned exploration of the principles a citizen reveres can shake that citizen's faith, but that risk is necessary to prevent citizens from becoming dangerously complacent.

There are obvious tensions among ideology, emotion, and interpretation as components of American citizenship. But they are tensions that appropriately reflect the delicate balance among creating a shared sensibility, sustaining democratic principles, preserving self-governance, and protecting rights. By contrast, two contending conceptions of citizenship—one culturally based, the other rooted in rights—would do away with this balance. Proponents of these views argue that restricting immigration or protecting immigrants' rights should take precedence over reforming naturalization policy.

II. Culture and Rights

Much of the debate over immigration in the United States revolves around questions of admission criteria in U.S. immigration and refugee policy. The issue at stake is who can become a member of the polity. The debate continues a long-standing dispute over whether immigrants are an asset or are an economic liability who take jobs from citizens and burden the welfare state.

What is new or, rather, what has reemerged in the present debate is a variety of commentators who advocate restricting immigration because they see the link between immigration and multiculturalism as threatening the nation-state. These observers celebrate the notion that a distinct culture defines what it means to be an American. They assert that the United States suffers because of its shift from a monocultural to a multicultural conception of belonging. Peter Brimelow captures this view in declaring that a nation-state is "a sovereign structure that is the political expression of a specific ethno-cultural group."[27] As a result, he worries that a large influx of immigrants from a wide variety of cultures threatens to undermine the cultural homogeneity that makes democratic politics possible. For Brimelow, the Constitution is merely an instrument of a people already formed by their cultural affinity. The Preamble's aspiration to "secure the blessing of liberty to ourselves and our posterity" meant only "the specific posterity of those men who signed that document. They represented a full-fledged nation."[28]

Cultural conservatives who favor closing the borders represent an especially powerful force because they offer a coherent theory of membership that addresses profoundly felt concerns of the American public. "If we had to take a million immigrants in, say Zulus, next year, or Englishmen, and put them in Virginia," asked Patrick Buchanan, "what group would be easier to assimilate and would cause less problems for the people of Virginia?"[29] This view has deep historical roots in the American experience.

While the colonists took on a new identity that emphasized individual allegiance to a set of political principles, they also saw themselves as possessing an Anglo–Saxon cultural and racial heritage that made them especially suited for the rigors of free government. John Jay's claim to a natural, national homogeneity, for instance, constitutes the most memorable description of ethnicity in *The Federalist Papers*:

Providence has been pleased to give this one connected country to one united people—a people descended from the same ancestors, speaking the

same language, professing the same religion, attached to the same principles
of government, very similar in manners and customs.[30]

Benjamin Franklin expressed many Americans' concerns when he asked,
"Why should *Pennsylvania*, founded by the *English*, become a colony of
Aliens, who will shortly be so numerous as to Germanize us instead of
Anglifying them, and will never adopt our Language or Customs any
more than they can acquire our Complexion?"[31]

The only reason the United States has survived the influx of so many
immigrants, Brimelow argues, is precisely because the racially restrictive
quotas enacted in 1924 gave the country "time to digest" immigrants from
radically different cultures. We need, he says, to initiate such a period of
digestion again. From this perspective, naturalization policy is not very
relevant. The problem relates more to admissions policy than to naturalization policy. The threat that multiculturalism and immigration pose to
the American nation can be countered by limiting the number of applicants eligible to emigrate to the United States and by favoring European
applicants. To the extent that cultural conservatives like Brimelow pay
attention to naturalization policy, they advocate lengthening the residency requirement from five to ten or more years, rigorously enforcing
the English-language requirement for naturalization, abolishing exemp-
tions from such requirements, such as for the elderly, and generally dis-
couraging foreign residents access to the political community.[32]

While the popular debate over immigration has recently been dominated by a cultural conception of membership, an entirely different view
of membership has arisen in Supreme Court doctrine and in educational
practice, legal commentary, and social science. This view denies that the
link between immigrants and multiculturalism poses a threat to democracy in America. Indeed, from this perspective, the full flowering of multiculturalism that immigration makes possible fulfills the promise of
democracy. A truly democratic polity, in this view, depends on the inclu-
sionary provision of universal rights rather than the exclusionary solidarity generated by cultural homogeneity.

During the 1970s and 1980s, the courts increasingly deemed citizenship
irrelevant for the provision of various social benefits. In a series of decisions traceable to *Graham v. Richardson* (1971), in which the Supreme
Court struck down a state law denying welfare benefits to aliens, the
court deemed classifications based on citizenship "suspect" and placed
aliens in the protected category of "discrete and insular minorities." Decisions such as *Plyler v. Doe* (1982), which required a state to provide free
public education to the children of undocumented aliens, further established the importance of personhood and residency. As Peter Schuck has
argued, *Plyler* bestowed significant benefits on the basis of social bonds

that developed between illegal aliens and the communities in which they lived. Consequently, citizenship lost part of its value, since it was no longer required for aliens to establish membership in the polity.[33]

Rights' advocates distrust citizenship as a mechanism for inclusion because it links belonging to the nation-state. They worry that idealized versions of American identity will justify exclusionary definitions of who benefits from full standing in the community of citizens. In their view, fashioning citizens on the basis of citizenship in the nation-state will compel conformity to a "dominant liberal discourse [that] is neither neutral nor all-inclusive." It will result in the reemergence of exclusionary definitions of citizenship: the Alien and Sedition Acts and the Chinese Exclusion laws, Alexander Aleinikoff points out, reflected majority preferences for maintaining "communities of character." For Aleinikoff, claims about national community merely reflect "the norms and culture of dominant groups."[34]

Rights' advocates are especially critical of efforts to make citizenship a mechanism for inclusion in an increasingly transnational age. Some argue that the nation-state is obsolete in a time when people, images, ideas, capital, labor, and even government flow across borders. Sanford Levinson describes membership in the nation as becoming like membership in individual American states. Membership in the nation "might supply us with teams to root for . . . and a place from which to vote," he writes. "It is, though, ever more unlikely to be of any real import in structuring our identities."[35] Transnationality and dual citizenship, observes Portes, "may not be a sign of imminent civic breakdown but the vanguard of the direction that new notions of community and society will be taking in the next century."[36]

Some proponents of rights consider naturalization requirements, such as a civics and history examination, to be fundamentally objectionable. Others regard such requirements as simply less important than protecting immigrants' rights and actively engaging newcomers in politics. To the extent that strong communal feelings are valuable, some rights' advocates argue, they can develop only through social interaction in smaller, more intimate settings. According to Jamin Raskin, participation in local community affairs helps all persons to develop a sense of "empathy, virtue, and feelings of community." Raskin therefore counsels that the distinction between citizen and alien ought to be further weakened by giving noncitizens the right to vote in local elections. "The move toward local noncitizen voting," he contends, "can be seen as part of the trend of communities accepting responsibility for participating in the enforcement of global human rights norms."[37]

The Ford Foundation's Changing Relation Project bolsters Raskin's focus on local politics. The study identified exclusion of immigrants from economic, social, and political opportunities as one of the major barriers to more harmonious relations between newcomers and citizens, the latter of whom the project refers to as "established residents." The project contends that, among other policies, local political participation by noncitizens could best address economic, community safety, and environmental issues and overcome "ethnic alienation and nativism."[38]

Instead of linking citizenship to the nation-state, rights' advocates offer a conception of membership rooted in universal rights and participation in local politics. They regard U.S. legitimacy as resting less on a definition of peoplehood than on an assertion of personhood and the experience of being neighbors. In their view, a renewed emphasis on naturalization risks imposing a biased definition of American identity, while offering less civic instruction than would be gained by actively engaging in the affairs of smaller associations.

Englishmen and Cosmopolitans

Cultural conservatives who favor restricting immigration do so not simply because of their doubts about immigrants from non-European cultures. They draw on a more fundamental tradition in American politics, one traceable to the Anti-Federalists. For many of the Anti-Federalists, citizenship reflected a people's culture rather than shaped it.[39] The Anti-Federalists' emphasis on cultural homogeneity had its own logic in the context of a small republic. Today, proponents of restricting immigration rightly point out that too much diversity can pose difficulties. Yet the Federalists' idea of "extending the sphere" has prevailed over the Anti-Federalists' emphasis on preexisting local communities. We have become an irrevocably heterogeneous polity.

More important, by defending a conception of political identity as the result of "accident and force," cultural conservatives undermine the Founders' emphasis on maintaining a vital sense of self-government through "reflection and choice." The Federalists, in particular, did not understand the Preamble's reference to "our posterity" to refer only to their descendants. Rather, they saw the *creation* of a national sense of identity as critical to the success of their new enterprise. Indeed, as I have argued, they regarded that task as a continual challenge facing a polity defined by attachment to a constitution.

Cultural conservatives suggest that a primary source of disaffection in American life is the greater cultural diversity fostered by immigration over the last thirty years. But the sources of disaffection in American life are multiple. The restrictionist strategy of addressing concerns over national identity and citizenship by focusing solely on who is coming to the United States, rather than on what they will become, draws attention away from America's broader problems of membership. And it does so at the cost of our self-definition as a nation committed to the continual creation of a common identity.

By accenting local affairs, adherents of the rights' position underscore how many of the virtues important to a constitutional democracy must be acquired in concrete interactions with specific people and institutions. Yet, while civic capacities may be first awakened in neighborhoods, simply emphasizing participation does not mean that citizens will share the qualities necessary for a heterogeneous population to govern itself, such as toleration, concern for the common good, and a willingness to offer reasoned arguments accessible to all.[40] Local activism can lead to anything from repression to anarchy if not moderated by some sense of the individual conduct and communal purposes appropriate to the entire political order. The withering of decentralized, participatory institutions makes it particularly important that we forge links between whatever lessons are learned at the local level and the aims of the national community.

Real changes wrought by the integration of national economies and the increase in transnational migration have led subscribers to the rights' position to question the importance of the national community. Those subscribers correctly suggest that new conceptions of political community linking the local to the international may evolve in the twenty-first century. But combining commitment to others with respect for pluralism is an even more difficult project when moved from the national to the transnational level. The capacity to enforce rights depends on a sense of community that creates a recognition of such rights and a willingness to sacrifice for their achievement. Which conception of sovereignty develops and how it is ratified matters more than the pace of an advancing globalism, as the travails of the European Union attest.[41]

Adherents of the rights' position devalue any level of community between the local and the universal. Until and unless a transnational conception of sovereignty develops, their view provides a tenuous basis on which members will act to support one another. By separating rights from peoplehood, rights' advocates underestimate the extent to which a sense of peoplehood makes both liberty and justice possible. Many important issues remain stubbornly national in scope, like rights and defense. These are issues that require judgments by individuals about their commitment to others whom they have never met, judgments that are more easily made about fellow citizens than about all persons. States without nations can be dangerous places.

Indeed, in the United States, the popular response to immigration is increasingly restrictive. Businesses press for a free market in goods and in persons, while elites and courts emphasize rights and participation. Many Americans, however, have turned to our majoritarian institutions and instruments of rule—Congress and the initiative process—to "revalue" citizenship by restricting the entry of newcomers and the rights and benefits afforded to immigrants already here.[42]

These efforts are part of a broader movement to revalue citizenship. Concern over alienated residents and the contraction of the public sphere has raised questions about the meaning of membership among native-born citizens and sparked a variety of proposals to balance rights with obligations. These proposals range from character education and national service for the middle class to work requirements for the poor and corporate responsibility for the wealthy.

Rights' advocates need to recognize that the current slew of proposals to revalue citizenship by restricting the entry of newcomers and the rights and benefits afforded to immigrants already here are driven not simply by racial and economic fears. These proposals are motivated, in part, by genuine concerns over a loss of sovereignty and common culture and a sense that immigration policy is woefully insulated from public control. Unless polices that address these concerns are proposed, the rights perspective is likely to encourage that which it least desires, further restrictions on the entry of newcomers and the rights of immigrants.[43]

While the legal strategy to extend rights to noncitizens has made important gains in equal protection for immigrants, the passive nature of rights means that it's also done little to actively draw newcomers into a broader political life. It is also losing strategic ground, as *Plyler* may be overruled and Proposition 187 (the California initiative that limits the educational, medical, and welfare rights of undocumented aliens) may be upheld. Ironically, the argument that may doom Proposition 187 (and did so in district court) is the doctrine of preemption—the contention that only the nation can make decisions about membership, not the states.[44]

Curiously, both conservatives who fear immigrants as a threat to national identity and rights' advocates reflect the ascendence of a static conception of citizenship. Many proponents of restricting immigration defend a preexisting community that is defined in cultural terms. They worry that an influx of immigrants will undermine the homogeneity that they believe makes democratic politics possible. Cultural conservatives see no need to turn immigrants into citizens, or indeed to make native-born Americans into citizens, because the project of self-government is complete once a culturally defined people govern themselves.

Proponents of the rights' perspective offer a more inclusive vision, yet they do not encourage immigrants to see themselves as part of a new people. They do not ask immigrants to undergo any transformation of consciousness because immigrants already possess what is necessary to be a full member of the polity: their personhood and their capacity to discover common interests through local political interaction. For both groups, the fact of membership in a particular constitutional order is essentially irrelevant, since in their view a polity merely reflects rather than shapes political identity. The latter group insists that a culture of rights is sufficient to undergird democracy; the former believes that a democratic polity can only be sustained by a relatively homogeneous culture.

Neither cultural conservatives nor rights' advocates offers a vision of membership that adequately encompasses the ideational, emotional, and interpretive aspects of American identity. Their visions fail to preserve the delicate balance among creating a shared sensibility, sustaining democratic principles, preserving self-governance, and protecting rights. What would a naturalization policy suitable to that task look like? To begin answering that question we need first to examine the history and current state of the naturalization process.

III. The Purpose and Practice of Naturalization

In the view of civic conservatives, naturalization is a solemn process by which newcomers proclaim their adherence to the political principles of American democracy. This approach views the United States as a universal nation in which allegiance is defined by adherence to constitutional values of liberty and equality. "Preparation for the tests and the ceremony of citizenship has long been a powerful instrument of unity," comments John Miller, "an engine of assimilation that turns newcomers into citizens who understand our political traditions and are proud to be Americans."[45]

Miller acknowledges that "few immigrants come to the United States because they want to be Americanized. . . . The choice [to naturalize] is very difficult because it involves thorny questions of loyalty, identity, and family."[46] Georgie Anne Geyer, on the other hand, describes previous waves of immigrants as deeply committed to becoming Americans. She further contends that Americans have always thought that citizenship mattered tremendously. Until recently, she argues, the naturalization process rigorously tested applicants for their understanding of, and commitment to, an uncontested notion of American identity.[47] Despite this image, the naturalization process has not been administered uniformly, nor treated as sacrosanct.

After the Revolution, individual states developed their own naturalization policies. Most states offered lenient terms for naturalization so as to attract settlers. Applicants typically had to swear an oath of allegiance to the state government, prove their good character, fulfill a brief residency requirement, and renounce their allegiance to their homeland. Disputes that arose from the different naturalization policies among states led

James Madison to propose uniform citizenship standards. He also recommended that the new nation follow the British model of "graded" citizenship, granting rights piecemeal as applicants met the criteria for naturalization. "In the end," explains Reed Ueda, "the Constitution repudiated graded citizenship as well as any notion that native-born and naturalized citizens should possess different sets of rights, and confirmed the principles that U.S. citizenship, once conferred, would be uniform and complete."[48]

The Naturalization Act of 1790 limited naturalization to free white persons who had been resident for two years. The Federalists ceased encouraging immigration and naturalization in the late 1790s when they realized that naturalized immigrants often supported the Republicans. The Alien and Sedition Acts of 1798, although soon repealed, curtailed the swift naturalization and political activity of immigrants by extending the residence requirement to fourteen years, barring immigrants from countries at war with the United States, and requiring that aliens register within two days of their arrival. In 1801, the Jeffersonian Republicans established a residence requirement of five years. Jefferson opposed the Alien and Sedition Acts, Gerald Neuman argues, in part because they would create a class of residents subject to the arbitrary authority of the president. This authority could threaten the liberty of all citizens; moreover, it improperly made a class of residents subject to the law but not protected by it.[49]

In 1802, applicants for citizenship were required to file a "declaration of intent" to naturalize at least three years prior to doing so, a requirement reduced to two years in 1824. The Know-Nothings sought to extend the residency requirement to twenty-one years, but their success was short-lived. ("Despite their name," Michael Walzer observes, "the Know-Nothings thought that citizenship was something about which a great deal had to be known."[50]) Naturalization standards have varied widely at different times in different locales. In some cases, officials upheld a stringent set of requirements; in other cases, applicants who simply showed up became citizens. Political machines guided immigrants through the naturalization process, sometimes before immigrants had lived in the United States for five years, in return for their votes. Often, the machines paid witnesses to testify on behalf of an applicant's character, filled out naturalization forms, and paid any filing costs.

In the nineteenth century, Americans subscribed to what John Higham called a "cosmopolitan faith—a conviction that this new land would bring unity out of diversity as a matter of course."[51] By the turn of the century, however, conviction in the country's natural assimilative powers had begun to wane. The Naturalization Act of 1906 required that applicants be "attached to the principles of the Constitution" and that they speak and understand English. Under the rubric of "Americanization," a host of states, chambers of commerce, school boards, unions, and philanthropic organizations sought to establish a formal process by which to incorporate newcomers. The movement imposed a set of obligations on immigrants. It pressed them to learn English, study American history and civics, and assent to a specific conception of "Americanness." But the Americanization movement also urged immigrants who met those obligations to participate in a common, public life. Unlike those who did not think immigrants could become Americans, the Americanizers wanted immigrants to join the polity.

The Bureau of Immigration and Naturalization, established in 1906 as part of the Department of Commerce and Labor, was only slightly ahead of the Americanization movement. It opened an Americanization Section in 1907 to determine what the Naturalization Act of 1906 meant by requiring petitioners for citizenship to be "attached to the principles of the Constitution of the United States." Later, especially between 1915 and 1924, the naturalization agency initiated its own Americanization projects. More often, it reflected the purposes of private organizations. Throughout this period it also served as a clearinghouse for the massive efforts undertaken by state, local, and private agencies.[52]

How did the government construe the primary purpose of the naturalization examination, and what did the test actually require immigrants to know about the Constitution? In the period around World War I, the government wavered between self-assurance and anxiety. Generally, it stressed that immigrants should demonstrate a broad sense of allegiance to the Constitution rather than particular substantive understanding of the document. During the 1920s and 1930s the government placed greater emphasis on a clear declaration of loyalty.[53] In 1950, Congress raised the standards for naturalization by requiring that applicants read and write English, not just speak and understand it, and that they demonstrate a basic knowledge of U.S. civics and history. Despite these new requirements, few public or private institutions paid sustained attention to naturalization in the second half of this century.

Name One Benefit of Being a Citizen of the United States

Although naturalization has not always been treated as sacrosanct, many immigrants and Americans have regarded it as such. Indeed, the ambivalence many immigrants have felt toward naturalization testifies to their sense that such a change has had significance. They have rightfully understood that joining this polity entails a transformation in their sense of self and membership. While naturalization has been far from sacrosanct, critics of the current process correctly assert that the process is more oriented toward processing applicants than it is to conveying any substantive knowledge or sense that citizenship has meaning.

In 1986, the Immigration Reform and Control Act (IRCA) enabled more than three million illegal aliens to legalize their status by taking special programs in American history and civics. Over a weekend, two INS officers developed one hundred questions and answers to be provided to applicants preparing for the exam. The substance of these questions and answers certainly needs improvement. Some of the approved answers themselves suggest an instrumental conception of citizenship, such as one that only lists government jobs, traveling with a U.S. passport, and petitioning for close relatives to come to the United States as acceptable responses to the question "Name one benefit of being a citizen of the U.S." Other answers are intellectually controversial, such as the claim that free speech comes from the Bill of Rights, that the Constitution guarantees rights to "everyone," defined as "citizens and non-citizens living in the U.S.," or that "American Indians (native Americans) helped the Pilgrims in America."

For some applicants, boredom not controversy hinders their preparation for citizenship. Many of the questions cover the same ground and so confuse applicants, because they assume each question is trying to elicit different information. "What is the date of Independence Day?" (A: July 4th), for instance, is followed by "What is the 4th of July?" (A: Independence Day). Other questions ask for largely irrelevant facts, such as "What is the 49th state of the Union?" Whatever lesson this question seeks to impart, if any, is lost without some broader context. Alaska was the 49th state to join the union, but how significant is Alaska's statehood to a prospective citizen? A question about the status of Puerto Rico might at least lead to a discussion about citizenship, statehood, and self-government.

These problems with the examination indicate the need to thoroughly reassess it. Its questions should be more coherent and contextual. For example, those answers that suggest that the Constitution and the process of becoming an American are largely about rights could be altered or expanded. Some analysts, however, question whether any set of naturalization questions is appropriate. "Which traditions are the ones that the alien must appreciate and understand?" asks Gerald Rosberg. "The tradition of those who were once slaves or once masters; those who won the Mexican–American War or those who lost it; those who came from Ireland or those who despised the Irish and would have sent them back?"[54]

Other observers propose that we make the naturalization examination far more substantive, asking questions about "values, self-government, and limited government."[55] Still others suggest that the qualities of American citizenship are so difficult for immigrants to learn, especially for those from Latin America, that we need to extend the residency requirement to provide enough time for newcomers to be properly inculcated in the values undergirding American citizenship.[56]

All these critics fail to understand the purpose of the naturalization examination, its limits, and its promise. The naturalization process is and always has been a poor test of prospective members' loyalty. As with most loyalty tests, applicants can easily lie. "Anyone who intends to be loyal will be so without a specific promise," observes Levinson, "and those who are in fact disloyal will further demonstrate their perfidy by cheerfully lying about it and making promises that they have no intention of carrying out."[57]

The naturalization test also serves as an inadequate measure of civic knowledge. A typical examination requires that an applicant answer seven out of ten or twelve questions correctly from a list of one hundred questions and answers provided in advance. In effect, the examination tests memory more than knowledge. Clearly, most applicants have sufficient memories for this exercise, as few applicants for citizenship are denied citizenship because they fail the exam. Most applicants get 80 to 90 percent of the questions right and many score a perfect 100 percent.[58] Indeed, while immigrants still regard the naturalization examination with trepidation,[59] immigrants who actually go through the process report that the exam is easy. Further, almost 80 percent found the examiner helpful. (Examiners often accept several different answers to a question.)[60]

The more difficult we make the test, the more we must first answer a fundamental question: Why, simply because they were born in the United States, should legal residents be entitled to the rights of citizenship, especially participation in governance? In particular, why should alienated residents, citizens who know little and care less about the polity, be entitled to citizenship, while committed and knowledgeable aliens are denied it? As Levinson points out, whether being born and raised in the United States actually means that one absorbs the polity's dominant values is an empirical question on which we could compare native-born citizens and immigrants.[61] Alienated residents may even have been born outside the country or raised by non-citizens. Representative Edward Roybal (D-Calif.) challenged his colleagues on this issue during the debate over IRCA when he asked why immigrants should have to meet higher standards than citizens, especially when, he asserted, many citizens could not pass the naturalization examination. "Real quick," he said, "what powers does the Senate have that the House of Representatives does not have? I do not think there are too many who can answer that."[62]

Roybal's claim points out the many deficiencies in the civic education of native-born citizens. But his charge also has its limits. Many ostensibly alienated residents remain fundamentally shaped by our constitutional order. Critics of American politics often register their critiques in the language of the Constitution. Citizens who claim to be unwilling to ratify the Constitution often make such a claim in the name of a more perfect vision of the Constitution. The Constitution thus is binding "to the extent that it continues to make a political people by providing the grammar by which they speak authoritatively about their public values and continues to define the institutions by which they exert their collective identity."[63] The connection between constitutional norms and the values Americans hold, writes Christopher Eisgruber, "does not depend on a fanciful claim that most Americans regularly read the *U.S. Reports* or that they would recognize the Bill of Rights if presented with it."[64] Alienated residents need not be naturalized because the Constitution is already natural to them.[65]

Still, the point remains that treating a certain minimum of civic knowledge as the basis for American citizenship seems a dubious proposition. This point helps us to see that the primary purpose of naturalization should not be to ratify newcomers' loyalty and civic understanding. It should be an instrument for fostering immigrants' identification with their new and complex identity, a link between old and new immigrants, and an opportunity to encourage both native-born and naturalizing citizens to explore the meaning of their shared identity.

Immigrants have always come to the United States for a mixture of economic, ideological, and personal reasons. Some become citizens as quickly as they can, others soon return home, whereas still others regard permanent adjustment to American life with ambivalence. In 1920, fewer than 30 percent of Italian and Polish immigrants had become naturalized citizens. By 1950, over 70 percent of Italian and Polish immigrants had naturalized.[66] For many immigrants, becoming a citizen is a painful psychological and spiritual process. A *New Yorker* cartoon that depicts two pilgrims arriving in Massachusetts Bay captures the complex combination of motivations behind emigration. "In the short run I'm here for religious freedom," one pilgrim remarks, "but in the long run I'm thinking of getting into real estate." Although worrisome, the largely instrumental interest in citizenship of today's naturalization applicants does not represent a radical break with tradition.

Despite immigrants' amalgam of instrumental and idealistic motivations for becoming citizens, most have become full participants in American life, committed to the broader community and supportive of its constitutional values. Indeed, although many Americans feared earlier waves of immigrants as a threat, a significant expansion of democracy has often taken place after the arrival of newcomers, as it did following the surge of immigration earlier in this century. Moreover, when the effect of recent immigrants is accounted for, some evidence suggests various ways in which immigrants are becoming incorporated into the United States.

A majority of Mexican Americans, Puerto Rican Americans, and Cuban Americans report that they are more concerned with U.S. politics than with the politics of their country of origin. Significant majorities in each group say they feel a very strong love for the United States and they are very proud of this country.[67]

There is, however, nothing automatic about these developments. Today, Americans' doubts about their own national identity and the weakening of many institutional capacities for incorporating newcomers have introduced greater uncertainty into whether new arrivals and current citizens will regard one another as equals who bear mutual obligations. The decline in local government, abandonment of public schools by whites, dissolution of common military service, the rise of a rights-oriented culture, and the celebration of individual consumption unconnected to social ends threaten the notion of a public sphere into which immigrants can become incorporated. Moreover, the 1960s and 1970s left a legacy of doubt about the fact or value of a common national identity, doubts seen most clearly in those versions of multiculturalism that describe American history as a story of ethnic oppression and characterize American society as one held together by few common bonds. The decline in U.S. civic life has thus made it especially difficult for immigrants to understand what a committed form of citizenship might entail.[68] Further, the churches, unions, and political machines that once played major roles in helping newcomers to forge links between the intense localism of family and neighbors to engagement in the broader society's political life are now far more attenuated.[69]

There is a growing awareness that the naturalization process needs to convey more than information. In the absence of strong institutional mechanisms for incorporating newcomers into American life, the naturalization process could help forge a communal sense of obligation. This mutual commitment then would derive from an emotional attachment to a shared identity as well as an abstract set of principles. It will issue, in part, from a sense of shared history and fate, a sentiment that, as George Fletcher puts it, "provides some basis for group cohesion, for caring about others, for seeing them not as strangers who threaten our security but as partners in a common venture."[70] As the pledge of allegiance aims to connect young Americans to the nation, a formal process of incorporation could encourage newcomers to see themselves as part of a new people. They would view naturalization as a serious endeavor, a process in which they take on, as Justice Rehnquist put it, "a status in and relationship with a society which is continuing and more basic than mere presence or residence."[71]

We could begin shoring up this part of the naturalization process by improving our swearing-in and oath-taking ceremonies. These ceremonies, as Gary Rubin, public policy director for the New York Association for New Americans, observes, should convey "the feeling of joining an important community. We need, in short, to think not only of knowledge *about* America, but how to publicly express allegiance *to* the country as well."[72] Many judges conduct remarkably moving naturalization ceremonies. Yet pressure to streamline the process has made many ceremonies more of an administrative procedure. We should make the citizenship process more efficient, but, as judges who resisted efforts to move naturalization out of the courts understand, we ought not to undermine the symbolic aspects of citizenship. It may not be possible for the courts to play the dominant role in the naturalization process, but the INS must treat the symbolic aspects of citizenship as central.

IV. Participation and Interpretation

Some scholars and advocates for ethnic groups and immigrants worry that making the naturalization process more substantive and symbolic will further burden newcomers. They fear such changes will create additional hurdles in an already bureaucratic process. Like the rights' advocates, these commentators focus primarily on rights and participation. Unlike the rights' advocates, they accept the framework of the nation-state and of citizenship as an appropriate category. In their view, political participation as a citizen is key to protecting one's rights and advancing the political position of one's ethnic group. They focus less on the role of participation in shaping local community and more on participation as a key to political power and influence at the state and national levels.

From the participatory perspective, most new citizens find naturalization ceremonies deeply moving events. Contrary to the transnational perspective, this view treats most immigrants who apply for citizenship as already deeply committed to the new polity. In this view, the fundamental threat to citizenship stems from an overly bureaucratic naturalization process that has discouraged many applicants from attempting or completing the process. Louis DeSipio and Harry Pachon report that as many as one-third of Latino applicants do not complete the process.[73] The capacity to maneuver through a bureaucracy, DeSipio points out, functions as an informal requirement for naturalization.[74]

Many advocates for immigrants regard criticism of the naturalization process as an attempt to accomplish via citizenship policy what anti-immigrant forces have not been able to accomplish by restricting the entry of newcomers. Why, they wonder, are so many citizens paying attention to naturalization after years of neglecting it? In their view, the major problem is not newcomers' lack of knowledge about, or commitment to,

the polity, but, rather, the discrimination they suffer. Immigrant advocates worry that emphasizing the need for newcomers to undergo a transformation of consciousness and to learn more about U.S. principles and
history will increase divisiveness. They object to critics who focus on
immigrants as the source of America's problems rather than emphasizing
the need for American citizens to more fully embrace the principles of
tolerance and respect for diversity.[75]

DeSipio observes that the context of naturalization is important to understanding what kind of citizens we can expect to result from the process. Naturalization, for instance, has not significantly spurred Mexican
Americans into electoral or organizational politics, since Mexican Americans have tended to naturalize for individual reasons. For Cuban Americans, on the other hand, naturalization has often been part of community-
wide initiatives where ethnic leaders link naturalization to larger goals of
political empowerment.[76]

DeSipio criticizes the current naturalization process for emphasizing
attitudinal rather than behavioral attachment. He emphasizes the importance to good citizenship of participation in electoral and organizational
politics and contends that our current naturalization process does not
create such citizens. The mistaken impression that naturalization necessarily leads to participation has been fostered, he argues, by studies that
have paid too much attention to two exceptional periods in American
history, the New Deal and the era of machine politics.[77]

What, then, should be done? DeSipio applauds the arguments advanced
on behalf of noncitizen voting rights by rights' advocates. But, he notes,
the demographic characteristics of most Latino noncitizens suggest that
they would not exercise the franchise. Noncitizens have had the right to
vote in New York school board elections since 1968, but few have done
so.[78]

DeSipio suggests two naturalization strategies to increase the political
participation of Latinos. First, he and Rodolfo de la Garza propose an
additional way for immigrants to naturalize. They suggest "that a limited
five-year noncitizen voting privilege be granted to new immigrants. If
during this five-year period, the immigrant regularly exercises the vote,
he or she will have been deemed to have demonstrated the behavior of a
good citizen and will have the naturalization examination requirements
waived." Thus, in addition to the knowledge-based route currently offered by the naturalization exam, DeSipio and de la Garza suggest a behavioral route by which immigrants can manifest their dedication to the
polity.[79]

DeSipio calls the second strategy, to promote naturalization, a civil
rights strategy. This approach has only recently been taken up by many
Latino organizations and immigrant-aid associations. Latino leaders

should emphasize that the large number of Latino noncitizens limits their ethnic political power and contributes to the exclusion of Latinos from politics. Latino leaders should demand federal support for naturalization as a way to overcome this exclusion.[80]

Ethnic and immigrant advocates regard most changes to the naturalization process, other than proposals to further streamline it, as threats to immigrants' chances to become citizens. We can see this concern in their treatment of the civic education programs required by IRCA. In proposing these programs, House Majority Leader Jim Wright argued that the goal of the amnesty program should be informed citizenship, not merely legalization. He claimed that requiring applicants to demonstrate their dedication to a new community by studying democratic principles would strengthen a common conception of citizenship. His program would steer a course between homogenization and balkanization by "test[ing] the sincerity and the seriousness of purpose of the immigrant who would cast his or her lot with our nation for the rest of his or her life."[81]

Wright's programs did not emphasize assimilation to a single standard of membership; nor did they require that an alien demonstrate any particular level of proficiency in civics or American history. Yet even these programs were severely criticized for propounding too demanding a conception of membership. Some immigrant advocates regarded the forty hours of civic education required for those seeking amnesty under IRCA as a hardship foisted on immigrants by thinly disguised nativists. They worked first to defeat these requirements and then to limit the amount of education required to ten hours.[82]

Advocates of participatory citizenship championed naturalization when it was neglected by the INS, the political parties, and most private, voluntary organizations. Their approach reminds us that naturalization and participation have always played important roles both in the advancement and incorporation of ethnic groups and in the general health of a democratic society. Just as adherents of rights stress engagement in local affairs, those who subscribe to the participatory conception of citizenship emphasize the importance of actual politics in developing civic virtues.

But, as with the emphasis on local affairs, this participatory vision reduces citizenship to electoral and organizational politics. The participatory view assumes that newcomers already possess the values, habits of mind, and sense of belonging that are integral elements of citizenship and so does not attempt to shape citizens in any fundamental sense. It gives immigrants the false impression that memorizing a few random facts and engaging in ethnically based politics is all the polity requires of them. Yet citizens are not simply born; they must be actively fashioned. This is especially the case for newcomers who may be unfamiliar with constitutional conceptions of self-government and who enter a polity beset by weakened political institutions and a fragile sense of public commitment.

A program that highlights the substantive and transformative aspects of American citizenship does not mean simply teaching reverence for shared values. Some critics of the naturalization process seem to suggest that naturalization is entirely a one-way process by which newcomers learn to venerate American ideals and history. But an emphasis on unthinking allegiance can only lead to the creation of citizens at odds with the requirements of our constitutional order. As the political scientist Charles Merriam observed in 1931, this approach creates citizens who lack the capacity for "invention, adaptability, and adjustment in a changing world."[83]

A fresh approach to naturalization could therefore invite prospective citizens to see themselves as part of a new people, but a people who continually interrogate the nature and purpose of their commitments. An expanded citizenship program could engage native-born and naturalizing citizens in an exploration of American values and aspirations. Such a program can simultaneously address concerns about resident aliens and alienated residents. It can contribute to the revitalization of our own public life and emphasize the contributions new and old immigrants make to one another.[84]

Not all new citizens will suddenly become constitutional theorists. Most citizens, naturalized and native-born, find it difficult to think theoretically about complex political issues. That difficulty is precisely why it makes sense to foster an emotional attachment to the polity, an attachment that does not depend on a sophisticated understanding of political concepts or American history. In doing so we should also emphasize the importance of critical judgment. At swearing-in ceremonies, new citizens need to receive copies of the Constitution as well as the miniature American flags they are currently given by the Daughters of the American Revolution. The flag properly emphasizes what Felix Frankfurter called the "binding tie of cohesive sentiment."[85] But the flag can be paired with the Constitution, which is, after all, to what new citizens swear an oath of allegiance.

Indeed, the applicant who swears "true faith and allegiance" to the Constitution does not become the subject of a government, an ideology, a nation, or a flag. Rather, the applicant becomes what Will Harris calls "a citizen of the text."[86] New citizens who try to understand what "true faith and allegiance" means explore fundamental questions about what binds a people.[87] The oath of allegiance thus commits new citizens to a continual process of constructing a political community or, as *Federalist* 1 puts it, to maintaining a vital sense of self-government through "reflection and choice."

One should not construe this emphasis on the interpretive aspects of citizenship and naturalization as abstract academic thinking. The process of preparing for the naturalization examination offers one of the best opportunities for immigrants and citizens to explore the meaning of American identity. An applicant for citizenship reminded me of this point the other day when she asked "Why do we call it *the* U.S.? We don't say *the* Europe or *the* Canada." As we puzzled through what is essentially a grammatical conundrum, we began to discuss the fundamental shift in American identity that took place in the nineteenth century.

We did not always call our country the United States. Before the Civil War many referred to it as *these* United States. Indeed, throughout much of the nineteenth century Americans debated whether membership in the nation or membership in individual states came first. So fraught was this issue that the pre-Reconstruction Constitution avoided any explicit definition of who was a citizen. A question about grammar thus sparked a difficult but rewarding discussion about American history.

Barriers and Bonds

Not all barriers are harmful. As Alan Wolfe points out, some barriers are "necessary for achievement and growth, as rites of passage that make an identity worth having."[88] A naturalization process that treats citizenship as a valued and substantive status gives applicants a reason to prize their new standing. Moreover, naturalization requirements can provide immigrants with valuable educational opportunities that foster their development as full members of the polity. Advocates predicted that IRCA's programs in civic education would fail to attract participants. Yet, these programs were oversubscribed. Applicants valued what they were learning. They often attended class well beyond the required forty hours. After three times as many students as expected showed up for classes, the Los Angeles School District established a twenty-four-hour school for citizenship.[89]

A more serious naturalization process need not mean fewer successful applicants. The Americanization courses pressed on immigrants in the 1910s and 1920s also presented serious obstacles for newcomers who worked at night or were exhausted by their day's labor. Yet, as Reed Ueda notes, although the average course lasted seven months and met nearly every day, attendance rates remained high.[90] Ueda also points out that, when in 1952 applicants for citizenship were required to read and write as well as speak and understand English, the number of failed applicants after 1952 was two-thirds lower than over the previous decade.[91]

For immigrants, the whole process of applying for citizenship can help them enter into American life through regular meetings with tutors.[92] A more substantive and symbolic naturalization process can also serve as a ritual that helps bind new and old citizens. It proclaims to citizens immigrants' commitment to their new identity, thereby strengthening the importance of citizenship as a category of mutual obligation. The Americanization movement in the 1910s and 1920s offers an example of how the commitments newcomers make increase support for their inclusion.

An equilibrium between commitment and support also characterized the debate over IRCA in the 1980s. Jim Wright confronted an impasse between representatives who wanted to close the border to illegal aliens and representatives who sought, primarily, to legalize undocumented workers. He convinced the proponents of increased border enforcement to support amnesty by stressing that a commitment to citizenship would be expected of qualified applicants. By emphasizing the process of civic education and the obligations aliens would undertake, Wright overcame the reluctance of some representatives to support the newcomers.[93]

Yet, while citizens have expressed concern over the naturalization process, they have not helped newcomers become a part of a common civic culture. They have done little to introduce immigrants to concepts fundamental to American political life, to emphasize the importance of making a commitment to a new political identity, and to welcome them to our deliberations over the public good. The purpose of making the naturalization process more substantive and symbolic should not be to increase the number of applicants who fail the exam. A process that fosters commitment and learning rather than ratifies loyalty and knowledge will be judged by how well it strengthens citizenship, not by how many immigrants it renders permanent resident aliens. To accomplish this task, Americans would need to take the responsibilities of citizenship more seriously, including the obligation to assist newcomers in becoming part of a shared political identity.

The Americanization movement of the 1910s and 1920s constituted the last major effort to formally incorporate immigrants into the polity. The Americanization movement, which was part of the broader Progressive effort to make everyone new citizens of a new society, urged immigrants to adopt an understanding of politics that had both a political and a cultural component. On the one hand, many Progressive Americanizers defined citizenship as attachment to the principles of liberal democracy. They affirmed a core set of beliefs in liberty, equality, individualism, constitutionalism, and democracy. Further, they emphasized that to become an American meant engaging actively and independently in the common public sphere. Some Progressive organizations saw Americanization not as "uniformity, not a dose of English and civics injected into the immigrants, not [just] naturalization, but participation in a common life."[94]

On the other hand, many Progressives also associated the survival of democratic institutions with the predominance of Anglo–Saxon culture. Hence, immigrants were instructed that to be good Americans they had to adopt a particular set of moral values, habits, and practices that included everything from the American way to brush one's teeth to the Protestant value of self-control. Some Americanizers taught new arrivals to forget their linguistic and cultural heritage and to associate their new nation's culture with its English heritage.

The Americanizers' tactics also varied significantly. The National Security League and the American Legion feared contamination by "alien cultures" and advocated restricting access to citizenship and a coercive program of Americanization. These views exerted significant influence in the Americanization movement. But other supporters of Americanization invested the proceedings with quite different meanings. The Foreign Language Information Service saw immigrants as carriers of important virtues who should be converted, not coerced, into the liberal democratic faith. They helped the new arrivals learn English and improve their health while preparing them for their naturalization examinations by exploring the democratic process, the nature of constitutional rights, and how the economy functioned.[95]

Americanization was often crude and coercive; even the most appealing programs established too static a conception of identity. They proclaimed as completed the project of defining what it means to belong to America. This approach risked creating citizens shaped only by acquiescence and not by the force of their own understanding of, and contribution to, a shared identity. But, at its best, Americanization offered immigrants an invitation that is often absent today, an invitation to think deeply about their new identity and to take seriously their role in the public life of a new country.

Today, there is an unhealthy division in the United States between groups that work directly with immigrants and groups concerned about the declining value of citizenship. Many organizations that aid newcomers focus on protecting immigrants' rights and easing their adjustment to American life. In their view, naturalization is a means to protecting those rights, not a transformative experience that commits immigrants to a new identity. On the other hand, organizations that decry the dissolution of a common American identity, the erosion of citizenship as a meaningful category, and the weakened civic attachment among all members of the polity have very little to do with newcomers.

Both these groups could take citizenship as seriously as they do helping immigrants become full members of the polity. Civic and community groups who do not aim to increase their political power via naturalization can still help ensure a more substantive and symbolic process. Ethnic associations and rights' organizations can ensure that citizen education programs do not become barriers to naturalization or simple programs of indoctrination into the glories of American citizenship. (To be sure, this is too crude a division of labor and does not adequately reflect either type of association's full set of concerns.) Joint projects of the National Association of Latino Elected Officials (NALEO) and the American Legion or the Rotary Club can make clear that the process of citizenship education and national self-definition is not simply a matter that takes place between native-born and naturalizing citizens, but among those who are already citizens as well.

Conclusion

Americans did not conceive of citizenship in the last century as we do today. In the same way, over the next one hundred years, we may develop very different ideas of membership and belonging. Significant changes are possible in the mix of political principles, emotional attachment, and interpretive judgment that constitute the meaning of American citizenship. We live in a time when both subnational and transnational forces challenge the dominance of a single, national sense of citizenship as the primary category ordering political membership. I have argued that a single complex sense of constitutional identity is necessary to integrate our allegiances to the multiple communities to which we belong. We need citizens who feel an emotional attachment to the polity, who are committed to its basic values, who share certain qualities and attitudes, and who are willing to interrogate those values and deliberate over the meaning of their shared identity.

A naturalization process for the twenty-first century should therefore stress the transformative identity of being an American, not simply induce immigrants to become citizens for purely instrumental reasons or empty citizenship of meaning. Such a process should bind new and old citizens without unduly burdening those who willingly meet the obligations asked of them. A more substantive and symbolic naturalization process cannot ensure the habits that cause individuals to recognize one another as fellow citizens who share a bond. Government policy is a blunt instrument; so nurturing a common identity must often be accomplished in smaller settings. Yet to guide this work we need a conception of citizenship that stresses the new and complex identity of being an American. The term "naturalized citizen" implies the importance of manufacturing political commitment. To "make natural" suggests the artifice in shaping a citizen in a constitutional order.

Notes

1. *Statistical Yearbook of the Immigration and Naturalization Service, 1996* (Washington, D.C.: U.S. Government Printing Office, 1997). Applications for citizenship jumped from 342,000 in fiscal year 1992 to 1,277,403 in fiscal year 1996. This increase can be attributed to a number of factors: a "Green Card Replacement Program" which required aliens to replace their permanent resident aliens cards, at a cost of $75, encouraged some long-term residents to apply for citizenship, which cost only $95; the naturalization eligibility of 2.68 million undocumented aliens who were granted permanent resident status under the Immigration and Reform Control Act of 1986; and the Citizenship USA initiative of the Immigration and Naturalization Service, which sought to streamline the naturalization process. Legislative efforts to deny immigrants public benefits also likely played a significant role in the rush to citizenship.

2. Lamar Smith, as quoted on *Morning Edition*, National Public Radio, 25 March 1997.

3. U.S. Commission on Immigration Reform, *Becoming an American: Immigration and Immigrant Policy* (Washington, D.C.: U.S. Government Printing Office, 1997), 28, 73–75; for a summary of these views, see Noah M. J. Pickus, *Becoming American/America Becoming: Final Report of the Duke University Workshop on Immigration and Citizenship* (Durham: Terry Sanford Institute of Public Policy, 1997), 20–21; in this volume, see Hiroshi Motomura, "Alienage Classifications in a Nation of Immigrants: Three Models of 'Permanent' Residence."

4. Harry Pachon, "U.S. Citizenship and Latino Participation in California Politics," in *Racial and Ethnic Politics in California*, ed. Bryan O. Jackson and Michael B. Preston (Berkeley: IGS Press, 1991).

5. For a wide-ranging analysis of the language, oath, ideological, and other requirements for citizenship, see Gerald Neuman, "Justifying U.S. Naturalization Policies," *Virginia Journal of International Law* 35, no. 1 (Fall 1994): 237–78.

6. The different positions I identify in this chapter—civic, cultural, rights, and participatory—are not monolithic. Significant differences exist among proponents of a single view; nor are these four positions mutually exclusive. The rights and participatory views, for instance, share much in common, and the civic and cultural cases against current naturalization policy overlap in some instances. Nevertheless, each position represents a distinct view of the meaning of membership in the late twentieth century.

7. Americans have, of course, disagreed sharply over the centrality of that definition of belonging. See Charles R. Kesler, "The Promise of American Citizenship," and Juan F. Perea, "'Am I an American or Not?' Reflections on Citizenship, Americanization, and Race," both in this volume.

8. For similar analyses, see David A. Hollinger, *Postethnic America: Beyond Multiculturalism* (New York: Basic Books, 1995); and William Rogers Brubaker, "Introduction," in *The Politics of Immigration and Citizenship in Western Europe and North America*, ed. William Rogers Brubaker (Lanham, Md.: University Press of America, 1989).

9. See Iris Marion Young, "Polity and Group Difference: A Critique of the Ideal of Universal Citizenship," *Ethics* 99, no. 2 (January 1989): 250–74; Will Kymlicka, *Multicultural Citizenship: A Liberal Theory of Minority Rights* (New York: Oxford University Press, 1995); and Joseph H. Carens, "Citizenship and Aboriginal Self-Government: Is Deep Diversity Possible?" (Paper delivered at the Ninety-second Annual Meeting of the American Political Science Association, San Francisco, 29 August–1 September 1996).

10. For some analysts, multicultural and national identity can be reconciled because the demand for group representation and cultural rights is a demand for inclusion. "Groups that feel excluded," observe Will Kymlicka and Wayne Norman, "want to be included in the larger society, and the recognition and accommodation of their 'difference' is intended to facilitate this." If this is true, we need to assess carefully the difference between assimilation to an existing national identity and requiring that the collective identity accept a radical change in its principles as the price of having minorities feel included. If the latter case, is it a demand for inclusion or for transformation? Will Kymlicka and Wayne Norman, "Return of the Citizen: A Survey of Recent Work on Citizenship Theory," in *Theorizing Citizenship*, ed. Ronald Beiner (Albany, N.Y.: State University of New York Press, Albany, 1995), 307.

11. The phrase is Michael Walzer's, from "Political Alienation and Military Service," in *Obligations: Essays on Disobedience, War, and Citizenship* (Cambridge: Harvard University Press, 1970), 114. I discuss some of these problems in "Does Immigration Threaten Democracy? Rights, Restriction and the Meaning of Membership," in *Democracy: The Challenges Ahead*, ed. Yossi Shain and Aharon Klieman (New York: St. Martin's Press, 1997), 137–41. See also Michael J. Sandel, *Democracy's Discontent: America in Search of a Public Philosophy* (Cambridge: Belknap Press of Harvard University, 1996); Christopher Lasch, *The Minimal Self: Psychic Survival in Troubled Times* (New York: W.W. Norton, 1984); and Mary Ann Glendon, *Rights Talk: The Impoverishment of Political Discourse* (New York: Free Press, 1991).

12. Hollinger, *Postethnic America*, 149.

13. Sanford Levinson, "Lawyers as Citizens: An Inquiry into National Loyalty and the Professional Identity of Lawyers," in *Diversity and Citizenship: Rediscovering American Nationhood*, ed. Gary Jacobsohn and Susan Dunn (Lanham, Md.: Rowman & Littlefield, 1996), 17–43.

14. Roger Rouse, "Mexican Migration and the Social Space of Postmodernism," *Diaspora* 1 (March 1991): 8–23; Robert C. Smith, "'Los Ausentes Siempre Presentes': The Imagining, Making, and Politics of a Transnational Community Between Ticuani, Pueble, Mexico, and New York City" (Ph.D. diss., Columbia University, 1993); Nina Glick Schiller, Linda Basch, and Christina Blanc-Szanton, *Toward A Transnational Perspective on Migration: Race, Class, Ethnicity and Nationalism Reconsidered* (New York: Annals of the New York Academy of Sciences, July 1992), vol. 645.

15. Alejandro Portes, "Global Villagers: The Rise of Transnational Communities," *The American Prospect*, March–April 1996, 77.

16. David Jacobson, *Rights Across Borders: Immigration and the Decline of Citizenship* (Baltimore: Johns Hopkins University Press, 1996).

17. I develop this argument in greater depth in "'Hearken Not to the Unnatural Voice': Publius and the Artifice of Attachment," in *Diversity and Citizenship: Rediscovering American Nationhood*, ed. Gary Jacobsohn and Susan Dunn (Lanham, Md.: Rowman & Littlefield, 1996), 63–84.

18. Michael Walzer, "What Does It Mean to Be an 'American'?" *Social Research* 57 (September 1990): 594–614.

19. James Kettner, *The Development of American Citizenship, 1608–1870* (Chapel Hill, N.C.: University of North Carolina Press, 1978).

20. Rogers M. Smith, *Civic Ideals: Conflicting Visions of Citizenship in U.S. History* (New Haven: Yale University Press, 1997).

21. Peter H. Schuck and Rogers M. Smith, *Citizenship Without Consent: Illegal Aliens in the American Polity* (New Haven: Yale University Press, 1985).

22. Pickus, "'Hearken Not,'" 64–68.

23. Pickus, "'Hearken Not,'" 68–73.

24. George P. Fletcher, *Loyalty: An Essay on the Morality of Relationships* (New York: Oxford University Press, 1993), 104.

25. Ronald Takaki, "Reflections on Racial Patterns in America," in *From Different Shores: Perspectives on Race and Ethnicity in America*, ed. Ronald Takaki (New York: Oxford University Press, 1987), 26–37.

26. Pickus, "'Hearken Not,'" 73–80; Hadley Arkes, *Beyond the Constitution* (Princeton, N.J.: Princeton University Press, 1990), chap. 4.

27. Peter Brimelow, "Time to Rethink Immigration," *National Review*, 22 June 1992, 34. See also Lawrence Auster, "The Forbidden Topic: Link between Multiculturalism and Immigration," *National Review*, 27 April 1992, 42–44.

28. Peter Brimelow, "Un-American Activities," *National Review*, 16 June 1997, 44.

29. Stephen L. Carter, "Nativism and Its Discontents," *New York Times*, 8 March 1992.

30. Alexander Hamilton, James Madison, and John Jay, *The Federalist Papers*, ed. Clinton Rossiter (New York: New American Library, 1961), no. 2.

31. "Observations Concerning the Increase of Mankind, Peopling of Countries, Etc.," in *Benjamin Franklin's Autobiography and Selected Writings*, ed. Larzer Ziff (New York: Holt, Rinehart and Winston, 1959), 210 [Franklin's italics].

32. Peter Brimelow, *Alien Nation: Common Sense About America's Immigration Disaster* (New York: Free Press, 1995), 264–67.

33. Peter H. Schuck, "Membership in the Liberal Polity: The Devaluation of American Citizenship," in *Politics of Immigration*; and Peter H. Schuck, "The Transformation of Immigration Law," *Columbia Law Review* 84, no. 1 (January 1984): 54–58.

34. T. Alexander Aleinikoff, "Citizens, Aliens, Membership and the Constitution," *Constitutional Commentary* 7, no. 1 (Winter 1990): 9–34. See also Pickus, *Becoming American/American Becoming*, 10, 16; Linda S. Bosniak, "A National Solidarity?: A Response to David Hollinger" and Joseph H. Carens, "Why Naturalization Should Be Easy: A Response to Noah Pickus," both in this volume.

35. Sanford Levinson, "Lawyers as Citizens: An Inquiry into National Loyalty and the Professional Identity of Lawyers," in *Diversity and Citizenship*, 27.

36. Portes, "Global Villagers," 77.

37. Jamin Raskin, "Legal Aliens, Local Citizens: The Historical, Constitutional and Theoretical Meanings of Alien Suffrage," *University of Pennsylvania Law Review* 141, no. 4 (April 1993): 1391–1470.

38. Robert L. Bach et al., *Changing Relations: Newcomers and Established Residents in U.S. Communities* (New York: Ford Foundation, 1993), 58–59.

39. Pickus, " 'Hearken Not,' " 68–73.

40. See Kymlicka and Norman, "Return of the Citizen"; and Sandel, *Democracy's Discontent*.

41. Josef Joffe, "Europe's Colossal Coin Toss," *New York Times* 1 May 1998, A27.

42. Peter H. Schuck discusses a similar point in "The Re-Evaluation of American Citizenship," *Georgetown Immigration Law Journal* 12, no. 1 (Fall 1997): 1–34.

43. Peter H. Schuck, "The Message of 187," *The American Prospect*, Spring 1995, 85–92.

44. *League of United Latin American Citizens v. Wilson*, 1998 WL 141325 (C.D.Cal. 1998); *League of United Latin American Citizens v. Wilson*, 908 F. Supp. 755 (C.D.Cal. 1995).

45. John J. Miller, "The Naturalizers," *Policy Review*, July-August 1996, 50.

46. Miller, "The Naturalizers," 52.

47. Georgie Anne Geyer, *Americans No More: The Death of Citizenship* (New York: Atlantic Monthly Press, 1996), especially chapters 2–4.

48. Reed Ueda, "Naturalization and Citizenship," in *Harvard Encyclopedia of American Ethnic Groups*, ed. Stephen Thernstrom (Cambridge: Belknap Press of Harvard University, 1982), 736–37.

49. Gerald L. Neuman, *Strangers to the Constitution: Immigrants, Borders, and Fundamental Law* (Princeton: Princeton University Press, 1996), 57–60.

50. Walzer, "American," 600.

51. John Higham, "Integrating America: The Problem of Assimilation," in *Send These to Me: Immigrants in Urban America* (Baltimore: Johns Hopkins University Press, 1984).

52. See especially John Higham's description of how the National Americanization Committee influenced the INS's civic education programs through subsidizing the Bureau of Education. Higham, *Strangers in the Land: Patterns of American Nativism 1860–1925* (New Brunswick: Rutgers University Press, 1955), chap. 9. See also John F. McClymer, "The Federal Government and the Americanization Movement, 1915–1924," *Prologue*, Spring 1978, 23–41.

53. Michael Kammen, *A Machine That Would Go of Itself: The Constitution in American Culture* (New York: Knopf, 1986), 235–48.

54. Gerald M. Rosberg, "Aliens and Equal Protection: Why Not the Right to Vote?" *Michigan Law Review* 75 (April–May 1977): 1092–1136.

55. John Fonte, testimony given at U.S. Senate, Committee on the Judiciary, Subcommittee on Immigration, *Hearing on Naturalization Requirements and the Rights and Privileges of Citizenship*, 22 October 1996.

56. Lawrence Harrison, testimony given at *Hearing on Naturalization Require-

ments. See also Dan Stein, testimony given at *Hearing on Naturalization Require-ments*; and Stein, "Oaths, Allegiance, and the Loss of Common Understanding" (Paper delivered at the National Issues Forum, Brookings Institution, 8 December 1997).

57. Sanford Levinson, *Constitutional Faith* (Princeton: Princeton University Press, 1988), 110.

58. John J. Miller and William James Muldoon, "Citizenship for Granted" (Washington, D.C.: Center for Equal Opportunity Policy Brief, October 1996).

59. Doris Meissner, "Putting the 'N' Back Into INS: Comments on the Immigration and Naturalization Service," *Virginia Journal of International Law* 35, no. 1 (Fall 1994): 1–11.

60. Louis DeSipio and Harry P. Pachon, "Making Americans," *Chicano–Latino Law Review* 12 (1992): 63.

61. Levinson, *Constitutional Faith*, 105.

62. Edward Roybal, *Congressional Record*, 19 June 1984, 6068.

63. William F. Harris II, *The Interpretable Constitution* (Baltimore: Johns Hopkins University Press, 1993), 118.

64. Christopher Eisgruber, "Justice and the Text: Rethinking the Constitutional Relation between Principle and Prudence," *Duke Law Journal* 43 (1993): 20–27.

65. There is also an important distinction between denationalization and denying citizenship to a member of another nation-state. The former case exposes an individual to the misfortune of statelessness, although the rise in rights granted to persons rather than citizens makes even this status less dire than it once was.

66. Ueda, "Naturalization and Citizenship," 746.

67. Rodolfo O. de la Garza et al., *Latino Voices: Mexican, Puerto Rican and Cuban Perspectives on American Politics* (Boulder, Colo.: Westview Press, 1992), 80, 101, 102. See also Aida Hurtado et al., *Redefining California: Latino Social Engagement in a Multicultural Society* (Los Angeles: UCLA Chicano Studies Research Center, 1992), chap. 6.

68. Pickus, "Does Immigration Threaten Democracy?," 137–41.

69. See Peter Skerry, *Mexican-Americans: The Ambivalent Minority* (New York: Free Press, 1993).

70. Fletcher, *Loyalty*, 21.

71. *Sugarman v. Dougall*, 412 U.S. 634 (1973).

72. Gary E. Rubin, personal correspondence with author, 28 July 1997. See also Gary E. Rubin, *The Assault on Citizenship* (New York: NYANA Policy Series, 1998), 25–26.

73. DeSipio and Pachon, "Making Americans," 62.

74. Louis DeSipio, "Making Citizens or Good Citizens?" *Hispanic Journal of Behavioral Sciences* 18, no. 2 (May 1996): 197.

75. Rubin, *The Assault on Citizenship*; see also Gary E. Rubin, *The War on Immigration: Why It's Hurting America* (New York: NYANA Policy Series, 1997); Harry P. Pachon, "New Citizens are the New Target," *Los Angeles Times*, 23 July 1996.

76. DeSipio, "Making Citizens," 201–11.

77. DeSipio, "Making Citizens," 197–99.

78. DeSipio, *Counting on the Latino Vote: Latinos as a New Electorate* (Charlottesville: University of Virginia Press, 1996), 130–31.

79. Rodolfo O. de la Garza and Louis DeSipio, "Save the Baby, Change the Bathwater, and Scrub the Tub: Latino Electoral Participation after Seventeen Years of Voting Rights Act Coverage," *Texas Law Review* 71, no. 7 (June 1993): 1479–1539.

80. DeSipio, *Latino Vote*, 181–83.

81. *Congressional Record*, 19 June 1984, 6066.

82. I describe in greater depth the wrangling over the civic education component of IRCA in " 'True Faith and Allegiance': Immigration and the Politics of Citizenship" (Ph.D. diss., Princeton University, 1995).

83. Charles Merriam, *The Making of Citizens: A Comparative Study of Methods of Civic Training* (Chicago: University of Chicago Press, 1931), 301. See also Richard M. Merelman, "Symbols as Substance in National Civics Standards," *PS: Political Science & Politics* (March 1996): 53–57.

84. On deliberation as a central component of citizenship, see Amy Guttman and Dennis Thompson, *Democracy and Disagreement: Why Moral Conflict Cannot be Avoided in Politics, and What Should be Done About It* (Cambridge: The Belknap Press of Harvard University Press, 1996).

85. *Minersville School District v. Gobitis*, 310 U.S. 586 (1940).

86. Harris, *The Interpretable Constitution*, 119.

87. For an example of this process by a native-born citizen, see Levinson, *Constitutional Faith*. Levinson describes his exploration as issuing in "a commitment to take political conversation seriously" (193).

88. Alan Wolfe, "The Return of the Melting Pot," *The New Republic*, 31 December 1990, 27–34. See also Wolfe, *Whose Keeper? Social Science and Moral Obligation* (Berkeley: University of California Press, 1989), 246–56.

89. Pickus, " 'True Faith and Allegiance,' " chap. 4; Susan Baker Gonzalez, *The Cautious Welcome: The Legalization Programs of IRCA* (Santa Monica, Calif.: Rand Corporation, 1990).

90. Ueda, "Naturalization and Citizenship," 745.

91. Reed Ueda, *Postwar Immigrant America: A Social History* (Boston: Bedford Books of St. Martin's Press, 1994), 52.

92. In "Making Naturalization Matter," I describe how the efforts of one recent applicant for citizenship have proved rewarding to her and to her family. *Freedom Review* 28, no. 3 (Fall 1997): 55–63.

93. Pickus, " 'True Faith and Allegiance,' " chaps. 4, 6.

94. Reed Lewis, director of the Foreign Language Information Service, quoted in Daniel Weinberg, "The Ethnic Technician and the Foreign-Born: Another Look at Americanization Ideology and Goals," *Societas—A Review of History*, 215.

95. Lawrence Fuchs, *The American Kaleidoscope: Race, Ethnicity, and the Civic Culture* (Hanover: University Press of New England, 1990), 61–67; and Philip Gleason, "American Identity and Americanization," in *Harvard Encyclopedia of American Ethnic Groups*.

Why Naturalization Should Be Easy:
A Response to Noah Pickus

Joseph H. Carens

I approach this topic as an American who lives in Canada—and as a Canadian who spent his first forty years in the United States. Both characterizations are accurate, and in some contexts I might put the second one first. I'm not yet legally a Canadian, but psychologically I have become one. At the same time, I have not abandoned either my legal status or my identity as an American. So questions about identity, loyalty, naturalization, dual citizenship, and so on have a personal resonance for me.

When I was first asked to reflect on the naturalization exam in the United States, I asked my ten-year-old son, Michael, what he thought about the issue. He responded almost incredulously, "You mean someone wouldn't be allowed to be a citizen and to participate because he didn't pass a test? That sucks! People who do not have a good education or who are just not good at taking tests have the right to be citizens too." I have concluded that Michael is entirely right. Most of what I have to say is simply an elaboration—probably superfluous—of his insight.

I'll start with a few comments about the problems with the naturalization exam and then try to take the argument to a deeper level. Naturalization exams are ostensibly designed to make sure that prospective citizens have the competence to participate in an informed and intelligent way. But this sort of test never works very well regardless of the particular questions it asks. The tests are usually set at a very low level and so screen out very few people anyway. That's good from my perspective because it means the tests do less harm than they would if they were highly selective, but it also suggests that the tests don't actually function very effectively

This essay was written in response to a draft of Noah Pickus's chapter, presented at the Duke University Workshop on Citizenship and Naturalization, October 30–November 1, 1997.

as screens. What about the few who do fail? Are we confident that they are not competent? My guess is that most who fail do so because of nervousness as much as lack of knowledge. But even if they don't know the answers, does that mean they are not competent to participate as citizens? The knowledge required for wise political judgment is complex, multifaceted, and often intuitive. It's not something that can be captured on a test of this sort. Moreover, we know that formal tests of this kind always have built-in biases that inappropriately favor some class and cultural backgrounds over others, even if that is not intended. The literacy tests that were formerly used to distinguish citizens competent to vote from those who were not had these sorts of biases even when they were not deliberately manipulated, as they often were, to exclude African Americans. There are many highly literate people who are deeply ignorant and many illiterate people who are profoundly wise.

In sum, I am deeply skeptical about the capacity of any naturalization exam to measure the competencies required for citizenship. All tests have flaws, of course, but sometimes we need them because we are obliged to sort and rank people for various purposes. But here we have another alternative. We don't have to sort and rank. We can treat everyone equally.

Let me turn now to the broader question of what it is appropriate to expect of people who want to become citizens. I suggest we distinguish among requirements, norms, and aspirations in the naturalization process. "Requirements" refer to legally enforceable standards that must be met as a condition of naturalization (such as length of residence, demonstrating a certain level of language proficiency, passing a test on the country's history and institutions, etc.). "Norms" refer to social expectations regarding the behavior and attitudes of immigrants. These social expectations are not enforced legally, but they do have sanctions attached. Failure to meet them may evoke disapproval, perhaps even public criticism from other members of society, but will have no impact on legal eligibility for naturalization. Finally, "aspirations" refer to hopes the receiving society has for the ways in which immigrants will adapt and the kinds of adaptation the society tries to foster without thinking it appropriate or even acceptable to criticize those who do not adapt in these ways. Broadly speaking, I want to argue that most of the things people advocate when they talk about strengthening or improving the naturalization process belong in the third category (aspirations), and many of the things that are currently treated as legal requirements really belong in the second (norms).

With respect to requirements, I think the standards should be set very low. Indeed, I think that length of residence is the only standard that is ultimately justifiable for permanent residents. I recognize that the standard I am proposing is not adopted as a general rule by any liberal democratic state and that, in comparative perspective, the American requirements for naturalization are relatively modest (though more demanding in some respects than the requirements of other countries of immigration like Canada and Australia). Nevertheless, I want to argue that, as a matter of fundamental justice, anyone who has resided lawfully in a liberal democratic state for an extended period of time (e.g., five years or more) ought to be entitled to become a citizen if he or she wishes to do so.

Why should the legal requirements be limited to residence? Fundamentally, this is an argument about the moral priority of civil society in relation to political society. Living in a society is what makes a person a member of civil society. In living in a society, one inevitably becomes involved in a dense network of social associations and acquires interests and identities tied up with other members of the society. Legal citizenship offers one important means by which those interests and identities can be protected and expressed. For many people it will seem an essential means.

But citizenship should be more than a means to private ends, some will say. Such a limited, instrumental conception of citizenship does not do justice to the political community and its needs for an active, engaged, committed citizenry. This is certainly a concern that shapes Noah Pickus's chapter, and I understand and agree with the concern in many ways. But this more demanding conception of citizenship is not fit material for legal requirements either of current citizens or of potential ones. These are the sorts of concerns that we can make the subject of our aspirations and perhaps, to a lesser extent, of our expectations—but not of our requirements.

At the heart of the liberal democratic conception of politics is the notion that the state exists for the sake of the members of society and that the fundamental interests of some members should not be sacrificed even if a majority would find that to their advantage. What makes a person a member of society with these kinds of claims against the state cannot depend on the state's own categories and practices. It depends instead on the social facts.

Let me cite an example from another country. In Germany the descendants of Turkish guest workers have been generally excluded from citizenship. These are people who have been born and brought up in Germany, whose parents may have been born and brought up in the same society, who may speak no other language than German and know no other home, but are nonetheless denied access to citizenship. In the United States the existence of a birthright citizenship rule precludes this kind of anomaly, but it may be useful for us to consider why such a policy is morally objectionable. The answer, I think, is that these people are so obviously members of German civil society that it is wrong to exclude them from full political membership. Indeed, the Germans have begun to reform their citizenship laws in partial recognition of such claims.

The same sort of principle applies to people who have lived in the United States for a long time even if they were not born there. Of course, to set five years as the threshold for this sort of membership is obviously arbitrary, but whatever the length of time, there must be some sort of threshold after which additional time is unnecessary. And it is important to remember that I am talking about people who have been admitted on a permanent basis, i.e., with the right to live there as long as they want.

I have already given my reasons for opposing tests of civic and historical knowledge. My claim that competence in English should not be used as a requirement for naturalization is apt to be equally or more controversial. In my view, individuals who have functioned in American society for several years without knowing English should be presumed to be capable also of participating in the political process without knowing English. They will have many forms of information available from friends and neighbors and media in their own language, and that should be enough. One may wish and hope that citizens will be better informed, but it would be unreasonable to insist on a knowledge of English for the sake of an idealized form of political information that the average English-speaking citizen does not possess. The political knowledge of most citizens is heavily filtered through friends, neighbors, and other trusted local sources, regardless of the language they speak. Moreover, we should not assume that minority language communities are monolithic in their political views or that local English-speaking communities are typically open to unconventional ideas and vigorous debate.

Some people may find length of residence a bit thin as a criterion of membership in civil society and prefer to emphasize labor market participation, participation in neighborhood associations, or other forms of more active engagement in civil society. These sorts of examples can certainly serve to bring home some of the many ways in which people are connected to one another in civil society and thus reinforce the sense of why access to citizenship may be both instrumentally necessary and associationally appropriate. Nevertheless, I want to be cautious about unduly emphasizing forms of involvement in civil society that may be gender-biased. Of course, many women also participate in the labor market or in neighborhood associations, but some women are primarily involved in child rearing and household maintenance. These are forms of work that have generally been undervalued and sometimes excluded altogether from accounts of civil society through the construction of the family as a separate, private sphere, distinct from both civil society and political community. In fact, more careful attention to the way child rearing and household maintenance actually work would undoubtedly show that these activities, too, normally engage people in a dense network of social associations outside the immediate family. However, it seems to me that it would be a normative mistake to make a person's membership in civil society, and hence entitlement to citizenship, depend in any fundamental way on an empirical assessment of the number or quality of one's social interactions. It is one thing to construct social policies with the goal of helping people to escape from unwanted forms of social isolation and quite another to use social isolation, wanted or unwanted, as a criterion justifying exclusion from citizenship.

To avoid any misunderstanding let me distinguish the position I am defending here from what is sometimes—as I think in Pickus's chapter—described as a cosmopolitan view. Nothing in my argument rests on the proposition that we have to treat all human beings alike, that we cannot distinguish between members and strangers. My argument does not depend in any way on a claim that we are obliged to admit any immigrants who want to come. On the contrary, it rests on the fact that we have chosen to admit certain immigrants as permanent residents, and having admitted them to live among us on an ongoing basis, we are obliged not to marginalize them, not to exclude them from participating in shaping the choices and directions of society or from enjoying the fuller security and rights that citizenship brings. In sum, long-term membership in civil society creates a moral right to political membership.

So, I would set the requirements threshold very low. What about the expectations imposed on immigrants? What sorts of norms can we establish? It is in the realm of norms rather than requirements that some of the concerns about language and values can be pursued. It is perfectly reasonable, in my view, to expect immigrants to send their children to schools where—if all goes well and as it is supposed to—they will learn English and will be encouraged to adopt liberal democratic values like toleration, mutual respect, and so on. Of course, we all know that what students learn about liberal democratic values from the behavior and attitudes of their teachers and fellow students is far more important than what they are taught in lectures and textbooks. Thus we need to be cautious about assuming that everything is fine if the right courses are in place, but in principle it is possible to justify this sort of expectation. I think it is also reasonable to expect that adult immigrants will try to learn English, so long as reasonable opportunities are provided and allowances made for the many different circumstances that affect people's capacities to acquire a new language. Finally, it is reasonable to expect immigrants to accept liberal democratic values as the principles that govern public life. (I deliberately use the term "liberal democratic values" to describe the kinds of commitments it is reasonable to expect because I do not think there is anything distinctively American about the kinds of principles and norms the Commission on Immigration Reform identifies as the ones it wants immigrants to adopt.) That is about all we can reasonably expect, either of immigrants or citizens, as a matter of socially enforced norms.

What about loyalty, patriotism, and identity? Can't we expect immigrants to become attached to America? As an empirical matter we can, of course, because most do. But as a normative matter, we should not try to impose such an expectation, much less make it a legal requirement. This is the sort of thing we can try to encourage and foster, but it's not the sort of thing we should try to command. In any event, such commands are probably doomed to failure. The heart does not normally respond well to coercion. If dual loyalties are a problem—and I think they rarely are a real problem—prohibitions of dual citizenship will do little to resolve them. People's feelings and identities may well remain divided, whatever legal status they choose.

We can also hope to foster a more active form of citizenship. Again aspiration rather than requirement or norm is the right way to approach this sort of concern, which is important, but in tension with liberal norms about people's rights to choose their own ways of life and set their own priorities. Because of those liberal norms, even our aspirations ought to be severely limited. It would not be right, for example, to hope that Muslim immigrants would convert to Christianity or that gay immigrants would become straight. The commitment to respect individual freedom that is such a central part of liberal democratic ideals sets severe limits on the sorts of things that are an appropriate subject for collective concern, even in the form of aspirations.

I conclude with a methodological point. I put my arguments forward without any effort to estimate the political feasibility of the policies I recommend, and feasibility is, of course, something that public officials—whether elected, appointed, or career—have to take into account. Nevertheless, I judged it appropriate for me to focus here on what I think is the right course in principle and to leave to others the important task of judging how we might need to modify that course to take account of political realities.[1]

Notes

1. For an elaboration of this methodological point see Joseph H. Carens, "Realistic and Idealistic Approaches to the Ethics of Immigration," *International Migration Review* 30, no. 1 (Spring 1996): 156–70.

Part III:

Multiple Memberships?

5

Plural Citizenships

Peter H. Schuck

To reflect deeply on citizenship is to enter a bewildering gyre of reasoning. It is common ground that citizenship entails a kind of membership, but there the consensus ceases and the contention begins. Membership in what? Why, in the polity of course. And what is a polity? It is a community of citizens. Oh. And does the polity include those who are not citizens? Well, it includes them in some senses but not in others. If it is the citizens who decide on the nature and conditions of noncitizens' inclusion, by what right did they acquire that power and under what limitations do they exercise it? Hmmm.

One cannot really answer these questions without some theory that can either justify or criticize existing practice. Failing that, a metaphor can sometimes serve as a placeholder or surrogate for theory; it is a kind of theory manqué whose power to persuade lies in its compressed, immediate, deeply felt associations and imagery. For this reason, citizenship-talk usually unleashes a high-stakes rhetorical battle of metaphors. One portrays citizens as members of a family of origin, individuals who are linked to one another irrevocably by blood or by some equally binding historical integument. Another conceives of citizenship as a normative fellowship of belief, a dense community of shared values, what Robert Cover called a *nomos*. A third depicts citizens as members of a club who join and disaffiliate for their own purposes as and when they wish, so long as they meet eligibility standards and their dues are fully paid up. A fourth image of the civic relationship is that of a marriage—formalized through solemn

The author wishes to acknowledge the generous and useful comments by Alex Aleinikoff, Stephen Legomsky, David Martin, Gerald Neuman, and Peter Spiro on an earlier version, which was also presented at faculty workshops at Yale Law School and Case Western Reserve Law School. A slightly different version of this essay also appears as Chapter 10 of Peter H. Schuck, *Citizens, Strangers, and In-Betweens: Essays on Immigration and Citizenship* (Westview Press, 1998).

vows, designed to be permanent, and dissolved only with the consent of the state and upon certain proofs.[1]

Each of these metaphors captures certain features of constitutive relationships like that between citizen and state. The idealized family imagery evokes our desire for security, permanence, and unquestioning devotion in a web of mutual commitments beyond choice or calculation; yet it also presupposes a common experience and affinity of descent that are infrequent in a society as radically heterogeneous and open as ours. The *nomos* metaphor, like that of marriage, draws much of its rhetorical power from our yearnings for commitments that are so intense and unique that they occupy our spiritual domain. The consensuality of marriage, however, preserves room for considerable self-definition and autonomy, whereas the totalizing tendency of religion and the ascriptive tie of family tend to constrict such a space. The club is the most instrumental of these communal forms. Like marriage, club membership is contractual in nature and may generate affective ties but arises out of more calculating, reversible choices. Like markets, clubs require only a partial, episodic commitment from a member; they lay claim to a relatively narrow part of a member's identity.

When the debate turns to dual citizenship or nationality[2] and the question of divided loyalty arises, these metaphors continue to both clash and converge. For those who invoke the family or *nomos* as the dominant image, dual citizenship[3] is an impossibility, a condition utterly at war with the logical, spiritual, emotional, and psychological presuppositions of such communities. For those who liken the polity to a marital relationship, dual citizenship amounts to polygamy, a diffusion of allegiance and affection that threatens the integrity of both relationships. In contrast, those who prefer the club metaphor are quite comfortable with multiple memberships, each for limited purposes defined by the member himself or herself. Alternatively, one might abandon these relational metaphors altogether and view acquired citizenship as a "new political birth"[4] or, focusing on citizenship's traditionally territorial-spatial dimension, regard it as a more or less permanent home.

This debate, of course, will not end there. One remains free to question the appropriateness of each of these metaphors as applied to a political community. One can also challenge the metaphors' normative integrity by pointing to certain inconsistent social practices that seem to compromise their coherence—for example, our separation of the religious and political domains; the multiplicity of family groupings to which we belong; the blending of families and the generation of new ones through marriage and remarriage; and the cessation of relationships through divorce.[5] Such challenges invite the suspicion that although each of these images captures some significant aspect of citizenship, none provides an adequate account of it.

In this chapter, I hope to move beyond these metaphors by focusing instead on how we might think about dual citizenship without being distracted by such familiar, freighted, and powerful images. This discussion will underscore the profoundly value-laden character of an increasingly incendiary dual citizenship debate that threatens to polarize Americans in positions that will be difficult to compromise.

Section I begins by explaining why dual citizenship is becoming both more common and more controversial. This requires some discussion of the legal and social contexts in which dual citizenship has been liberalized[6] and citizenship itself is being reassessed. Others have ably and recently covered this ground, so my summary can be brief.[7] Section II develops some distinctions that can add texture to our understanding of dual citizenship and help us to identify some leverage points for possible policy change. Section III, the heart of the chapter, analyzes the arguments for and against permitting dual citizenship; it explores both the normative claims and the often-suppressed empirical issues that underlie the normative debate.

Based on this analysis, section IV considers how dual citizenship law might be reformed. I generally applaud the recent trend in U.S. law to accept dual citizenship and believe that this emerging regime should be refined rather than being either rejected or extended. I focus on two problems with existing dual citizenship law that deserve reformers' attention. First, the statutory requirement that a naturalizing citizen "renounce and abjure absolutely and entirely all allegiance and fidelity to any" other state, language that dates back to 1795, is broader than necessary to secure the loyalty that the United States needs and has a right to expect of its citizens. This broad, indiscriminate formulation obscures what the oath should clarify: the kinds of ties to other states that are inconsistent with American citizenship and must therefore be renounced. It may suggest to new citizens that they are being asked to renounce more than a liberal polity should demand. Second, the renunciation requirement applies only to naturalizing citizens, not to those dual citizens who acquired their U.S. citizenship by birth or descent. This difference creates an inequality among citizens that is difficult to justify and that appears to contradict fundamental constitutional principles. This inequality warrants public scrutiny and debate. By refining and clarifying the renunciation requirement and by calling on Congress to make the rights and obligations of citizens—old and new alike—as equal as possible, I hope to remedy both problems.

I readily acknowledge that even if my approach to the first problem were adopted—that is, if the oath were modified to require new citizens to renounce only the core political allegiance that they bear to another state—our dual citizenship policy and practice might change little. Americans (whether single or dual citizens) might continue to view their political rights and duties much as they do now, naturalization officials and the courts might interpret the standards as before, and aliens' incentives and propensity to seek naturalization might remain largely unaffected. Even if my proposal would change little in practice, however, this is hardly ground for objection. Because I do not regard the current permissive dual citizenship policy as being fundamentally "broke," I see no strong reason to "fix" it except for refining the renunciation language in the oath. On the other hand, my approach to the second problem—that is, reducing the inequality among citizens with respect to their right to acquire dual citizenship—would affect the right of existing U.S. citizens to acquire additional nationalities in the future and to act accordingly.

Some commentators on citizenship issues, including me, have expressed doubts about the dominant conceptions of citizenship, the distribution of rights and responsibilities among those who reside in the polity, and the justifications advanced to support this distribution.[8] While these criticisms raise interesting and important issues concerning citizenship, none of us doubts the fact that strong normative arguments can be made for retaining some distinctive citizenship status, although disagreement exists about which arguments are most persuasive. In what follows, I shall assume the essential validity of the status of citizenship,[9] even as I question certain conventional ways of thinking about and regulating it.

I. The Contemporary Debate and Context

It is only a matter of time before Congress takes up the dual citizenship issue. A number of structural changes are stoking Americans' anxieties about the course of our political development and about the coherence of our national identity. These changes include the globalization of the economy; easier travel; instantaneous and inexpensive communications; increased immigration, especially by the undocumented; diminished American autonomy in the world; the expansion of multinational corporations and the emergence of influential transnational nongovernmental organizations; growing multicultural pressures prompting concerns about immigrant assimilation and English language acquisition; the loss of a unifying ideology; dizzying technological changes; the expansion and consolidation of the welfare state; and what many perceive to be a devaluation of American citizenship.

In analyzing these developments, I have suggested that together they are already precipitating a reevaluation of the meaning of citizenship and of the legal and political practices that give shape and texture to that meaning.[10] This reevaluation of citizenship is broader, more robust, and more radical[11] than perhaps any consideration of the subject since the Nineteenth Amendment was adopted in 1920. It is even more remarkable because much of the law governing citizenship is both old and relatively stable. With several extremely important exceptions—the 1798–1801 period when the Alien and Sedition Acts were in effect, the elimination of racial and gender barriers to eligibility in 1870, 1920, and 1952, and the more durable ideological exclusion and English language requirement added in 1906[12]—the legal requirements for naturalization have changed little since the First Congress. The principle of birthright citizenship (*jus soli*) was established even earlier; indeed, its English roots have been traced back to 1290.[13]

Despite (or perhaps because of) their antiquity, both naturalization and birthright citizenship principles are now under active reconsideration. In the wake of the political and legal imbroglio arising out of the naturalization of thousands of ineligible aliens shortly before the 1996 elections,[14] as well as prosecutions of private naturalization testing organizations for large-scale fraud,[15] Congress is investigating the administration of the naturalization program and reviewing the naturalization standards themselves. Legislation to limit birthright citizenship for native-born children of illegal aliens is also under active consideration.[16]

Because dual citizenship is a product, among other things, of naturalization and birthright citizenship rules, controversy over those rules necessarily implicates dual citizenship as well. But dual citizenship raises a host of other controversial questions that extend well beyond the issues raised by naturalization and birthright citizenship. The context in which dual citizenship operates, moreover, is being transformed. It is not surprising, then, that prominent academics and policy-oriented foundations are now taking a lively interest in the subject and are publishing important critiques of existing practices.[17] The Immigration and Naturalization Service (INS) itself has commissioned an outside consultant to study the possibility of "reengineering" the naturalization process.

No reliable data exist on the number of Americans holding dual citizenship, but there can be little doubt that the total is growing rapidly. With current legal and illegal immigration approaching record levels, naturalization petitions quintupling in the last five years to almost two million annually, and legal changes in some of our largest source countries that encourage (and are often designed to encourage) naturalization in the United States, dual citizenship is bound to proliferate. This fact alone would justify Congress in reconsidering U.S. dual citizenship policy.

But this reassessment reflects more than simply the growth of dual citizenship. Modern transportation and communication technology make residence and effective participation in two polities easier than ever, converting many merely "technical" dual nationals into functional ones.[18] Many Americans believe that immigrants today are naturalizing for "selfish" reasons—for example, to obtain social benefits for which only citizens are eligible—and that the rules should be changed to require, or at least encourage, purer motives for naturalization. A decade ago, many commentators expressed consternation over Rupert Murdoch's naturalization, which appeared to be prompted primarily by Murdoch's desire to qualify under Federal Communications Commission rules limiting ownership of multiple media properties to U.S. citizens.[19] More recently, controversy over the judicial decision to free convicted rapist Alex Kelly on bail led critics to allege that he and his parents had acquired Irish citizenship for the sole purpose of facilitating his flight from the United States should he decide to become a fugitive rather than face prison.

The government does not maintain a registry documenting the incidence of dual citizenship (much less indicating how and why it is acquired), so the purported increase in its "opportunistic" use is far from clear.[20] But there is a more fundamental reason why we cannot answer this question. Even if it were possible to discern and disentangle the complex mix of feelings that surround a decision to naturalize, no social or political consensus exists on the normative question of which motives are and are not legitimate; indeed, this issue has scarcely been discussed.

Whatever aliens' motives for naturalizing may be, the road to dual citizenship seems easier to travel today than it was in the past. Both of the social behaviors that create new opportunities for dual citizenship—marriage between individuals with different nationalities, and international migration by individuals—have become more common, and the legal rules that govern dual citizenship are also changing in ways that permit migrants to exploit these opportunities. The interaction between these behaviors and rules, then, has increased the dual citizen population.[21] Many of the principal countries of origin for immigrants to the United States have amended their nationality laws to enable their nationals in the United States to acquire American citizenship more easily.[22] Mexico, the Philippines, the Dominican Republic, Canada, and India, for example, now confer their nationality on children born to their nationals in the United States and thus acquiring birthright citizenship here.[23] The Council of Europe is also moving in this direction; its draft convention would permit those who become dual nationals in member states by birth to retain both nationalities.[24] To the extent that states like Germany that traditionally have accepted few permanent immigrants and refugees begin to accept more of them (a course that the United States increasingly urges upon them), they will be under greater pressure to liberalize their policies toward dual citizenship in order to facilitate the assimilation of these new-comers.[25]

More important for present purposes, major source countries are also making it easier for their nationals to retain that nationality when they naturalize in the United States, as well as making it easier to reacquire it thereafter if it is subsequently lost through mandatory renunciation of it in the course of naturalizing in the United States. Some of these countries have repealed provisions that required those wishing to naturalize there to renounce their other nationalities, while others decline to give effect to their own nationals' renunciations if those renunciations are required by the second state as a condition for naturalizing (as in the United States).[26] Moreover, many countries of origin that might be prepared to effectuate their nationals' renunciation of citizenship may nevertheless fail as a practical matter to learn of the renunciations and thus will continue to treat them as their nationals.

An important instance of this liberalizing trend—at least in terms of the number of individuals who may be affected—is a new Mexican law that took effect in March 1998. It reverses long-standing constitutional limitations on Mexican dual nationality and enables Mexicans who naturalize in the United States (approximately 100,000 did so in 1996) to retain or reacquire their Mexican nationality, which confers many economic rights in Mexico but not the franchise. (Mexico would continue to require, as does the United States, that those who naturalize there must renounce their other citizenships.) A second change limits its *jus sanguinis* transmission of citizenship/nationality to the first generation; children born in the United States to Mexican citizens will be Mexican nationals but their children will not (unless, of course, they naturalize there).[27] Although estimates of the number of Mexicans eligible to do so range from 2.3 to 5 million,[28] the new balance of incentives created by this law, coupled with legal and policy developments in the United States that are prompting record levels of aliens to petition for naturalization, strongly implies that the number of Mexicans seeking to naturalize will be much larger than would be predicted from the group's traditionally low rate of naturalization in the United States.[29] In India, another major source country, a major political party supports similar liberalization of its dual citizenship law.[30]

These changes clearly demonstrate the most significant change of all: other states increasingly *want* their own nationals to acquire U.S. citizenship, a striking departure from the historical pattern.[31] Approximately 60 percent of Swiss nationals now live abroad as dual citizens, a fact evidently desired by the Swiss state.[32] Sending states in Central America attach enormous importance to the remittances by their nationals of funds earned in the United States, which are likely to increase if those migrants can acquire dual citizenship.³³ The "transnational communities" created through their nationals' dual citizenship in the United States—communities often reinforced by multinational enterprises and international nongovernmental organizations—increase the flow to these states not only of remittances but of technology, skills, and tourism.³⁴ These states also welcome the growing prospect that their nationals, once naturalized and able to vote in U.S. elections, may succeed in influencing American politics in ways that will serve the interests of the states of origin.³⁵

The growth in the U.S. dual citizen population, however, reflects changes in domestic law as well as foreign law developments. The United States has acquiesced in these external changes by not attempting to counter them, but it has also magnified their effects simply by its growing toleration of dual citizenship. For example, the INS has steadily increased the resources and visibility that it devotes to the promotion of naturalization. Yet the United States has also refrained from taking any meaningful steps to assure that its new citizens' renunciation oaths are legally effective in their countries of origin (which, as just noted, usually make little or no effort to do so).

Since the 1960s, moreover, the Federal courts have limited the government's authority either to denationalize its citizens or to denaturalize those who have acquired citizenship through misrepresentation.³⁶ Congress might have responded to these limits by framing narrower standards capable of surviving judicial scrutiny but it has not done so. Indeed, it has enlarged dual citizenship over time by narrowing the severe gender bias in prior law that made it easier for females to lose their U.S. nationality by marrying foreigners and made it harder for females to transmit *jus sanguinis* citizenship to their children born abroad.³⁷ By substantially raising the level of legal immigration, the United States has multiplied the number of aliens who will eventually naturalize and who will, despite the renunciation requirement, retain or reacquire their prior nationalities. The State Department, bowing to such realities, has gradually shifted its official policy from one of opposition to dual citizenship to one of grudging acceptance.³⁸

These liberalizations in law and policy advance important humanitarian goals. They reflect efforts by countries of origin to facilitate their nationals' naturalization in the United States (and elsewhere) by not automatically denationalizing them when they do so, and they reflect efforts by the United States to reduce the tension between the unwanted growth of dual citizenship and a commendable desire to avoid the potentially harsh effects of denationalization and denaturalization on individuals who often possess strong ties to this country.

Noteworthy as these liberalizations have been, they do not necessarily mark an inexorable trend. Because they also entail some risks to the polity's interests (discussed in section III), they could generate a political reaction and reversal. Canada has recently had some second thoughts about its liberalized law,[39] and the United States is likely to reconsider its own changes in the light of new developments, especially the new Mexican nationality law, which heighten the doubts and anxieties about dual citizenship that many Americans harbor.

II. Some Policy-Relevant Distinctions

Before turning to the putative advantages and disadvantages of dual citizenship, it is worth briefly considering five distinctions that may help to clarify the debate over the effects, merits, and possible reform of dual citizenship policy. These distinctions concern 1) who is affected by dual citizenship; 2) the role of consent in citizenship law; 3) how Congress may regulate political and nonpolitical rights; 4) the different treatment of original and newly acquired citizenship; and 5) the effectiveness of renunciation of prior citizenships.

Entities Affected

Different entities may be affected by dual citizenship policy and will therefore seek to shape the rules governing it. (An appraisal of these effects is deferred until section III.)

Dual citizenship most obviously affects the *individuals* who may acquire, or be denied, that status. Many procedural and substantive rights turn on whether one is a citizen of the polity in which one lives or does business. Moreover, polities define the specific content of those rights differently, although international law seeks to reduce those differences. For example, one's ability or willingness to migrate and to work or receive public benefits in the destination state will vary with the state (or states) in which one can claim and exercise those rights.

Dual citizenship affects the interests of *states* quite apart from its impact on individuals. Because dual citizenship rules affect the incentive and opportunity to migrate to and remain in the destination state, they help to shape the political identities of states and their inhabitants, as well as the contours of public programs and budgets. Historically, at least, dual citizenship policies have also had far-reaching impact on the military, diplomatic, political, and commercial relationships among states, which has occasioned bilateral and multilateral conventions seeking to regulate dual citizenship.[40] For these reasons, dual citizenship also affects the interests of the states' existing citizens. They will have strong feelings, of course, about who belongs to their community and under what terms. Like stockholders facing a possible dilution of their shares, they do not wish to see their own membership devalued by extending membership to others "too cheaply." As taxpayers, they want to ensure that their fiscal burdens are not increased unduly.

Finally, the *international community* possesses a discrete interest in dual citizenship rules insofar as it hopes to minimize the risk that individuals will be rendered stateless, a goal that it has long sought to achieve through international agreements. States' general, ex ante interest in a system that minimizes statelessness, of course, is not inconsistent with the ex post reality that particular states, when confronted with a potentially stateless individual's claim for citizenship in their polity, may decide to oppose his claim. Although this interest might seem superfluous—dual citizenship, after all, presupposes an existing nationality in some other state—it is not. In a world of mass migration, poor record-keeping, uncertain citizenship rules, and state incentives to deny nationality to some individuals who may claim it or to withdraw it from some who already possess it, the international community may view dual nationality as a kind of safety net for those who might otherwise fall between the cracks of the state system.[41]

Consent

Broadly speaking, one may acquire or lose citizenship consensually or nonconsensually. Naturalization, of course, is the paradigmatically consensual mode of acquisition, at least for adults. (Parents' naturalization can confer nationality on children without the latter's consent.) The more nonconsensual modes of acquisition include citizenship conferred at birth and descent through the operation of *jus soli* and *jus sanguinis*. Marriage is a hybrid mode of acquiring citizenship; one might view it as either consensual or nonconsensual, depending on whether one focuses on the individual's awareness of the nationality consequences when marrying or on the automaticity of citizenship upon marriage (where that is the rule). Citizenship may be lost consensually through expatriation where one has renounced citizenship or performed some other act that has that legal effect. (Under U.S. law, one must also *intend* that it have that effect.) It may be lost nonconsensually through a state's denationalization or denaturalization of its citizens without their knowledge or assent, where the state's rules permit this.

The perceived consensuality of one's acquisition or loss of dual citizenship may affect the way in which it is evaluated by others and hence the consequences that they may wish to attach to that acquisition or loss. This is not to say that consent is the only criterion of legitimacy, only that it is, in some form, the most widely accepted and important.[42]

On one view of the matter (and other things being equal), a citizenship that one actively seeks through naturalization—especially if accompanied by an express renunciation of another allegiance—is likely to be viewed as more genuine, deliberate, and morally deserving of recognition than if one acquires it adventitiously and without some measure of personal commitment or at least continuing connection to the polity. The perceived fairness and legitimacy of a citizenship acquired passively and automatically through one's parents may vary depending on whether the nationality-conferring event is defined as birth in a state to which the parents are significantly linked (what might be termed "qualified" *jus soli*), birth in a state where the parents simply happen to find themselves at nativity (absolute *jus soli*), or birth to these parents *wherever* they may be located (*jus sanguinis*). By the same token, a loss of citizenship caused by a voluntary, knowing act of expatriation will probably be perceived as fairer and more legitimate than an involuntary, state-imposed denationalization. This is not to deny that one's political or national identity may be powerfully shaped by a citizenship that one acquired nonconsensually; it is merely to call attention to the normative appeal of consent as a norm legitimating many of our most important social practices.[43]

If the consensuality of an acquisition or loss of citizenship is viewed as an important indicator of its legitimacy, then the methods that a state uses to regulate acquisition and loss are likely to be designed to test its knowing, voluntary character. Requiring the individual to take a naturalization oath is one such technique; mandating that he or she elect one nationality, as through renunciation of other allegiances or designation of one nationality as "primary,"[44] is another. Some states are more lenient in permitting their nationals to retain a second citizenship if it was acquired involuntarily (as through *jus soli*) rather than through naturalization. This same purpose of measuring and assuring consent explains the requirement that a parent (or under now-repealed law, the individual in question) establish some period of residence in the United States in order to acquire *jus sanguinis* citizenship, a requirement that the Supreme Court has held to be constitutional (*Rogers v. Bellei*).[45] It also explains the constitutional (and now statutory) requirement that expatriation occur only through an unambiguous act and formal procedures giving some assurance that the relinquishment of citizenship will be both knowledgeable and voluntary.[46]

Regulating Political and Nonpolitical Rights

Political membership in the polity is the hallmark of citizenship, and political rights are usually limited to citizens.[47] The most important of these, of course, is the right to vote, but other political rights such as eligibility to hold high public office and to contribute money to political campaigns may also be restricted to citizens. Congress defines political and nonpolitical rights and decides how they are to be distributed among citizens, noncitizen nationals, and aliens; in this way it establishes the functional significance of these statuses.

This power is subject to constitutional constraints. The two most important ones are the mandate that naturalization rules be "uniform" and the equal protection principle, which the Supreme Court has interpreted to preclude distinctions between naturalized and other citizens, at least in the expatriation context.[48] On the other hand, these principles might not prevent Congress from providing that U.S. citizens who subsequently naturalize in other countries may not exercise political rights there, so long as Congress does not discriminate unfairly among groups of U.S. citizens. Indeed, Congress might possess the constitutional power to prohibit U.S. citizens from naturalizing elsewhere at all, even though *Afroyim v. Rusk* (1967) might preclude it from enforcing this prohibition through the harsh, constitutionally limited sanction of expatriation.

Original versus New Nationality

The coexistence of these congressional powers and constitutional constraints renders even more doubtful the continuing differences between those who already possess U.S. citizenship and those who wish to acquire it through naturalization, with respect to their opportunities to enjoy dual nationality. After all, the latter are required as a condition of naturalization to renounce their earlier allegiances and thus be limited to a single citizenship, while the former are free to acquire new ones as they wish. How can this be justified in light of the *Schneider v. Rusk* principle of legal equality between all citizens? The truth is that little or no attention has been devoted to the question.

In both the debate about and the practice of dual citizenship, the assumption seems to be that one's original nationality is more binding and deeply felt and thus less problematic than one's subsequently acquired nationality. We seem to worry much more about the divided loyalties of people who are nationals of other states and wish to naturalize in the United States than we do about those of the many American citizens who choose to naturalize in other countries while retaining their American citizenship (as other states increasingly permit them to do). This interesting premise seems to drive the renunciation requirement that is at the heart of our dual citizenship law. Why else would we require naturalizing citizens to renounce other national allegiances while permitting U.S. citizens to acquire other nationalities without constraint?

Yet the basis for this premise is far from clear. Recall that one can only naturalize in the United States by actively and solemnly renouncing one's original nationality—an act that provides some affirmative evidence of loyalty and commitment to the United States. In contrast, an American who naturalizes elsewhere may have never been obliged to acknowledge or even confront seriously his or her sentiments about the United States; rather, we simply infer that allegiance from his or her continued residence and minimal law-abidingness—surely weaker indicia of loyalty and commitment. As Sanford Levinson puts it, "American law tolerates political bigamy so long as the second political marriage follows, rather than precedes, the acquiring of United States citizenship."[49]

The explanations for this practice may be more chauvinistic than rational.[50] Perhaps Americans imagine that fellow citizens who naturalize elsewhere (or who take up residence in their country of origin) without renouncing their U.S. citizenship must be taking this step not out of dissatisfaction with American society but in order to serve some instrumental purpose (say, retirement or business) or to affirm a religious or ethnic tie (as with Ireland or Israel), and that doing so is not inconsistent with retaining their political loyalty to the United States. Only if they use their new citizenship to shirk obligations to American society, such as avoiding taxes or military service, do their fellow Americans begin to question their suitability for continued citizenship.[51]

A more psychological explanation would be that the first allegiance (like first love?), because it grows out of an earlier acculturation in another society, is the dominant, deeper, and more durable one unless it is renounced (and perhaps even then); a newer allegiance thus seems more opportunistic and shallow, thus less legitimate. The opposite assumption, of course, also seems plausible. That is, an allegiance explicitly acknowledged during maturity and after some study of American institutions is likely to be more genuine than one for which no acknowledgment has been required and which may have never been put to a serious test. Even if the premise is true on average (how would we know?), it is surely both underinclusive and overinclusive. After all, many of those who naturalize do so after having resided in the United States for quite long periods of time during which they may have become fully assimilated, while birthright or *jus sanguinis* citizens may have spent little or no time in the United States. (The requirements of physical presence and residence in the United States that sometimes condition the transmission of *jus sanguinis* citizenship now apply to the parents, not to the child who thereby gains citizenship.)

The Supreme Court has also played its part in creating and legitimating this asymmetry by refusing in *Afroyim* to recognize the effectiveness of congressionally defined expatriating acts unless they are voluntarily performed with the specific intention of relinquishing U.S. citizenship, a ruling that Congress accepted and codified in 1986. Although the Court primarily invoked textual and rights-based justifications for this position, it may well have been influenced by the assumptions that a first citizenship is less vulnerable to dilution than a subsequently acquired one and that Congress can always assure the integrity of the latter by prescribing standards for naturalization if it wishes.

Formal versus Effective Renunciation

U.S. law requires those who wish to naturalize to renounce their other political allegiances as a formal matter. Unlike Germany, however, it does not require that they make that renunciation legally effective by successfully expatriating themselves under the other state's law, much less that they provide proof of such expatriation to the naturalization court. As Gerald Neuman has shown, even the German practice provides for exceptions (such as when expatriation is not possible or is unreasonable), and in any event this requirement is far from foolproof.[52] Evasion (by the naturalizing citizen, the country of origin, or both) and nonenforcement are likely to be common in any such system. The arguments for and against requiring a truly effective renunciation are of course the arguments for and against dual citizenship, a subject to which I now turn.

III. An Assessment of Dual Citizenship

Dual citizenship, like other complex social-legal phenomena, is difficult to evaluate. It is not simply that the normative criteria to be applied to it are deeply contested, although they are. It is also that the empirical consequences of the current regime of dual citizenship, and of the various reforms that might be adopted, are highly uncertain. We know what the rules of dual citizenship are (they are admirably clear, except for the standards for denaturalization),[53] but we lack any reliable information concerning how those rules actually affect the sensibilities and behavior of would-be and existing citizens and how those effects might change if the rules were altered in one way or another.

To render the evaluative enterprise manageable, one is tempted to elaborate models designed to capture the disparate values that might be brought to bear on it. In an earlier effort to appraise naturalization policy, for example, Gerald Neuman did just that, sketching four "simple normative models" or perspectives which he called unilateral and bilateral liberal, republican, and communitarian.[54] Although Neuman's article contained some very useful insights, his models did little analytical work for him. What was interesting in his analysis did not derive from the models, in part because they were characterized at so high a level of generality that many naturalization practices could be justified under several or all of the models.[55]

I doubt that an effort to develop more rigorously specified normative models of dual citizenship would be worth the trouble. Instead, I shall employ the less systematic but perhaps more effective approach of canvassing the advantages and disadvantages for the American polity of dual citizenship (in various possible forms), drawing on a variety of normative perspectives including those suggested by Neuman's models. In each case, I shall try to highlight the most important but unanswered empirical questions on which the integrity of such evaluations may ultimately depend. The answers to such empirical questions will obviously determine, from a given normative perspective, the magnitude of benefits and costs that the evaluator will assign to some aspect of dual citizenship. Obviously, the variety of possible normative perspectives merely compounds these uncertainties by raising a further, more fundamental question of whether one should characterize dual citizenship as a benefit or as a cost in the first place.

In light of the indeterminacy of any overall assessment under these (quite common) conditions, it should not be surprising that I do not reach any crisp, rigorously derived evaluative conclusions. Nevertheless, at the end of the day I am inclined to think that the growth of dual citizenship is on balance a good thing. Moreover, I am able in section IV to recommend a nontrivial (or so it seems to me) policy change that seems broadly consistent with *all* of the leading normative perspectives.

Benefits of Dual Citizenship

As noted in section II, dual citizenship's benefits flow to a number of different entities. For individuals who hold dual citizenship, the status is advantageous because it provides them with additional options—an alternative country in which to live, work, and invest, an additional locus and source of rights, obligations, and communal ties.[56] Despite the growing and enthusiastic literature on transnational communities,[57] it is a fair question whether the quality of the dual citizen's relationships to his polities and civil societies is diluted by the possible diffusion of attention, affection, and commitment that dual citzenship may entail. People who commute between two communities, for example, often report that they feel a bit alienated from both and fully attached to neither. On the other hand, many people who are members of two nuclear families (perhaps through divorce and remarriage) seem to feel intense ties to both. Even if the quality (somehow defined) of each relationship were diminished, it might well be that the total satisfaction derived from the two families taken together is greater than before.

It is hard to know how to answer such questions, just as it is hard to know which of these (or other) analogies to dual citizenship is most appropriate in thinking about it. What is clear, however, is that the individual's choice is always a necessary, albeit not sufficient, condition of dual citizenship. Because it is usually acquired voluntarily and can be renounced when it is not (or no longer) desired, no individual is compelled to be a dual citizen against his will for very long (although the law may prevent some who wish to be dual citizens from becoming or remaining one). The individual who perceives dual citizenship to be a benefit will become (or remain) one if he or she can (i.e., if the law permits it); otherwise, not. From a liberal perspective, and perhaps under some versions of republicanism and communitarianism as well, this is justification enough for dual citizenship.

U.S.-based business firms also benefit from dual citizenship. Employees, by acquiring dual citizenship, become more valuable to a firm because they can travel and work abroad more easily, are more likely to be bilingual, and can more readily build transnational market networks that will advantage the firm. By the same token, other states and their citizens benefit from the liberal availability of dual citizenship in the United States. I have already noted that the steady flow of remittances from the United States is essential to the social and economic viability of many other societies, but the dynamic is a more general one. Just as genuinely free trade among nations tends to benefit all participants in the long run, so too does the international flow of human, financial, and technological capital that dual citizenship facilitates. For the same reason—and also because (as noted earlier) dual citizenship reduces the risk of statelessness which all countries have a strong interest in minimizing—the international community of states benefits.

Finally, dual citizenship confers significant benefits on American society as a whole. In addition to the economic advantages (including tax revenues) generated by a population with many dual nationals, there are exceedingly important social and political advantages. Citizenship probably facilitates (as well as reflects) the assimilation of newcomers by imparting a sense of welcome and belonging, reinforcing their attachment to American values and improving their English language skills.[58] Citizenship also helps to legitimate the exercise over them (and others) of governmental power by reducing the risk that they will be subject to discriminatory treatment. To the extent that a liberal dual nationality policy encourages long-term immigrants to naturalize—a causal relationship whose existence most commentators assume[59]—it advances the essential democratic value of full political and social participation by all individuals who are subject to the polity's coercive authority.

Even a liberal state, which more than republican and communitarian polities values individuals' rights to decide for themselves whether and how to participate, may nevertheless have a strong interest in actively encouraging resident aliens to naturalize. The reason, I have noted elsewhere, is that "at some point . . . the ratio of aliens to citizens might become so high that aliens' lack of direct or indirect political participation and representation would present a serious problem for democratic governance."[60] Sanford Levinson put the point this way: "one must ask if a country consisting primarily of resident aliens can sustain itself as a community with ideals worth professing."[61] Such a scenario, I suggest, is by no means far-fetched; if current trends continue, almost one-third of Germany's population by 2030 will consist of non-German foreign nationals, and in large cities the figure could reach 45 percent.[62]

Peter Spiro sees an additional attraction of dual citizenship. Citing as an example the 1996 elections in the Dominican Republic in which many U.S. dual citizens voted, he imagines that if those who acquire U.S. citizenship thereby absorb American constitutional values, they "may put those values to work not only in the U.S. but also in the country of origin. . . . Dual nationality . . . could become a part of the U.S. strategy to enlarge global democracy." The desirability of having U.S. citizens who retain their political links to other countries is thus an argument for eliminating the renunciation requirement in U.S. law.[63]

Costs of Dual Citizenship

Were these benefits the only consequences of dual citizenship, it would hardly be the contentious public issue that it is—and will increasingly become. A liberal dual citizenship policy entails costs, however, and they must be taken into consideration in evaluating its merits.

Some of these costs are rather mundane and unlikely to have much weight in any overall evaluation of the merits of dual citizenship policy. For example, dual citizenship can magnify legal uncertainties and hence the transaction costs associated with resolving them. Under conventional conflict of laws principles, an individual's citizenship can be a factor in determining the jurisdiction whose law applies to his or her conduct, transactions, or status. This determination becomes correspondingly more difficult where he or she possesses two nationalities.

A more significant cost of dual citizenship, which arises from the 1996 welfare reform statute, is fiscal in nature. Under this statute, which departs radically from prior law, most aliens—including many who have lived in the United States for many years—are no longer eligible for some valuable public benefits and services to which citizens may be entitled. Providing these benefits and services to resident aliens imposed a substantial fiscal burden on the federal government, which was a major reason why aliens were targeted as part of the deficit reduction effort in the first place.[64] (Assumption of some of these fiscal burdens by the state and local governments, which have moved with surprising speed to narrow the gap created by the federal statute,[65] has merely shifted the costs rather than eliminating them.) To the extent that a liberal dual citizenship policy confers public benefit entitlements on individuals who, if they remained aliens, would not otherwise receive them, those budgetary costs would again be borne by government.[66] And to the extent that those marginal costs are occasioned by individuals who did not contribute commensurate taxes to the United States, this fiscal effect will be even more objectionable to many existing citizens.[67]

Less quantifiable is the effect of dual citizenship on the state's obligation to provide diplomatic protection to its citizens. Peter Spiro recently analyzed this consideration, noting that the traditionally unfettered right of a state to treat its own citizens pretty much as it likes sometimes clashes with the second state's right and obligation to protect its citizens (single or dual) when they are abroad, including when they are in their other country of nationality where the second state's protection responsibility was traditionally not applicable.[68] He maintains, however, that the establishment of a regime of general international human rights, in which a state may protest another state's mistreatment of individuals regardless of whether or not they are nationals of the protesting state, effectively reduces the protesting state's diplomatic protection burden. Spiro acknowledges that dual citizenship may intensify such interstate conflicts but asserts that this "will be more a matter of politics than of law, and in any event the factor is unlikely to push anyone over the brink." He also argues that one state is unlikely to hold another state responsible for the actions of its (their) citizen because "states so clearly have lost the capacity to control the international activities of their citizens."[69]

Spiro's assertions concerning tendencies and probabilities may well be correct as a general matter. It seems plausible that when compared with other factors that influence state actions in the international sphere, the motivational significance of dual citizenship may have declined. At the margin, however, it also seems plausible that a state will intervene more readily and energetically on behalf of its own nationals than on behalf of strangers to whom it owes no special duty of protection, and thus where the state's arguments for intervening are closely balanced, the existence of such a duty might furnish a real or pretextual reason that could affect, or even tip, the balance.[70] Ultimately, the magnitude of the protection burden posed by dual citizenship is one of those empirical questions to which we simply have no reliable answers, especially since it is likely to depend on many factors and thus vary from situation to situation.

In the debate over liberalizing dual citizenship, the most divisive and worrisome concerns are of a fundamentally political nature. The fact that they are perhaps the most speculative and least quantifiable of the impacts of dual citizenship does not mean that they are insubstantial and thus easily dismissed. Indeed, it is precisely the elusiveness of these political concerns that makes them such powerful rhetorical weapons in the hands of partisans.

Consider first the electoral implications of dual citizenship. Assume that a dual citizen is eligible to vote in the elections of both countries.[71] Should this be troubling to Americans? To the extent that the interests of the United States and those of the other country do not conflict, it is hard to see any good reason for objecting to a situation in which the individual asserts one set of interests in the American election and another, not inconsistent set of interests in the other election. Here, Spiro's speculation seems plausible.

Sometimes, however, those interests will conflict in the sense that the other state's election may shape that state's policies—on trade or foreign policy, for example—in ways that either benefit or adversely affect the United States. It is true, indeed *increasingly* true given the growing national origins diversity of the U.S. population, that American citizens/voters often have policy preferences that accord some weight to the interests of other countries. This has always been the case, and always a source of concern to other members of the polity who think themselves exempt from such conflicts. Such preferences in fact exist whether or not the citizens/voters are also citizens of those other countries, and whether or not the other-country interests might, under some views of America's national interests, be adverse to those American interests.

Somewhat more controversially, I believe that we should conceive of the national interest of the United States as including those preferences. After all, if the national interest is in some fundamental democratic sense an (indeterminate) aggregation of the interests perceived by citizens/voters,[72] then this aggregation cannot exclude preferences that accord some weight to other-country interests. As Spiro puts it,

> A dual Mexican–American who advocates policies that benefit Mexico is little different from a Catholic who advocates policies endorsed by the Church or a member of Amnesty International who writes his congressman at the organization's behest. There are no questions here of disloyalty, only of interests and identities and of different modes of social contribution.[73]

This seems correct, at least within very broad limits—that is, so long as Mexico, like the church and Amnesty International, is not an enemy of the United States capable of doing it great harm.[74]

Spiro also posits the harder case in which the Mexican government endorses candidates in American elections and seeks to influence the votes of its dual nationals in the United States. (Given Mexico's well-publicized protests against Governor Pete Wilson's position on Proposition 187 in California's 1994 elections, this example is not at all fanciful.) Spiro dismisses this concern, arguing that states of origin have little leverage over their nationals in the United States and even less inclination to use it and that retention of Mexican nationality would add little to the dual national's existing propensity, shared with other "hyphenated" Americans, to give weight to ethnic affiliations. Again, this seems persuasive, at least given the current U.S.–Mexico alliance, the long-standing attitudinal differences among groups of people in the United States with Mexican ancestry,[75] and the propensity of voters, including hyphenated Americans, to focus on local issues.

Voting, of course, is not the only form of participation in U.S. elections by dual citizens. Like other citizens and legal resident aliens, they may contribute to political campaigns, make independent expenditures, and otherwise seek to shape public opinion. Although recent congressional hearings concerning apparently illegal campaign contributions by foreign companies and individuals fronting for them may eventually lead to additional restrictions on these practices (in fact, proposals to limit or ban legal aliens' campaign contributions are pending in Congress), extending such restrictions to dual citizens would be unwise and almost certainly unconstitutional. Their full participation benefits American politics for the same reasons that the participation of other citizens (and legal aliens) does.[76]

The reverse situation, in which U.S. citizens participate in elections in countries where they hold dual citizenship—conduct that once triggered denationalization under U.S. law but no longer does due to the Supreme Court's ruling in *Afroyim*—also seems unproblematic from the American point of view, at least so long as this participation does not embroil the United States in unwanted disputes with the other country or involve situations in which the voter subordinates the interests of the United States to those of the other country, as distinguished from merely taking the latter into account in determining the former. Indeed, Spiro's point bears repetition here: This participation could help to disseminate abroad the liberal democratic values that the American polity seeks to inculcate in its citizens.

This analysis suggests that the electoral conflicts engendered by dual citizenship are in principle quite consistent with the aggregation of preferences that we call the national interest. It is true, of course, that the government will ordinarily find it impossible as a practical matter to discern, much less prove in a denaturalization or expatriation proceeding, that the voter has in fact preferred another country's interests to those of the

United States (properly defined). Accordingly, we must assess the risk of disloyalty in this sense on the basis of probabilities and magnitudes—that is, the probability that a U.S. voter will subordinate American interests, and the number of Americans who are likely to go to the trouble of voting in foreign elections. Both seem exceedingly low.

All of this, of course, still begs the most basic question raised by dual citizenship: Who should be permitted to become a U.S. citizen and thus to vote and have his or her preferences counted in that aggregation process? In order to address that question, we must look beyond possible electoral conflicts to more transcendent concerns having to do with political unity, identity, community, and loyalty.

If citizenship is anything, it is membership in a political community with a more or less distinctive political identity—a set of public values about governance and law that are very widely shared by those within it. As already noted, we do not require birthright and *jus sanguinis* citizens to affirm a commitment to those values and that identity, yet we permit U.S. citizens to acquire other citizenships without limit and without affirming their continuing solidarity with and loyalty to American society. How, then, might dual citizenship threaten this American political identity?[77]

One answer is that although all citizens who are also members of other polities may threaten this identity, the government is in a position to minimize that danger by exerting a leverage (the oath requirement) over the individual who wishes to naturalize that it lacks over its existing citizens. This answer, however, ignores several possibilities. Congress could require existing U.S. citizens also to take a loyalty oath,[78] as they now do when they apply for passports and certain jobs. It might also limit their freedom to naturalize abroad or, if they are allowed to naturalize, might limit their freedom to take certain actions, such as voting in other countries' elections. As discussed earlier, such legislation should not raise constitutional difficulties so long as Congress neither discriminates among citizens in this regard nor seeks to enforce its restrictions by expatriating them.

One can also argue that dual citizenship threatens America's political unity and identity regardless of whether one thinks that it is inconsistent to require only naturalizing citizens to swear an oath. In this view, dual citizenship dilutes America's political identity by adding members who are committed to other polities with other values. Put another way, in terms elaborated by Albert Hirschman, dual citizenship weakens loyalty by making exit easier.[79] To be sure, citizens in a federal system may owe simultaneous allegiance to two polities but if both share essentially the same values, as in the American case, the danger of disunity would be less than where they are members of two polities with quite different political cultures.

At least two responses to this claim are possible. One is to deny that this identity is unique; the claim is that the polities from which most immigrants come today are committed to the same principles of governance to which the United States subscribes. This claim, however, is not convincing, at least in practice. Of the ten leading source countries in 1996, only Mexico, the Philippines, India, Dominican Republic, and Jamaica even arguably qualify.[80] Another response, conceding that American values are indeed unique, might nevertheless despair of our ability to reduce them to a verbal formulation that can serve as more discriminating naturalization criteria than the existing standards, tests, and oath. In this view, we have little choice but to continue administering them in essentially their current form. This position assumes, however, that we know what it is we are asking the individual to affirm and renounce. I challenge this assumption below.

Two variations on these disunity and dilution themes should be noted. The first was made by the Canadian parliamentary committee which expressed a fear that dual citizens might "import and perpetuate their strident ethnic or nationalistic self-interests here in their new country"; they might "bring foreign quarrels to Canada."[81] Insofar as this is not simply another way of voicing the electoral concerns discussed earlier, it seems to envision a more general threat to political civility and accommodation posed by certain types of conflicts that dual citizens are thought more likely to inflame.

The second variation is that many dual citizens naturalize for the "wrong" (i.e., selfish or opportunistic) reasons.[82] This characterization is already being made of the flood of naturalization petitions in the wake of the 1996 welfare reform law and that will likely be used to disparage naturalizations by Mexicans once the new Mexican law becomes effective. There is evidence that many aliens are indeed naturalizing to preserve or obtain welfare benefits,[83] and this perception has had powerful political ramifications. In addition, Aleinikoff cites a study of a 1994 change in the Dominican Republic's citizenship law similar to that being adopted in Mexico, which shows that the desire to facilitate Dominicans' naturalization in the United States without reducing their ties to the home country was an important argument for the change.[84]

Nevertheless, it is not clear what we should make of this "wrong reasons" argument. It implies that we know and can define what the "right" reasons for naturalizing are, that right and wrong reasons either do not coexist or can be disentangled, that we can render transparent through evidence the motivational mix that particular individuals possess, and that existing citizens do not value *their* (our) citizenship, at least in part, for instrumental reasons. None of these propositions, however, has been demonstrated or appears likely. It is true—as public opinion surveys and the political support for the 1996 welfare reform law suggest—that most Americans are repelled by the notion that some aliens are naturalizing in order to gain access to the welfare system. But as Aleinikoff points out, other instrumental reasons, such as a desire to integrate and actively participate in American society and politics, are not only viewed as praiseworthy but reflect values that "we look for in native-born citizens."[85] Lines that are both morally satisfying and administrable are exceedingly difficult to draw here.

This leads to a final complaint about the relation between dual citizenship and political community and identity, which goes to concerns about the social assimilation of immigrants.[86] Dual citizenship, the argument goes, retards assimilation by encouraging newcomers to cling to old ties and refrain from unequivocally casting their lot with the United States. Dan Stein, a leading opponent of dual citizenship, states that immigrants "ought to get on board or get out."[87] Naturalization and assimilation are surely correlated, if only because one must have already achieved some level of English proficiency and knowledge about American society in order to qualify in the first place. But naturalization does not merely reflect assimilation; it probably also accelerates it, as discussed earlier. For this reason, one can argue that the government has an interest in promoting naturalization more energetically than it does, rather than essentially relying on individual aliens' initiative.[88]

For present purposes, however, the relevant question is not how naturalization affects assimilation, but how *dual* citizenship, as distinguished from single citizenship, affects it at the *margin*. It may be, as Spiro asserts, that "retention of former nationality will not in itself retard the process by which the new citizen deepens his identification with the community of his naturalized homeland," but he cites no evidence to support his assertion and I know of none one way or the other.[89] There are reasons, however, to question his claim. If it is true that dual citizenship helps to build and reinforce "transnational communities," that any individual possesses only limited affective and attentional resources, and that allocating those resources between two communities necessarily reduces the level of commitment to either one, then it seems to follow that this lower level of commitment to the American community will slow the rate of assimilation into it. To recur to the family metaphor, it is doubtful (although possible) that parents with two sets of children from different marriages manage to devote the same amount of time to each child as they would if they had only one set of children to raise.

Even if this is true, of course, countervailing considerations may nonetheless support a more liberal dual citizenship policy. Spiro immediately adds, for example, that "denying the possibility of naturalization (or of raising its price too high, by requiring renunciation) *will* retard that process and weaken the bonds of community, at least as delimited in territorial terms" (italics original).[90] Again, he cites no support for this important and plausible empirical claim about how the price of naturalization (including renunciation) affects the speed and quality of assimilation. But the opposite claim—that immigrants whom the law requires to make a firm, undiluted commitment to American society may assimilate sooner and better than those who can naturalize without having to affirm that commitment—is also plausible. In the end, we are left with no evidence but an important research issue. In my view, the question of the marginal effects of dual citizenship on assimilation is indeed pivotal, but alas it is also unanswerable at present except on the basis of supposition.

Beyond the concern about assimilation, the debate on dual citizenship revolves around the issue of dual nationals' loyalty to the United States. The anxiety, of course, is that their allegiance to the United States is wanting—at best divided and at worst subordinate to their initial allegiance. This is partly a concern about national security. In this view, people whose loyalties are either divided or lie elsewhere may be tempted to subvert the nation's safety and well-being in service to another state, even to the point of treason.

Traitors[91] do indeed dot our history, but it is doubtful that dual citizens or even aliens, who have not sworn allegiance to the United States, are disproportionately represented among them. Spiro believes that the national security risk posed by dual citizenship is minimal. As with diplomatic protection, he emphasizes historic shifts that have reduced the differential danger posed by dual citizens compared with others. Specifically, he argues that the spread of democracy in the world has lowered the prospect of war, especially the kind in which dual nationals might pose a security threat. "Lightning wars conducted by volunteer armies," he suggests, "present few opportunities for shadowy fifth columns." Moreover, the undemocratic regimes with which the United States might now go to war are "less likely to instill the real loyalties of dual nationals even where they command their formal ones."[92]

As with diplomatic protection, one can acknowledge the general tendencies that Spiro identifies while still doubting that they will apply in every case and reduce the risks to zero. Our world is one in which hostilities may take the form not only of formal military campaigns[93] but also of clandestine acts of terrorism or thefts of valuable technologies undertaken on behalf of undemocratic regimes that nevertheless can claim the fervent political and religious loyalty of their people.[94] Although legal or illegal aliens can also engage in such conduct, citizens probably have somewhat greater opportunities at the margin to do so. In such a world, Spiro's assurances may be too optimistic. The fact that few dual nationals pose any greater danger of disloyalty than those with only one nationality does not preclude the risk that the dual citizenship of those few may place them in a better position to wreak immense damage. This risk is a cost (to be discounted, of course, by its presumably low probability) that must be assessed against a policy of more liberal dual citizenship. Again, any effort to quantify it raises empirical questions for which there are no obvious answers.

But to view public concerns about the loyalty of dual citizens as being limited to the fear of treason is to risk trivializing those concerns. Even if divided loyalty does not culminate in active betrayal, it may create practical and moral conflicts, as when both countries demand military service of their citizens. Beyond such concerns, these divided loyalties surely offend common-sense conceptions of the desired citizen-state relationship. I have already alluded to the variety of competing metaphors that may plausibly frame those popular views. As I also noted, these metaphors should not impoverish a reflective deliberation about dual citizenship; our metaphors, after all, should serve us rather than rule us. At the same time, however, such a deliberation should take seriously the public values that are embedded in the metaphors that our society invokes.

My guess—and it is of course only a guess—is that most thoughtful Americans, if asked to characterize the relationship between citizen and state that naturalization and the oath ought to affirm and reify, would view marriage and the marriage vow as the most closely analogous. Americans simply do not think of their polity as a mere club, a transitory affiliation affording easy entry and exit for purely instrumental reasons with few strings attached;[95] but neither do they think of naturalizing citizens as entering an ideologically or spiritually defined *nomos* or a blood relationship.

If we think that naturalizing citizens are entering into a kind of marital relationship with the polity, it might seem natural and morally compelling to insist that they make a firm choice of one polity or another. The law, after all, sometimes obliges us to make a firm choice between competing claims on our allegiance and identity. We must choose one U.S. state of residence,[96] one political party,[97] one name,[98] and one marriage at a time. Why not require us to choose one national citizenship? In marriage, we expect a certain exclusivity or (where not exclusive) at least a clear priority of commitment. One who marries, of course, does not thereby renounce all nonmarital affections, obligations, and trusts; the vow surely contemplates the maintenance of other deep attachments and other duties of emotional or financial support. But virtually all marrying couples, not to mention the larger society, certainly expect that some of the most essential marital commitments, such as procreation and sexual intercourse, will indeed be exclusive, while others, such as friendships and Wednesday evenings, may be more widely diffused. Yet even here, we expect the spouse to enjoy unequivocal pride of place in the event of conflict.

Is the analogy of citizenship to marriage accurate? It is of course far from perfect. In particular, the intense intimacy that marriage entails is not always replicated in the relation of citizen to polity—and vice versa, as many unsuccessful marriages attest. Moreover, American political culture apparently does not regard dual citizenship as bigamous, for it now permits U.S. citizens to acquire other nationalities without constraint. It is also true that the "transformed consciousness" of which Levinson speaks in connection with marriage (drawing on Hegel and David Hartman) is not quite the same as the "new political birth" to which naturalization is sometimes likened. Likewise, it is hard to imagine the civic counterpart of procreation, unless it is citizens' inculcation of American values in their children.

Despite these differences, however, I believe that marriage probably comes closer than any other common relationship to capturing the quality of enduring loyalty and priority of affection and concern that most Americans expect from those who apply to become fellow citizens. And if this is true, certain implications might follow. First, the exclusive loyalty demanded of a citizen, like that demanded of spouses, would be a circumscribed loyalty, one limited to the domain of political loyalty appropriate to the relationship between citizen and state in a liberal democratic polity. Even within that domain, loyalty is perfectly consistent with the most severe public criticism of the polity and its officials, and outside that domain loyalty is simply not a question, as the citizen's only essential duty is to observe the law (which may of course impose other duties), not to love the country.

Second, just as marital duties apply to all married persons equally and categorically, the political loyalty required of naturalized citizens should be the same—no more, no less—as that required of all other citizens, regardless of how they acquired their citizenship. This principle, affirmed in *Schneider v. Rusk*, lies at the heart of any polity committed to equal protection of the laws. Such a polity, especially one whose civil society and public philosophy countenance large inequalities in private goods, cannot flourish unless its members regard and treat each other as political and legal equals. In this sense, second-class citizenship is a pernicious oxymoron. Deviations from the equality-among-citizens principle should be tolerated only for the most compelling reasons.

As already noted, naturalization imposes some requirements on would-be citizens that birthright and *jus sanguinis* citizens need not satisfy. Neuman calls these "asymmetries." Some are procedural and to that extent are inescapable in the case of naturalization, but others such as good moral character and the renunciation of prior allegiances are deeply substantive.

If the principle of equality among citizens means anything, it must mean that these substantive asymmetries demand justification. Neuman shows that some of the requirements themselves can be criticized from certain normative perspectives, but he does not view the asymmetries as problematic because the former do not yet possess U.S. citizenship and "a power to revoke is more dangerous than a power to withhold in the first place."[99]

Rather than justifying the asymmetries, however, Neuman's assertion begs the most significant questions about them.[100] First, the power to revoke is not always more dangerous than the power to withhold; for example, one who already has something may be in a better position to defend it (e.g., through political mobilization) than one who still lacks it.[101] Second, the persuasiveness of the revoke/withhold distinction depends on the nature of the asymmetry at issue. For example, the good moral character asymmetry probably strikes most people as less objectionable than, say, the ideological asymmetry which excludes otherwise desirable citizens simply because they subscribe to unpopular views that existing citizens are perfectly entitled to advocate.[102]

Third, different asymmetries may have different rationales, and no single justification is likely to work for all of them. The asymmetric requirements concerning knowledge of the English language and American government, for example, might be defended on the basis of a strong presumption—not true in every case, of course—that birthright citizens, by adulthood, have lived and been schooled in the United States long enough to acquire this knowledge and that *jus sanguinis* citizens acquire it through their families. The good moral character asymmetry might be justified by a presumption that living in American society nurtures such character (this would be quite a stretch) or by the intuition that anyone applying for membership in a community should be expected to satisfy so minimal a requirement.[103]

Finally, none of these rationales can serve to justify either the ideological or renunciation asymmetries. Many existing citizens hold ideological views that might preclude their naturalization, and many others have acquired plural nationalities along with the risk of divided loyalties which the naturalizing citizen must renounce. A defense of these asymmetries, then, must be based on something like the leverage argument that I noted earlier, which of course is less a justification than a raw assertion of power.

This analysis narrows, but does not resolve, the question of which forms of disloyalty other than treason should be counted as costs of dual citizenship. If (as I believe and Spiro does not) even a polity committed to a liberal dual citizenship policy can properly demand that new citizens affirm their exclusive political loyalty to the United States, we must still decide what we mean by "exclusive political loyalty to the United States" and which kinds of continuing commitments to other polities are deemed consistent with that loyalty. The answers, I believe, should be reflected in the content of the oath itself.

IV. Possible Reforms

Particular anxieties about dual citizenship imply particular questions that must be addressed and particular remedies that might then be proposed. Some concerns go to the standards and processes by which one may acquire and lose citizenship; others go to the rights and duties that attach to the status. Some concerns go to the criteria for naturalization, while others go to the criteria for dual citizenship. Overlap obviously abounds; as we have seen, the debate about dual citizenship today is largely a debate about what the appropriate standards for naturalization should be. Reforms directed at particular concerns, then, risk overbreadth and should be carefully targeted at the specific problem that is perceived.

One set of possible solutions is based on the premise that dual citizenship is now acquired too easily and/or for the wrong reasons. I have already expressed doubts about this premise, but if that is the diagnosis, then certain remedial options would follow. For example, we could fashion eligibility standards for dual citizenship that are more stringent than they are now or than they are for single citizenship naturalizations. Instead (or in addition), we could reduce the benefits flowing from dual citizenship. In either case, we might distinguish these standards and rights from those that apply to people who naturalize for single citizenship. Again, however, any effort to create distinct classes of citizens, particularly with respect to their legal rights,[104] would raise constitutional difficulties.

I shall not discuss these possibilities further here, as I believe that the reformers have not met the burden of proof, which I think they must bear, that a significant problem in fact exists as to either the standards or the motivations for acquiring dual citizenship. I shall instead focus my attention on the naturalization oath itself and on how it might be modified to address the threats to political identity and loyalty that I discussed in section III. I do so for several reasons. First, many Americans already take these threats seriously.[105] Second, these anxieties are likely to intensify in the future as the national origins of the immigration stream continue to diversify. Third, there is much merit, quite apart from whether these anxieties are justified, in attempting to be clearer about what it is we imagine we are asking new citizens to affirm in their oaths. The delightfully archaic formulation of the oath, as well as its ambiguities, together make for considerable uncertainty as to its meaning and practical effects.[106] If consent (as I believe) is the master concept underlying our political arrangements, that consent should be knowing, discriminating, and authentic.[107] I argue below that the current oath, particularly the renunciation provision, fails these tests.

Before turning to my proposal,[108] let me make certain premises explicit. First, it should go without saying that I take the naturalization oath requirement, and hence the content of the oath itself, seriously, as do most oathtakers.[109] Drawing on analogies to wedding and religious vows, Levinson has reviewed the arguments for and against loyalty oaths, including the inconsistency of their professions with certain social realities and their possible ineffectiveness, hypocrisy, and even cynical uses. He correctly notes, however, that oaths—at least when solemnly performed in an appropriately focused and dignified setting—have the capacity not only to bind one in a psychological sense but also to generate "a transformed (and socialized) consciousness."[110] Having observed naturalization ceremonies and discussed them with presiding judges and new citizens, this claim rings true to me.[111]

Second, I believe that an effort by some immigration proponents to eliminate the renunciation requirement in the oath would constitute a colossal, even tragic political blunder. Such an effort, which Spiro urges, would arouse intense, widespread political opposition and animus that would be directed against immigrants in general and naturalizing immigrants, especially Mexican–Americans and other Spanish-speaking groups, in particular. The renunciation requirement would swiftly be transformed into a sacred shibboleth, a symbol of the integrity and security of the American polity with a prominence out of all proportion to its genuine significance.

On the other hand, a suitably modified renunciation requirement should be embraced, even by those who now doubt its efficacy, as a useful instrument of immigrant assimilation regardless of how that controversial idea is defined. The reason is that, after all is said and done, after one acknowledges both the unpersuasiveness of some rationales for renunciation and the inconsistency between even the most persuasive rationales and some of our actual practices, few would seriously contest the notion that the United States may legitimately insist that those who naturalize here owe the United States a core political loyalty. They will surely disagree about which sorts of commitments constitute that core, which of these are exclusive and which merely primary, and which commitments lie outside the core and thus may be made to other polities without violating a properly refined renunciation oath. My own view is that this core is properly quite small, limited to those obligations that are essential to the flourishing of a polity as liberal as ours is; but that there is *some* core that the United States may demand in exchange for the rights and blessings of citizenship seems indubitable.

A third premise is that the current oath, which requires one to renounce "absolutely and entirely all allegiance and fidelity to" another polity, utterly fails to define any such core. As already noted, its terms are simply too archaic, broad, and unqualified to communicate which duties Americans would truly place within this core were they to deliberate about the question. Because of this overbreadth, the current renunciation oath cannot elicit the knowing, discriminating, and authentic consent of the oathtaker that is necessary both to confer full membership in the polity and to legitimate its exercise of power over him or her. People taking a solemn oath of renunciation should know what it is they are accepting and forswearing. Accordingly, the requirement should be reformulated to provide a clearer, more refined definition of the loyalties that must, and that need not, be renounced.

Finally, certain aspects of loyalty that the United States can legitimately demand of its new dual citizens are already encompassed by other parts of the naturalization oath. Hence they need not be among those aspects of loyalty to which a redefined renunciation requirement should apply. Specifically, these aspects of loyalty include the duty "to support and defend the Constitution and the laws of the United States," the duty "to bear true faith and allegiance to the same,"[112] and the duty to bear arms or to perform equivalent public service. These duties obviously (though they do not say it in so many words) encompass an obligation to obey U.S. law.

Which aspects of loyalty, then, does the dual citizen owe exclusively or primarily[113] to the United States such that there is something that he or she must renounce? I am inclined to place only two duties of loyalty in that core. First, the naturalizing citizen should be obliged to prefer the interests of the United States over those of any other polity. This duty to accept the primacy or superiority[114] of America's claim on its citizens will seldom come into question except in cases of war and other serious conflicts between the United States and the other country of nationality. In such situations, dual citizens may be obliged to make decisions (perhaps in voting or about military service) knowing that the interests of the two countries inescapably clash and that they must therefore choose between the two, as distinguished from simply taking the interests of the other state into account in forming their views about where U.S. national interests lie. Ordinarily, moreover, the oathtaker's true state of mind and affection cannot be challenged practically or legally. Since the government may not (and even if it could, should not) seek to control or punish its citizens' thoughts or feelings, the oathtaker's bad faith (if it exists) cannot be effectively sanctioned unless it relates to objective facts that he or she has misstated and that might be the subject of denaturalization proceedings. Still, these realities do not render the duty meaningless. The fact that it will generally be unenforceable does not distinguish it from many other significant duties that we owe to others but whose observance must ultimately rest on our conscientious moral commitments.

Even this relatively constrained duty of primary loyalty, however, can be challenged as going too far. Stephen Legomsky, for example, argues that naturalizing citizens should be required at most to accord *equal*, not greater, weight to U.S. interests in the event of a conflict, and he wonders how I think the United States should respond if other countries required primary loyalty from their dual nationals who are U.S. citizens and if such individuals took such an oath in the other country.[115] My answer, which presupposes that citizenship should be more demanding and hence exclusive than mere membership in a voluntary club, is that a nation has a legitimate claim to its citizens' primary loyalty (as I have narrowly defined it), and that one who cannot muster that minimal degree of loyalty should not be granted citizenship. Whether the government should be able to expatriate American citizens who voluntarily, knowingly, and solemnly pledge their primary loyalty to another state in derogation of their primary loyalty to the United States (again, as narrowly defined) is a separate question turning on several considerations; but in principle, and under current law as legitimated by the Supreme Court and confirmed by Congress in 1986, the answer might be yes.

The second core duty is that the new citizen must not hold a high public office in another polity.[116] Although this proscription is likely to be too broad in the sense that many official decisions that such an individual makes would not actually impinge on U.S. interests, a relatively clear prophylactic rule nevertheless seems warranted. Some of the official's decisions may create conflicts with his or her first duty to prefer the interests of the United States, the stakes to the United States in these decisions may be disproportionately great, and drawing distinctions in general or on a case-by-case basis would be very difficult. Even so, some line-drawing would be necessary. For example, the offices that are "high" enough to trigger this duty should probably depend on the breadth of their policymaking responsibilities, a familiar form of legal classification. Ordinary military service in another nation not at war with the United States would not necessarily implicate this duty, but perhaps a military leadership position should.

Plausible objections to this duty can be anticipated as well. One is that the government could not constitutionally (or now, even statutorily) expatriate or denaturalize U.S. citizens for holding office in another nation unless they specifically intended thereby to renounce their American citizenship. The Supreme Court, however, has never so held; *Afroyim* involved only voting in a foreign election, which as I have just noted poses a smaller risk of conflicting loyalties. But even if the Constitution does bar the government from depriving foreign officeholders of U.S. citizenship, it would probably not bar Congress from imposing other sanctions on them. The question, then, may be more one of appropriate remedy than of the power to implement a policy against foreign officeholding.

Stephen Legomsky makes another objection. Noting my belief that American citizens may properly take the interests of other groups and even countries into account in deciding where our national interest lies, he wonders why I should be troubled by a U.S. citizen holding high office in another nation any more than if that citizen were holding high office in a corporation or other interest group and favoring that group's interests at the expense of the U.S. national interest.[117] My answer is that the risk of conflict in the government-government situation is likely to be far greater, the stakes for the United States in how such conflicts are resolved far higher, and the number of individuals who would be burdened by this duty far fewer than in the government-private entity situation that Legomsky posits.[118] Like my first response, this one will not satisfy those who find no justification for citizenship as a distinctive status carrying certain rights and responsibilities denied to noncitizens. As I noted in my introduction, however, I am not such a person.

By solemnly affirming their primary loyalty to the United States and renouncing any inconsistent political allegiances in their naturalization oaths, new dual citizens would minimize any risks to the American polity that their divided loyalties might seem to pose. They should not be required to renounce any ties to their other country that do not pose these risks—for example, the intention to vote in foreign elections, serve in nonpolicymaking offices abroad, or seek to advance another country's interests. The naturalization oath can be easily and succinctly revised to express these principles. The revised oath can take the form of either a renunciation or an affirmation. What is essential is that it define the core aspects of loyalty that the new citizen must accept.

This change, however, would not remedy the anomaly in current citizenship law that naturalized citizens are obliged to accept these duties and renounce inconsistent allegiances, while citizens who are Americans through birthright or *jus sanguinis* are not and may indeed acquire new allegiances (short of treason) without taking, much less violating, any oath. Congress could address this anomaly (if anomaly it is)[119] by seeking to eliminate the differential treatment. It could do so by making these duties applicable to *all* citizens in two ways. First, it could oblige existing citizens to take the same loyalty oath. Precisely because many (like the author) would find such a requirement obnoxious, it would focus their minds on the troubling implications of demanding more of their new fellow citizens than they do of themselves.[120] Congress could also (or instead) limit their freedom to acquire new citizenships or to act upon them (as through voting) in ways that were not permitted for naturalizing citizens. If new citizens can be forced to affirm their loyalty publicly, then why not existing ones? If existing citizens are unwilling to do this, then they may conclude that they should not force new ones to do so either. This conclusion would demonstrate once again the value-clarifying, unfairness-constraining function that the principle of legal equality among all citizens can play in democratic discourse and politics.

Notes

1. See Robert M. Cover, "The Supreme Court, 1982 Term: Foreword: Nomos and Narrative," *Harvard Law Review* 97 (1983): 4; Michael Walzer, *Spheres of Justice: A Defense of Pluralism and Equality* (New York: Basic Books, 1983); and Sanford Levinson, "Constituting Communities Through Words That Bind: Reflections on Loyalty Oaths," *Michigan Law Review* 84 (1986): 1440.

2. Following convention, I use the terms "citizenship" and "nationality" interchangeably for most purposes in this discussion, although the legal distinction between the two concepts does become important below when I discuss how the law should treat the franchise; paradigmatically, citizens possess it but nationals do not. A recent essay urging that the two statuses be decoupled in order that their functional and normative aspects can be separated also observes that citizenship "attempts to encompass in one word a legal status, a state of mind, a civic obligation, an immigration benefit, an international legal marking, and a personal virtue." See Note, "The Functionality of Citizenship," *Harvard Law Review* 110 (1997): 1814.

3. I shall continue to refer to "dual" citizenship although, as noted below, triple and even more plural citizenships are becoming increasingly available to individuals as a result of the conjunction of modes for acquiring citizenship—and liberalizing ones at that—deriving from parentage, marriage, naturalization, and reacquisition of former nationalities.

4. Peter J. Spiro, "Dual Nationality and the Meaning of Citizenship," *Emory Law Journal* 46 (1997): 1435 (citing President Buchanan's Secretary of State, Lewis Cass).

5. In addition to the widespread adoption of no-fault laws for dissolving marriages, at least one state, Louisiana, has created a consensual, dual-track regime for regulating the conditions for divorce. See Kevin Sack, "Louisiana Approves Measure to Tighten Marriage Bonds," *New York Times*, 24 June 1997, 1.

6. Liberalization can occur in the country of first nationality (as when it does not denationalize its citizens for naturalizing elsewhere), in the country of second nationality (as when it does not require naturalizing citizens to renounce their earlier nationality), or in both.

7. See T. Alexander Aleinikoff, "Citizenship and Membership: A Policy Per-

spective" (Washington, D.C.: Carnegie Endowment for International Peace, forthcoming, 1998); Gerald Neuman, "Justifying U.S. Naturalization Policies," *Virginia Journal of International Law* 35 (1994): 237–78; and Spiro, "Dual Nationality."

8. See, for example, Rogers M. Smith, *Civic Ideals: Conflicting Visions of Citizenship in U.S. History* (New Haven: Yale University Press, 1997); Peter H. Schuck and Rogers M. Smith, *Citizenship Without Consent: Illegal Aliens in the American Polity* (New Haven: Yale University Press, 1985); Stephen H. Legomsky, "Why Citizenship?" *Virginia Journal of International Law* 35 (1994): 279; T. Alexander Aleinikoff, "Citizens, Aliens, Membership and the Constitution," *Constitutional Commentary* 7 (1990): 9; and Neuman, "Justifying U.S. Naturalization Policies."

9. In my view, citizenship can be justified, among other reasons, as creating an additional incentive to assimilate by acquiring a minimal competence in the dominant language, gaining a minimal understanding of (and hopefully a love for) the nation's institutions, and affirming a minimal allegiance to the polity. Such assimilation is of inestimable value both to American society and to the aliens. See Peter H. Schuck, Expert Testimony in *Lavoie v. The Queen*, Federal Court of Canada, Trial Division, October 1994.

10. Peter H. Schuck, "The Re-Evaluation of American Citizenship," *Georgetown Immigration Law Journal* 12 (1997): 1. Also in *Challenge to the Nation-State: Immigration in Western Europe and the United States*, ed. C. Joppke (New York: Oxford University Press, 1998).

11. I mean this in the etymological sense of the word; the debate is addressing questions at the very root of the notion of citizenship.

12. Neuman, "Justifying U.S. Naturalization Policies."

13. Schuck and Smith, *Citizenship Without Consent*; and Spiro, "Dual Nationality."

14. U.S. General Accounting Office, "Naturalization of Aliens: INS Internal Controls," Testimony before Subcommittee on Immigration, Senate Judiciary Committee, May 1, 1997, GAO/T-GGD-97–98.

15. Katharine Q. Seelye, "20 Charged With Helping 13,000 Cheat on Test for Citizenship," *New York Times*, 28 January 1998, A12.

16. U.S. Congress, "Societal and Legal Issues Surrounding Children Born in the United States to Illegal Alien Parents," Joint Hearing before Subcommittee on Immigration and Claims and the Subcommittee on the Constitution, House Judiciary Committee, 104th Congress, 1st Session, December 13, 1995, Serial No. 50 (Washington, D.C.: Government Printing Office, 1996); and U.S. Congress, Hearing before Subcommittee on Immigration and Claims, House Judiciary Committee, 105th Congress, 1st Session, June 25, 1997 (unpublished).

17. Neuman, "Justifying U.S. Naturalization Policies"; Spiro, "Dual Nationality"; Aleinikoff, "Citizenship and Membership"; Peter H. Schuck, "Dual Citizenship in an Era of Migration," forthcoming in Peter H. Schuck, *Citizens, Strangers, and In-Betweens: Essays on Immigration and Citizenship* (Boulder, Colo.: Westview Press, 1998); and Noah M. J. Pickus, ed., *Immigration and Citizenship in the Twenty-First Century* (Lanham, Md.: Rowman & Littlefield, 1998).

18. Gerald L. Neuman, "Nationality Law in the United States and Germany: Structure and Current Problems," in *Paths to Inclusion: The Integration of Immigrants in the United States and Germany*, ed. Peter H. Schuck and Rainer Münz (Providence, R.I.: Berghahn Books, 1998). Neuman points out that "before the 1860s the U.S. was full of dual nationals who thought of themselves as Americans."

19. William Safire, "Citizen of the World," *New York Times*, 16 May 1983, A31. The flip side of this selfishness—Americans who acquire foreign nationalities and renounce their U.S. citizenship in order to avoid paying U.S. taxes—aroused such public resentment that Congress enacted a statute in 1996 to address the practice. See Ted J. Chiappari, "Expatriation Tax: Income Tax Liability of Expatriates and Departing Lawful Permanent Residents," in *1997–98 Immigration and Nationality Law Handbook*, Vol. 2 (Washington, D.C.: American Immigration Lawyers Association, 1997).

20. Alex Aleinikoff estimates that half a million children acquire dual citizenship in the United States *at birth* each year. See Aleinikoff, "Citizenship and Membership," 26.

21. Alex Aleinikoff identifies six discrete combinations of rules that can lead to dual citizenship. See Aleinikoff, "Citizenship and Membership," 24–26. Peter Spiro notes that dual citizenship was expanded by the historical circumstances that states in the nineteenth century increasingly rejected other states' claims of perpetual allegiance, and that Europe's adoption of *jus sanguinis* in the nineteenth century coincided with the application by the United States of an almost absolute rule of *jus soli*. See Spiro, "Dual Nationality," 1411, 1436.

22. Spiro views this development as the third major challenge to the historical paradigms of nationality, following the spread of the principle of perpetual allegiance and the growth of liberal democratic states. See Spiro, "Dual Nationality," 1411, 1416.

23. Aleinikoff, "Citizenship and Membership," 25.

24. Spiro, "Dual Nationality," 1411, 1457.

25. See Schuck and Münz, *Paths to Inclusion*, "Introduction." Germany is sharply divided on this question. The Free Democrats, Socialists, and Greens support dual nationality for children born of foreigners in Germany, with the children required to choose between German and foreign citizenship at age eighteen. The Christian Democrats and Christian Social Union strongly oppose dual nationality.

26. Eugene Goldstein and Victoria Piazza, "Naturalization, Dual Citizenship and Retention of Foreign Citizenship: A Survey," *Interpreter Releases* 73 (April 22, 1996): 517.

27. Aleinikoff, "Citizenship and Membership," 30; and Jorge A. Vargas, "Dual Nationality for Mexicans? A Comparative Legal Analysis of the Dual Nationality Proposal and Its Eventual Political and Socio-Economic Implications," *Chicano-Latino Law Review* 18 (1996): 50. Aleinikoff believes that the net effect of these two changes, which trade off more dual nationals in the first generation against fewer in the second and future ones, will be to produce fewer dual nationals eventually than under the old rules. Whether or not he is correct about this, the changes will surely encourage more Mexicans to naturalize in the United States.

28. Spiro, "Dual Nationality," 1411, 1458; and Sam Dillon, "Mexico Woos U.S. Mexicans, Proposing Dual Nationality," *New York Times*, 10 December 1995, 16.

29. Some observers doubt that the new Mexican law will significantly affect naturalization rates in the United States, while arguing that discrimination against noncitizens in the United States is a more important factor driving naturalizations. See "Dual Citizenship, Domestic Politics and the Naturalization Rates of Latino Immigrants in the U.S.," Policy Brief, Tomas Rivera Center, June 1996.

30. Somini Sengupta, "Immigrants in New York Pressing Drive for Dual Nationality," *New York Times*, 30 December 1996, B1.

31. Until recently, as Spiro shows, states actively opposed and contrived to limit their nationals' affiliations with other states through military, legal, and diplomatic means. He also points to the inconsistencies of some states' positions on dual citizenship, "attempt[ing] a rule of nationality from other states that they would not have for themselves." See Spiro, "Dual Nationality," 1411, 1485 (n 35). I speculate that this practice is more difficult to effectuate today than it was when states were more willing to discriminate overtly in their legal regimes.

32. Rey Koslowski, Comments at roundtable discussion on plural citizenship, Carnegie Endowment for International Peace, 25 April 1997.

33. Neil Lewis, "Reno Acts to Suspend Deportations," *New York Times*, 11 July 1997, A13.

34. Alejandro Portes, "Divergent Destinies: Immigration, the Second Generation, and the Rise of Transnational Communities," in Schuck and Münz, *Paths to Inclusion.*

35. Indeed, Spiro notes that many states are now so eager for their nationals both to naturalize in economically advanced countries and to retain their ties to the state of origin that their nationality laws make it difficult or even impossible for their nationals to make an effective renunciation in the second state. In an arresting phrase, he calls this a "new perpetual allegiance," different from the old in that the states now *encourage* their nationals to acquire additional citizenships. He suggests that this development poses a dilemma for the second state if it wishes to minimize dual citizenship among its new members by requiring (as the United States now does *not* require) an effective renunciation. If it refuses to naturalize migrants from states that will not effectuate such a renunciation, then in effect no migrants from those states will be able to naturalize. This refusal would create political and diplomatic difficulties between the states and, by preventing those naturalizations, would impede the assimilation of these migrants. See Spiro, "Dual Nationality," 1483 (n 313); and Dillon, "Mexico Woos U.S. Mexicans."

36. T. Alexander Aleinikoff, "Theories of Loss of Citizenship," *Michigan Law Review* 84 (1986): 1471. See also *Kungys v. United States*, 485 U.S. 759 (1988).

37. Nancy F. Cott, "Marriage and Women's Citizenship: A Historical Excursion," unpublished manuscript, Yale University Department of History, 1996; and Spiro, "Dual Nationality," 1456 (n 203). The Supreme Court recently rejected, albeit in a highly fractured decision, a challenge to one aspect of this gender bias—the transmission of citizenship to illegitimate children. See *Miller v. Albright*, 1998 WL 186812 (U.S.).

38. "Advice about Possible Loss of U.S. Citizenship and Dual Nationality,"

U.S. Department of State, reprinted in *Interpreter Releases* 67 (1990): 1093. Indeed, as David Martin has argued, the State Department not only tolerates dual citizenship through naturalization elsewhere by U.S. citizens, but actually makes it more difficult for citizens to renounce their American citizenship by not effectuating renunciatory language in the other state's naturalization oath. David A. Martin, "The Civil Republican Ideal for Citizenship, and for Our Common Life," *Virginia Journal of International Law* 35 (1994): 301.

39. Aleinikoff, "Citizenship and Membership," 37.

40. Spiro, "Dual Nationality," 1428. Aleinikoff notes that some of the problems associated with dual citizenship today could be ameliorated through bilateral agreements between states. See Aleinikoff, "Citizenship and Membership," 34.

41. For another example of an ex ante interest that even an insular state may have in an international safety net regime (for refugees), see Peter H. Schuck, "Refugee Burden-Sharing: A Modest Proposal," *Yale Journal of International Law* 22 (1997): 243.

42. Schuck and Smith, *Citizenship Without Consent*; but see also Gerald L. Neuman, *Strangers to the Constitution: Immigrants, Borders, and Fundamental Law* (Princeton: Princeton University Press, 1996).

43. Schuck and Smith, *Citizenship Without Consent*; and Peter H. Schuck, "Rethinking Informed Consent," *Yale Law Journal* 103 (1994): 899.

44. A commission reviewing Canada's dual citizenship law recommended in 1994 that both new "involuntary" dual citizens and naturalizing citizens "accord primacy" to their Canadian nationality. Canada House of Commons, "Canadian Citizenship: A Sense of Belonging," Report of the Standing Committee on Citizenship and Immigration (June 1994), 15.

45. *Rogers v. Bellei*, 401 U.S. 815 (1971). Some have expressed concern that a liberal dual citizenship policy might encourage the proliferation of second- and third-generation dual citizenship in the United States by permitting those who naturalize in the United States to transmit their U.S. citizenship through *jus sanguinis* to children and grandchildren who live elsewhere and have no other ties to the U.S. Congress could respond to this risk, if it exists, by enacting the kinds of residency requirements for *jus sanguinis* citizens that *Bellei* upheld.

46. *Afroyim v. Rusk*, 387 U.S. 253 (1967).

47. Usually, but not always. Well into the twentieth century, aliens were permitted to vote in some states, and some municipalities permit them to vote in local elections—a practice that is common in Europe. Indeed, even undocumented aliens are entitled to vote in local school board elections in New York City. See Jamin Raskin, "Legal Aliens, Local Citizens: The Historical, Constitutional and Theoretical Meanings of Alien Suffrage," *University of Pennsylvania Law Review* 141 (1993): 1391.

48. *Schneider v. Rusk*, 377 U.S. 163 (1964).

49. Levinson, "Constituting Communities," 1465.

50. One possible explanation—that immigrants wishing to naturalize in the United States are aliens whose petitions give the government leverage over them that it lacks over Americans who are already citizens and wish to naturalize elsewhere—simply begs the central policy and perhaps constitutional questions of

which conditions the polity can and, as a moral matter, should impose on the acquisition of citizenship through birth or consent, and why the status difference between the two groups should matter insofar as the supposed dangers of dual citizenship are concerned.

51. The United States has become increasingly aggressive in pursuing those who expatriate—thus ending their dual citizenship status (if they had it)—in order to minimize their U.S. taxes. Tax law changes enacted in 1996 are designed to defeat this stratagem. See Chiappari, "Expatriation Tax."

52. Neuman, "Nationality Law in the United States and Germany."

53. The confusion about standards results from the Supreme Court's severely fractured decision in *Kungys v. United States* which had attempted to define them. These standards may become clearer as a result of denaturalization cases that are being initiated in the wake of revelations that the INS has erroneously naturalized many ineligible aliens. See Seelye, "20 Charged with Helping 13,000 Cheat."

54. Neuman, "Justifying U.S. Naturalization Policies," 238–42.

55. Peter H. Schuck, "Whose Membership Is It, Anyway? Comments on Gerald Neuman," *Virginia Journal of International Law* 35 (1994): 321.

56. For some parents of dual citizens, it also permits them to protect their children from the dangers of growing up in American ghettoes. Apparently, the children do not always want that option. See, for example, Larry Rohter, "Island Life Not Idyllic for Youths From U.S.," *New York Times*, 20 February 1998, A4 (describing "Dominican Yorks").

57. See Linda Basch, *Nations Unbound: Transnational Projects, Postcolonial Predicaments, and Deterritorialized Nation States* (Langhorne, Pa.: Gordon and Breach, 1985); and Portes, "Divergent Destinies."

58. Recent empirical research suggests that naturalization affects English proficiency more strongly than any other indicator of durable attachment to the United States. This effect, moreover, goes beyond the fact that one who naturalizes must already have acquired some English proficiency: "although there is a modest English prerequisite for U.S. citizenship, it is hard to image that this effect outweighs the substantial propensity for naturalized citizens to want to make long-term investments in many forms of U.S.-specific capital, including learning English." Thomas J. Espenshade and Haishan Fu, "An Analysis of English-Language Proficiency Among U.S. Immigrants," *American Sociological Review* 62 (1997): 300.

59. See, for example, Spiro, "Dual Nationality," 101–2. That the ease of acquiring dual nationality increases immigrants' propensity to naturalize in the second state seems self-evident and has been reported by some observers in some countries. See Sengupta, "Immigrants in New York." Participants in the Carnegie Endowment workshop reported that the average period taken by Italians who naturalize in Canada declined from seventeen to six years after Italy permitted dual citizenship, and that the naturalization rate of Irish immigrants increased when Australia eliminated from its naturalization oath an affirmation of loyalty to the British Crown. Mary Woods, Comments at roundtable discussion on plural citizenship, Carnegie Endowment for International Peace, 25 April 1997. But see Tomas Rivera Center, "Dual Citizenship."

60. Schuck, "Whose Membership Is It Anyway?" 329.

61. Levinson, "Constituting Communities," 1440, 1461.

62. Schuck and Münz, *Paths to Inclusion.*

63. Spiro, "Dual Nationality," 102–3.

64. The 1997 budget agreement will restore approximately half of these 1996 benefit cuts. See Robert Pear, "Legal Immigrants to Benefit Under New Budget Accord," *New York Times*, 30 July 1997, A17. President Clinton proposed in his January 1998 State of the Union message to fill much of the remaining gap. See Michael Fix and Wendy Zimmerman, "The Legacy of Welfare Reform" (working draft, The Urban Institute, February 1998).

65. Fix and Zimmerman, "Legacy."

66. Strictly speaking, of course, it is not dual citizenship *per se* that imposes these fiscal burdens, but rather the naturalization incentive created by a policy to deny benefits to aliens. Still, the effect is the same: A liberal dual citizenship policy will cost the government—*some* government—more in benefits. These costs, of course, should be offset by any corresponding social benefits, such as food stamps and SSI, that are generated by making these individuals eligible for these transfer programs.

67. The Canadian parliamentary committee cited this concern, among others. Canada House of Commons, "Canadian Citizenship," 15.

68. Recent examples are Sweden's effort to prosecute Argentine military officers for the death of a teenager who was a Swedish–Argentine dual citizen and Spain's effort to prosecute Argentine military officers for the murder of Spanish–Argentine dual citizens.

69. Spiro, "Dual Nationality," 1464.

70. Depending on how one views these complex imbroglios, China's increasingly bellicose protests against Taiwan, which governs millions of people whom China views as Chinese citizens, and Russia's threats against the Baltic republics for their discrimination against resident Russians might be considered examples. As Neuman points out, these are often cases not of dual nationality but of single-nationality individuals who reside outside their country but have ethnic ties to it. Neuman, "Nationality Law in the United States and Germany."

71. Under U.S. law, they can certainly vote in American elections. Whether they can also vote in the other state's elections depends on the law of that state. As noted earlier, the pending Mexican law will not permit Mexicans naturalizing in the United States to vote in Mexican elections, although Mexico could change its election law to allow them to do so, in effect rendering them citizens, not merely nationals, of Mexico. Mexico has already changed its election law to permit Mexican citizens who reside abroad to vote by absentee ballot.

72. The existence of Arrovian voting paradoxes does not really affect this argument.

73. Spiro, "Dual Nationality," 1477–78. Foreign politicians from major sending countries now frequently visit American communities in which their emigres live, seeking to woo remittances, investments, and political support. See, for example, Patrick J. McDonnell, "San Salvador Mayor Visits Expatriates in L.A.," *Los Angeles Times*, 19 November 1997, 1.

74. Although the possibility that the church might harm U.S. interests seems far-fetched, the risks of other nongovernmental organizations (NGOs) doing so may be worth considering at a time when NGOs can wield enormous influence, even qualifying them for the Nobel Peace Prize. As Spiro points out, NGOs enjoy the freedom of action to undertake certain conduct that states are unlikely to engage in because of the legal, political, or diplomatic constraints under which they operate.

75. Peter Skerry, *Mexican–Americans: The Ambivalent Minority* (New York: Free Press, 1993).

76. Peter H. Schuck and Bruce Brown, "Lessons from Lippo," *Wall Street Journal*, 27 February 1997, A16.

77. It is always possible to finesse the question by simply assuming that those who have already lived as U.S. citizens have accepted that political identity through a kind of tacit consent. This argument from tacit consent is plausible, but problematic. See Schuck and Smith, *Citizenship Without Consent*; and Levinson, "Constituting Communities."

78. I do not favor this approach, which is discussed in the final paragraph of this essay.

79. Albert O. Hirschman, *Exit, Voice, and Loyalty: Responses to Decline in Firms, Organizations, and States* (Cambridge: Harvard University Press, 1970).

80. Obviously, there is room for interpretation here; if the criterion of an independent judiciary were used, for example, it is not clear that any of these countries (except perhaps India) would qualify. The others, in order of the number of immigrants sent, are Vietnam, China, Dominican Republic, Cuba, Ukraine, and Russia.

81. Canada House of Commons, "Canadian Citizenship."

82. The suspicion that many who naturalize do so for opportunistic reasons seems to animate a recent proposal to decouple functional citizenship (concerned with rights and duties) and nationality (concerned with affirming one's affective ties to the polity). See "The Functionality of Citizenship," 1814.

83. Some other reasons for increased naturalizations include an intensified INS effort to encourage them, aliens' need to pay a fee for renewing their green cards that is only slightly lower than the naturalization fee, and the large cohort of those legalized under the amnesty provisions of the Immigration Reform and Control Act of 1986 who have only recently satisfied the time limits required for naturalization.

84. Aleinikoff, "Citizenship and Membership," 31.

85. Aleinikoff, "Citizenship and Membership," 19.

86. I shall not attempt here to define assimilation or to defend its importance as a preeminent value against which to assess immigration policy generally and dual citizenship policy in particular. I have discussed these matters elsewhere, and there is a large literature on the subject.

87. Sengupta, "Immigrants in New York."

88. Schuck, "Whose Membership Is It, Anyway?"

89. Spiro, "Dual Nationality," 1474.

90. Spiro, "Dual Nationality," 1474.

91. "Traitor" is used here in its colloquial sense—as someone who betrays the

nation—rather than its technical sense, which requires among other things that the traitor be a citizen of that nation. See *Kawakita v. United States*, 343 U.S. 717 (1952). For a nuanced discussion of treason and loyalty, including some cases in which citizenship was an issue, see George P. Fletcher, *Loyalty: An Essay on the Morality of Relationships* (New York: Oxford University Press, 1993), especially chapter 3.

92. Spiro, "Dual Nationality," 1462.

93. In such campaigns, of course, dual citizens are as entitled to serve in the armed forces as other citizens. Indeed, resident aliens may serve.

94. Indeed, Americans may also engage in such conduct on behalf of *democratic* regimes, even close allies of the United States, as is demonstrated by the fascinating case of Jonathan Pollard, who illegally transferred U.S. military secrets to Israel—apparently in the belief that there was no conflict of interest.

95. For the classic exploration of the different ways of thinking about and institutionalizing relationships in which loyalty plays some role, see Hirschman, *Exit, Voice, and Loyalty*.

96. My colleague Akhil Amar points out that U.S. citizens may not simultaneously be a citizen of more than one American state because this would give them two votes for Congress and the presidency rather than the one that their fellow citizens enjoy.

97. However, open primary states permit members of one political party to vote in the primary of another.

98. Many people, of course, use names that are different from their legal ones.

99. Neuman, "Justifying U.S. Naturalization Policies," 252.

100. Other asymmetries may not be far off. The Commission on Immigration Reform, for example, considered whether to limit future immigrant admissions by restricting the right of newly naturalized citizens to petition for admission of their relatives beyond the limits that apply to other citizens.

101. In fact, evidence from cognitive psychology strongly suggests that people who already possess a thing value it more than they would value the same thing if they did not yet possess it but hoped to acquire it. Hence, they are more likely to defend it effectively.

102. As Levinson puts it, native-born citizens "are free to regard the Constitution as an abomination and even support its violent replacement by a more agreeable substitute; naturalized citizens, however, are formally bound to swear that their new self-definition of being 'American' will include at least the propositions laid out in their oath." Levinson, "Constituting Communities," 1463. Neuman does seem to view this asymmetry as problematic; see his "Justifying U.S. Naturalization Policies," 253–63.

103. This assumes, of course, that good moral character is defined in a minimalist fashion. This has not always been the case.

104. As a glance at the naturalization statute reveals, we have long done so with respect to eligibility standards. Rights have not been exempt from discrimination. The most important example is voting rights, which were withheld from citizen women until the Nineteenth Amendment and are still withheld from citizen felons and citizen children under the age of eighteen.

105. Neuman suggests that their concerns may be pretextual and "often a tactic for preventing naturalization of Mexicans." Gerald L. Neuman, letter to author dated August 18, 1997. As noted earlier, Aleinikoff harbors the same suspicion. In any event, nothing in my analysis turns on whether or not they are correct.

106. Aleinikoff, "Citizenship and Membership," 18.

107. Schuck and Smith, *Citizenship Without Consent*.

108. After circulating several drafts of this essay containing my proposal, I learned that Lawrence Fuchs in recent congressional testimony had made a similar one and that the Commission on Immigration Reform had recommended an oath like the one favored by Fuchs. See U.S. Commission on Immigration Reform, *Becoming an American: Immigration and Immigrant Policy* (Washington, D.C.: U.S. Government Printing Office, 1997), 14. We all emphasize the requirement of a primary loyalty to the United States. I go beyond them, however, in seeking to specify (not necessarily in the oath itself) the duties that should define that primary loyalty.

109. Some evidence of oathtakers' seriousness, were it neeeded, appears in the report that Irish naturalization rates in Australia rose when applicants were no longer required to swear allegiance to the British Crown.

110. Levinson, "Constituting Communities," 1459.

111. For what it is worth, Congress seems to agree; only recently and reluctantly did it permit the INS, and not just judges, to conduct the ceremony and oath-taking.

112. This clause seems superfluous unless it means to affirm a state of emotion or veneration that might strengthen the inclination, already required, to support and defend the Constitution and laws.

113. Whether this duty should be characterized as "exclusive" loyalty to the United States or merely "primary" loyalty is not clear. It is exclusive in the sense that it overrides any other duties in the unlikely event of conflict, but it is primary in the sense that, precisely because conflict is unlikely, it can easily coexist with duties to others. In any event, nothing turns on the distinction.

114. The notion of a hierarchy of claims appears in the very same provision of the Immigration and Nationality Act that prescribes the naturalization oath. Section 337 of the statute, in defining "religious training and belief" for purposes of an exception to the duty to bear arms, provides that the phrase means a "belief in a relation to a Supreme Being involving duties that are superior to those arising from any human relation." The Canadian parliamentary committee, which as noted earlier would require that certain new dual citizens accord "primacy" to their Canadian nationality, does not define what such primacy means or would entail.

115. Stephen H. Legomsky, letters to the author dated 21 August 1997, and 2 September 1997.

116. There are at least two recent examples: an American who was briefly the president of Yugoslavia, and another who is now president of Latvia (but has relinquished his U.S. citizenship). While this duty is important, however, it is likely to be implicated so rarely that it need not be mentioned explicitly in the renunciation oath, which should retain its solemn dignity and lofty generality insofar as possible.

117. Legomsky, letters to the author dated 21 August 1997, and 2 September 1997.

118. To be sure, one can imagine a scenario in which a government-private entity conflict would be more troubling than a government-government conflict—for example, if the other state were an insignificant one which could not harm U.S. interests but the private entity were a multinational corporation with interests throughout the globe that could harm the United States. But such a possibility does not invalidate the prophylactic rule that I am proposing to govern the vast majority of situations.

119. Lawrence Fuchs writes, "I do not worry about the asymmetries required between naturalized citizens and native born Americans. Not every inconsistency can be fixed." Letter to the author dated 12 September 1997.

120. I wish to be clear that I am generally opposed to loyalty oaths, and I am not advocating them here. Indeed, my point is that one's revulsion against loyalty oaths should lead one to resist requiring them of others. Moreover, if Congress does require an oath of existing citizens, it must choose its words very carefully in order to avoid violating Justice Jackson's canonical precept: "If there is any fixed star in our constitutional constellation, it is that no official, high or petty, can prescribe what shall be orthodox in politics, nationalism, religion, or other matter of opinion or force citizens to confess by word or act their faith therein" (*West Virginia State Board of Education v. Barnette*).

Why Immigrants Want Dual Citizenship (And We Should Too): A Response to Peter Schuck

Michael Jones-Correa

Peter Schuck, in his discussion of dual citizenship, has pointed out that this status is likely to become more rather than less salient over time, not only for newly naturalized American citizens but for native-born citizens as well. With intermarriage, migration, and changes in the laws of immigrant-sending countries, there will be more instances of dual citizenship, leading to greater visibility and, most likely, greater controversy.

Despite this controversy, the fact is that dual citizenship is increasingly tolerated for the reasons Schuck points out: it doesn't seem to cause much harm and, on the contrary, may actually do some good. The old worries about conflicting jurisdictions and the possibility of dual loyalties during war seem less relevant in a world where international ties have proliferated and where the likelihood of war among liberal states seems remote.

Americans abroad increasingly adopt second nationalities, and Americans at home increasingly carry them. If American citizenship is, as Schuck suggests, a metaphorical "marriage," is the adoption of dual citizenship a besmirching of the marriage vows? A new citizen swears to "renounce and abjure absolutely and entirely all allegiance and fidelity to any other" state. But in many cases new citizens do not cease to have other loyalties and attachments. Are they, then, playing around on the side?

It is a rare citizen who doesn't have conflicting attachments and loyalties of one sort or another, and yet somehow or other we all still manage

This essay was written in response to a draft of Peter Schuck's chapter, presented at the Duke University Workshop on Citizenship and Naturalization, October 30–November 1, 1997.

to stumble along and fulfill our obligations as citizens. Certainly we allow multiple loyalties of native-born citizens; why shouldn't we allow them of our naturalized citizens? If native-born citizens can meddle in other countries' elections, raise money for insurgencies abroad, and lobby the U.S. government for special consideration for particular countries, why shouldn't naturalized citizens? It doesn't seem to me that there is a very good answer to this question. Should we hold naturalized citizens to a different standard than we do native-born citizens? If so, why?

One answer might be, as Bonnie Honig has argued in her work,[1] that Americans hold immigrants up as the exemplars they themselves are not. To paraphrase that ubiquitous army advertisement, we want immigrants to "be all that we *can't* be." We want them to be not just like us, but *better* than us. The less charitable answer might be that somehow we are less sure of them as Americans, and they have to prove themselves somehow. Neither of these expectations, it seems to me, is grounded in reality.

The second response is more easily rebutted than the first. If we are afraid that naturalized citizens will prove disloyal or unreliable, there is little evidence to prove it. In fact, the preponderance of the evidence is on the other side. From our earliest wars, immigrants, resident aliens, and what would now be called illegal immigrants have fought and died for this country. Recall the Irish and German regiments that fought for, and died en masse for, the Union in the Civil War; those of Italian and German descent that fought in both world wars; and most striking of all, native-born Japanese Americans who joined the armed forces in World War II, even as their friends and families were being interned in concentration camps. If anything does, this record in war demonstrates that having attachments to other countries does not preclude dying for this one.

On the other hand, if we expect immigrants to be better than us, then we had better learn to live with perpetual disappointment. What we can hope for, and expect, is that immigrants will be as good citizens as we ourselves are. What does this mean? Well, in part it means that they will take a full and active part in our civic and political life. I believe, and here I am in agreement with Schuck, that dual citizenship facilitates this active involvement.

I spent eighteen months in 1991 and 1992 talking to first-generation Latin American immigrants in Queens, New York City, about their political lives.[2] In particular I was interested in the question of why, at the time, so many of them hesitated before becoming citizens in this country. This question, by the way, is now increasingly moot; with the change in the climate toward immigrants, many of those who were wavering in 1992 have now probably become citizens. But at the time, many people were hesitating, sometimes for many years, before taking the plunge.

In my view, a large part of the hesitation stemmed from what immigrants saw as the high cost of immigration. Not only the literal cost—the time, effort, and money involved—but the *symbolic* cost. There's a story that circulates among immigrants about the oath required during the naturalization ceremony renouncing old allegiances and pledging allegiance to the United States. It's become a kind of urban legend—the kind of thing no one has seen, but everyone has heard about. I'll give you an example of this story, which I heard repeatedly in my interviews. This a Colombian immigrant talking about why Colombians were reluctant to take on U.S. citizenship:

> It started as an anecdote . . . that if you became an American citizen you had to renounce your country, and step on the Colombian flag. When I came to this country, they told me: ". . . you're going to have to stand on the flag of your country [*tu patria*], and spit on it." . . . there are still people who believe that if you've become an American citizen, it's because at some time you stood on the flag.

This story circulates widely among immigrants. It's not necessary that the story be true or even thought to be true among those who tell it. It serves to illuminate certain feelings about citizenship and the loss of homeland. The scenario juxtaposes the secular authority of the foreign state with the nationalist, almost religious symbolism of the home country's flag. An immigrant is asked to choose between desecrating the symbol to become an American or remaining an immigrant in a kind of martyrdom of marginality. The way in which the story is told makes clear, of course, what the choice should be.

Another fear that immigrants have is that traveling back to their home country with an American passport will mean being treated as a foreigner or worse. In a meeting of Ecuadorian immigrants with a visiting legislator from Ecuador, a woman said that she owned a house and property in Ecuador, but she was an American citizen. She resented the fact that when she went back she had her luggage searched at the airport (to check for what she was bringing back from the United States) and that she had to get a visa if she was going to stay for more than thirty days. Another participant at the meeting said she resented being treated as a foreigner when she went back and particularly resented having to get visas for her children to travel to Ecuador. Yet another Ecuadorian woman told me: "I have seen very sad cases of people who have changed nationalities and have come back to visit relatives and been very badly treated. People treat them very badly, saying, 'They are no longer one of ours.' " The fear of being treated as a foreigner in one's own country crops up repeatedly in conversations with immigrants, particularly from immigrants from countries who would automatically lose their nationality if they take on the nationality of another. For many immigrants, the loss of their original nationality substantially raises the cost of becoming a U.S. citizen.

During the time that I was in Queens, there were campaigns under way among immigrants to change the dual nationality laws of their countries of origin so that taking on U.S. citizenship would not result in the loss of their original citizenship. Up until that point, U.S. citizenship meant the loss of rights in their birth countries. Between 1992 and 1995, Colombia, Ecuador, the Dominican Republic, and Mexico all passed legislation allowing dual nationality. What's interesting to me about these changes is that they all originated in immigrant communities in the United States. Immigrants were interested in acquiring U.S. citizenship, but not at the cost of losing their original citizenship. So they used what leverage they had, which was not inconsiderable, to persuade their birth countries to allow dual nationality. Politicians from these countries were open to persuasion because they realized that immigrants contributed remittances, investment, and tourist income to their economies, and not least, campaign contributions as well. New York City in particular was a popular campaign and fundraising stop. There's another point to make here as well: The decision was almost costless for these politicians; there was no downside. Not only was it almost literally costless, but it really represented very little risk. We have to keep in mind that what these countries allowed, for the most part, is dual nationality, *not* dual citizenship. They allowed the retention of property and such rights as the right to hold a passport, but not the political rights that go along with citizenship. In general, these political rights can still be exercised, but they have to be exercised in the home country. Dual nationals have to fly back to vote.[3] Needless to say, this suppresses voter turnout.

I don't think this matters for the vast majority of immigrants. What dual citizenship does for them is reduce the cost of becoming naturalized as an American citizen. Some want to have dual citizenship to keep open the option of return, even while they continue their lives here. Others want to participate fully as American citizens without feeling they've betrayed their original loyalties. I've heard conversations among immigrants that represent both points of view. Sometimes a person will hold both views simultaneously. But the second view is held by far more immigrants.

When we evaluate dual citizenship, or dual nationality, as a policy, we should think not just about whether it's more or less risky, or more or less costless, but what end we think it serves. If it helps immigrants become fully participating members in the polity, then I'm all for it. The thing to remember is that, even if we accept the metaphor of citizenship as marriage and think of dual citizenship as the equivalent of having two spouses, immigrants at most send money to their other "spouse"—but they live with us.

Notes

1. Bonnie Honig, *"No Place Like Home": Democracy and the Politics of Foreignness* (forthcoming, Princeton University Press).

2. This fieldwork, which I draw on in the remaining discussion, is presented in Michael Jones-Correa, *Between Two Nations: The Political Predicament of Latinos in New York City* (Ithaca: Cornell University Press, 1998).

3. The exception is Colombia, although most recently the Dominican Republic in the fall of 1997 indicated that it would allow Dominican nationals abroad to vote in Dominican national elections and elect their own representative. However, even allowing voting from abroad does not guarantee interest and turnout. Colombians abroad, who have been able to cast ballots for national elections at Colombian consulates, have very low turnout rates. Fewer than 4,000 of the more than 100,000 Colombians in the New York City metropolitan area turned out to vote in either of the last three Colombian presidential elections.

6

Alienage Classifications in a Nation of Immigrants: Three Models of "Permanent" Residence

Hiroshi Motomura

In 1996, federal welfare legislation significantly changed what it means to be (or not to be) a citizen of the United States. For the first time, many noncitizens are now ineligible for food stamps and Supplemental Security Income (SSI).[1] Among those barred are many aliens who became lawful permanent residents long before 1996. The legislation also barred future legal immigrants from federal means-tested programs, most importantly food stamps and SSI.[2] In August 1997, Congress restored some benefits,[3] but the 1996 bars remain largely in place.

The 1996 welfare legislation renews difficult questions about the meaning of citizenship. How is being a citizen of the United States different from being a permanent resident alien, i.e., a noncitizen who is admitted as an immigrant and who may remain in that status indefinitely? What differences in our treatment of citizens and permanent residents are appropriate as a matter of public policy and constitutional law?

My purpose in this chapter is to offer a more textured understanding of alienage classifications than the account that prevails in policy analysis and constitutional law. The prevailing discourse on alienage classifications posits permanent residence and citizenship as two distinct statuses, then discusses how they should differ. It thus assesses alienage classifications in relation to citizenship in general. I call this the "affiliation model"— permanent residence is a form of affiliation with American society that

---

For their thoughtful and stimulating comments on earlier drafts, I thank Alex Aleinikoff, Linda Bosniak, Curtis Bradley, Carol Lehman, Sean McAllister, Noah Pickus, Victor Romero, Dan Tichenor, and Nadine Wettstein.

199

grows over time. Under this model, long-term permanent residents merit a status close to that of citizens, if not identical. Thus, the inquiry reduces to the question, "how close"?

Here I suggest that citizenship in general should not be the only reference point and that the affiliation model is not the only model. I propose two other models that view permanent residence as something less than citizenship but more than the minimum status that all noncitizens enjoy by virtue of their basic human rights. A second model of permanent residence I call the "contract model." The attributes of permanent residence may be bargained for. Under the contract model, anything is permissible if a new immigrant has notice before accepting the bargain, but thereafter the terms of the bargain are fixed. A third model views permanent residence not in contrast to citizenship generally, but rather as a stage toward naturalization in which the permanent residents are prospective citizens. I call this the "transition model." Much of this chapter explores how our thinking about alienage classifications would change if we were to adopt it and the idea on which it is based—that we should view alienage by reference to naturalization, not to citizenship generally.

These three models all protect permanent residents, but they do so in different ways and for different reasons. Although the protections under each model are limited, they are complementary, not contradictory, ones. Together, they explain the complexities of permanent residency much more clearly than any one model alone. At a more normative level, the combined effect of these three models suggests certain shortcomings in the protections for permanent residents in both statutory and constitutional law—particularly in the period before they become eligible to naturalize. Adding the transition model to prevailing discourse exposes the primary flaw in our current treatment of permanent residents: that it fails to recognize that permanent residency is part of the naturalization process, and that permanent residents are prospective citizens.

I. "Permanent Residence" versus "Citizenship"

How Do We Treat Citizens and Permanent Residents Differently?

Some differences are matters of immigration law itself, which, as traditionally defined, concerns the admission of noncitizens to the United States and the terms under which they may remain. A citizen must be admitted to the United States, while a noncitizen may be refused admission.[4] Citizens may not be removed from the United States,[5] unless they first lose their citizenship through renunciation or denaturalization. In contrast, noncitizens—including permanent residents—may be removed on various deportability grounds.[6]

Other differences between citizens and permanent residents go beyond immigration law. They are matters of alienage law, which as traditionally defined concerns the status of aliens in the United States. Noncitizens, including permanent residents, generally may not vote in public elections. They generally may not hold federal civil service jobs, and their access to certain state and local public employment is restricted. And as mentioned above, Congress has limited noncitizen access to federal public benefits.

Permanent residents also have fewer opportunities than citizens to sponsor their relatives for admission as immigrants.[7] Citizens may sponsor their spouses, minor unmarried children, and parents (if the petitioning citizen is twenty-one years of age) as "immediate relatives" exempt from numerical limits. Citizens may also sponsor relatives in three additional categories: adult sons and daughters and siblings of any age, subject to numerical limits. In contrast, permanent residents may sponsor only their spouses and unmarried children, not their married children or siblings.[8]

Do We Need "Permanent Residence"?

Sound public policy sometimes calls for treating citizens and noncitizens differently. The text and history of the Constitution support the distinction between citizens and noncitizens. More fundamentally, the distinction rests on the idea that a liberal democracy, in order to shape itself as a community of interests and shared values, must have the power to grant or refuse membership to prospective new members.[9] This power may be limited, but some power must remain. This inevitably leads to a distinction between insiders and outsiders, between members and nonmembers, and between citizens and noncitizens.

Permanent residents are noncitizens, but why not treat them entirely like citizens, leaving noncitizens to a lesser status only if they are not permanent residents? We could eliminate a functionally distinct concept of permanent residency by treating permanent residents and citizens identically. But making permanent residence entirely indistinct from citizenship would lead to two undesirable consequences.

First, if permanent residence were tantamount to citizenship itself, the process of choosing new citizens would be unwisely constrained. In effect, we would choose new citizens rather than new permanent residents from the large applicant pool. By analogy, suppose universities could hire new faculty only with tenure. The selection process would have much more momentous consequences, yet be carried out with much less information than it would be if some lesser status were available—call it permanent residence or untenured faculty. Because permanent residence is less than citizenship, entails treatment different from a citizen, and may be revoked, we may use it to make tentative choices, to be confirmed at a later point in time. Thus, we have tenure reviews for faculty, and we admit students to law school before we admit them to the bar. Permanent residence that is something less than citizenship promotes better choices of new citizens, wholly apart from how we answer the question of how many or how few are chosen.

A second, alternative consequence of eliminating permanent residence as a distinct category may be two categories of citizenship, one fuller than the other. Prevailing doctrine says that there is only one form of citizenship.[10] The only recognized exception is the express constitutional requirement that the president be not only a citizen, but "natural born Citizen."[11] Yet, we have distinctions among citizens, even if we do not usually think of them that way. For example, *jus soli* principles confer citizenship on children born in the United States, regardless of the immigration law status of their parents. But these child citizens may not petition for their parents to immigrate in the favored "immediate relative" category; only adult citizens may.[12] A second example: we recognize the abstract principle that citizens may not be removed from the United States. But we tolerate de facto removal of citizen children when the government removes their alien parents.[13]

These age-based distinctions among citizens have developed in order to limit the consequences of conferring birthright citizenship on the children of undocumented aliens. Otherwise, noncitizens would have a strong incentive to come to the United States (illegally if necessary) to give birth to a child who could then immediately petition for his or her parent(s) to immigrate legally. In short, we are willing to confer citizenship, but not completely. So we divide citizens into two groups in order to limit the citizenship that we do confer. If permanent residence and citizenship were identical, similar distinctions would likely arise, for example between new permanent residents and those of longer standing. This is not necessarily better or worse than distinguishing between permanent residents and citizens in the first place. But this will not eliminate permanent residency as a distinct status, just rename it "new citizen."[14]

II. Three Models of "Permanent" Residence

Limits on alienage classifications fall into two general categories: institutional and substantive. By institutional, I mean the question of *who* may adopt alienage classifications. For example, may only the federal government do so, or does it share this authority with states and localities? And within each level of government, may only certain actors adopt alienage classifications?

The institutional questions are important and complex, but I have started to address them elsewhere,[15] and they are not this chapter's primary concern. Here I focus primarily on *substantive* limits on alienage classifications. Assuming that we may sometimes treat permanent residents and citizens differently, then when and how?

The discussion in this section applies the contract, affiliation, and transition models to answer this question as a matter of legislative policy constraints on alienage classifications. In section III, where I discuss the transition model more fully, I will sketch answers to the separate question of whether certain policy constraints are also judicially enforceable as a matter of constitutional law.

The Contract Model

One of the political compromises evident in the current package of restrictions on permanent resident welfare eligibility is that noncitizens who were already permanent residents in August 1996 are treated much more favorably than new arrivals. Why? The intuitive appeal of a cutoff date suggests one model of permanent residence, as a form of contract. When immigrants come to the United States as permanent residents, they enter into a bargain. They accept certain conditions of permanent residency as part of that bargain. The cutoff date protects the original expectations of those who are already permanent residents. At the same time, it serves adequate notice that new arrivals must make do under less favorable conditions. New permanent residents will knowingly enter into a bargain that is less favorable, but still attractive enough that they choose to immigrate.

While the contract model protects the expectations of those who are already permanent residents, it sets essentially no substantive limits on alienage classifications for future permanent residents. Is anything wrong with approaching alienage classifications using only this model? Can citizens bargain with new permanent residents for an agreement to forsake a welfare safety net, for example?

The problem with relying on the contract model alone is that the conditions of permanent residence do not exist solely for the benefit of the permanent resident, to be bargained for or bargained away. This explains our cautious attitude toward guest worker programs and other admission policies that assume that the workers "agree" to come for "temporary" stays to meet short-term labor needs. Notice and contract are relevant and important, but other concepts and values need to play a role as well.

Here we need to stop and think about what alienage classifications are and what they do. There is a traditional distinction between immigration law and alienage law, or put differently, between the law of immigration and the law of immigrants. This distinction is important for two reasons. First, the plenary power doctrine has traditionally foreclosed serious constitutional judicial review in immigration law.[16] In contrast, the traditions and analyses of domestic, mainstream constitutional law have been more readily applied to alienage law than to immigration law.[17] Second, any state law directly regulating immigration triggers garden-variety federal preemption.[18]

The immigration-alienage line is important, but it is elusive because immigration and alienage law overlap functionally.[19] Alienage rules may be surrogates for immigration rules. Often, the intended and/or actual effect of an alienage rule is to affect immigration patterns. California's Proposition 187 is a good example. While it does not directly regulate admission to the United States, its clear intent is to deter undocumented immigration to California and to encourage emigration by undocumented aliens already there. Similarly, immigration rules may be surrogates for alienage rules. For example, deportability grounds traditionally belong to immigration law, since they regulate admission after the fact. Yet they also govern the everyday lives of permanent residents, no less than do rules governing access to public benefits.

The reason for the functional overlap between immigration and alienage rules is that both types of government decisions belong to the broader project of determining who belongs to American society as full members or as something less. This is a project of national self-definition that will consist not only of traditional immigration law but also alienage classifications, as long as permanent residency is a status between complete outsider and full citizen-member. This national self-definition project involves not only the power to admit and expel, but also the power to define the attributes of alienage status. So defined, it is at least likely that there are some policy constraints on alienage classifications beyond the minimal constraint of notice inherent in the contract model. To determine what these constraints might be, we should examine the affiliation and transition models.

The Affiliation Model

Another interesting feature of current bars to welfare eligibility is the rule exempting permanent residents who have worked forty quarters. The model of permanent residence that explains this rule is the dominant model in prevailing discourse—what I call the affiliation model. Permanent residence, while something less than citizenship, represents a form of "affiliation" with American society.

The affiliation model draws support from the idea that America is a nation of immigrants. This image suggests that we should recognize the stake that immigrants acquire over time and that this recognition implies policy constraints on alienage classifications. Longer affiliation means treatment closer to citizenship. Besides sheer length of time, permanent residents may acquire their stake through tangible contributions, such as taxes and draft eligibility, as well as intangible ones, such as community participation.[20]

An expression of the affiliation model is this passage from the Supreme Court's decision in *Mathews v. Diaz:* "The decision to share . . . bounty with our guests may take into account the character of the relationship between the alien and this country: Congress may decide that as the alien's tie grows stronger, so does the strength of his claim to an equal share of that munificence."[21] Consider also from *Mathews v. Diaz:* "It is unquestionably reasonable for Congress to make an alien's eligibility depend on both the character and the duration of his residence."[22] Similarly, the court wrote in *Johnson v. Eisentrager:* "The alien . . . has been accorded a generous and ascending scale of rights as he increases his identity with our society."[23]

The recognition of permanent residents' stake in the United States also reflects their declining attachment to their country of formal citizenship. This decline is often due to quirks of family history rather than personal choice. It is unjust, the reasoning goes, to deny them some form of membership in their adopted country even if they never naturalize. They would be denied not only formal rights, but also the completeness of personal identity that comes from community membership.[24]

The affiliation model reflects the interests not only of permanent residents, but also of citizens.[25] To be sure, a liberal democracy depends in part on closure through its rules of membership. Yet, the existence of a substantial population that is a permanent part of the community but can never acquire a voice in its governance is, over time, a serious threat to liberal democracy for all. As Michael Walzer has explained, unless "the same standards apply to naturalization as to immigration, that every immigrant and every resident is a citizen, too—or, at least, a potential citizen," then "the state is like a family with live-in servants."[26] That, he adds, "is—inevitably, I think—a little tyranny."[27]

The affiliation model is important, but it, like the contract model, has limited explanatory power. It suggests that we should treat long-time permanent residents more like citizens. But as a corollary, it suggests that we may treat new permanent residents less like citizens. This means that the affiliation model removes an incentive to naturalize. To explain: a permanent resident generally becomes eligible for naturalization after five years. Under the affiliation model, this five-year point should mark the approximate time that the permanent resident should enjoy a citizen-like status *without* naturalizing. Under this reasoning, then, eligibility for the public benefit is no longer a reason to naturalize.[28] The affiliation model assumes that removing this incentive is not troubling.

This incentive problem reveals a deeper aspect of discourse about permanent residency. If removing the incentive is not troubling, it is because we accept (at least tacitly) that permanent residence may be permanent. After some period, the permanent resident becomes an almost-citizen and may remain so indefinitely. Over time, permanent residence resembles citizenship enough that naturalization, even if easy and routine, is not necessarily attractive, advantageous, or perhaps even meaningful. Against this background, the affiliation model focuses the central inquiry on the permissible degree of discrimination against permanent residents. Put differently, the attributes of permanent residency are determined by reference to citizenship generally.

If instead we viewed permanent residence as a temporary transition to citizenship, first our basic vocabulary would change. When the affiliation model compares permanent residence and citizenship, the differences look like "discrimination." But if we view permanent residence in relation to naturalization rather than citizenship generally, it is much harder to distinguish invidious discrimination from a benign (or at least well-intentioned) incentive to naturalize. This is why I am avoiding the term "alienage discrimination" in favor of the more neutral "alienage classification."

All of this suggests that the affiliation model fails to capture all of the policy constraints on alienage classifications. It may protect long-term permanent residents more than they deserve, if they can acquire that same protection through the alternative means of naturalization. At the same time, the affiliation model does not capture the quite different reasons why newer permanent residents should be protected in policy and constitutional law.

The Transition Model

Once we assess permanent residence in relation not to citizenship generally, but rather to naturalization, a third model emerges. Under what I call the transition model, permanent residence is not *permanent* at all, but rather a transition to citizenship—part of the naturalization process. This model does not suggest that immigrants become full members of American society upon arrival—far from it. But with time, immigrants must be able to become full members easily, through both formal naturalization and socioeconomic integration.[29]

Like the affiliation model, the transition model draws on the nation of immigrants idea. Both models reflect concern with the permanent residents themselves. In addition, both models posit that a permanent group of marginalized residents—who are governed but cannot acquire a voice in governing—impairs our self-interest in liberal democracy. The difference is that the affiliation model does not focus on naturalization. Rather, it recognizes a permanent approximation of citizenship. In contrast, the transition model focuses on the acquisition of actual citizenship through naturalization.[30]

Under the transition model, permanent residents must have routine access to citizenship through naturalization, even if a waiting period is required. Alienage classifications are inconsistent with the transition model if they unduly impede naturalization. In addition, permanent residents must have access to socioeconomic integration, without which formal naturalization loses much of its practical significance. Thus, alienage classifications are also inconsistent with the transition model if they impose disabilities that handicap permanent residents after they have navigated the transition to full membership.[31]

The transition model's emphasis on naturalization means that it does not protect the same group of permanent residents as the affiliation model. While the affiliation model protects permanent residents after a significant term of residence, the transition model assumes that such permanent residents can naturalize. The transition model protects permanent residents *until* they can naturalize. Permanent residents who decline routine naturalization choose to forego the advantages of citizenship, and the transition model no longer protects them.[32]

In practice, the transition model must protect permanent residents for longer than the formal eligibility period of five years (three years for spouse of citizens), to account for the time the naturalization process takes. Eligible permanent residents may file their applications three months before they have been permanent residents for the required time period,[33] but it typically takes much longer than three months from application to taking the oath of citizenship.[34] Additional time for the potential citizen to decide to naturalize may be appropriate.

The incentive issue operates quite differently in the transition model than the affiliation model. We can speak of meaningful incentives to naturalize only if the permanent resident is eligible. Because the transition model protects permanent residents only while naturalization is unavailable, it removes no incentives to naturalize. On the contrary, it creates incentives to naturalize for the permanent resident who wishes to continue the protection that the transition model has provided up to the time he or she becomes eligible.

The availability of dual citizenship for naturalized citizens is relevant here. If permanent residents may naturalize in the United States without relinquishing their original citizenship, permanent residents have one more reason to naturalize. The availability of dual citizenship reinforces the idea that the transition model's protections should end when naturalization becomes available. Conversely, if we view permanent residence as a transition to citizenship, then we should tolerate or encourage dual citizenship, since it encourages naturalization and thus maximizes the number of permanent residents who choose to become citizens.[35]

III. Applying the Transition Model

Each of these three models places only limited policy constraints on alienage classifications, but they are cumulative. All protect permanent residents, but in different ways and for different reasons. Of course, even under the combined constraints of the contract, affiliation, and transition models, many alienage classifications are unobjectionable. But for example, a newer permanent resident, who has not been here long enough to invoke the affiliation model, might persuasively argue that a certain alienage classification unduly impedes her transition to citizenship. Or a long-term permanent resident who cannot invoke the transition model might persuasively argue that an alienage classification inadequately recognizes his stake in American society. And a classification may be consistent with both the transition and affiliation models, yet change the immigration bargain enough that it is inconsistent with the contract model.

Most writing about alienage classifications has adopted some version of the affiliation model. This chapter tries to contribute by adding both the contract and transition models to the discourse, but I will devote most of my attention to the latter. The contract model comes into play under narrowly defined circumstances. In contrast, the transition model should make a difference in a wide variety of situations that tend to be addressed with only the affiliation model in mind. Thus, the rest of this chapter discusses how the transition model constrains alienage classifications in ways that differ from the constraints under the other two models. I will continue to focus on policy constraints, but where appropriate I will also address whether these constraints would be judicially enforceable as a matter of constitutional law. Generally, adding the transition model serves to identify certain shortcomings in our treatment of permanent residents in the period before they become eligible to naturalize.

To decide how the transition model might constrain alienage classifications, we should first ask what transition implies. The transition period is partly a probationary period. Unless a permanent resident violates the conditions of that probation, he or she is presumptively worthy of naturalization. Permanent residence is also a period of socioeconomic integration in preparation for naturalization. The probationary and integrative concepts of permanent residence are consistent and have a common basis: the idea that permanent residence is a transition to naturalization and citizenship.

Another key aspect of the transition model is that naturalization must be routine. This does not mean automatic, and it does not foreclose a naturalization process that imposes meaningful tests, educates new citizens, or solemnizes the attainment of citizenship through ritual. But the transition model does not tolerate difficult obstacles for the permanent resident who wants citizenship in an earnest way. For example, a basic English language requirement would be consistent with the transition model, but an English fluency requirement would not. When does a particular type of alienage classification "unduly impede" the transition to citizenship? Admittedly, this is a difficult line to draw, but the concept is important and worth an attempt to give it content.

Public Education

Let me begin with what may be an easy case, but one that illustrates the basic principles underlying the transition model. Consider a law that denies public elementary and secondary education to permanent resident children. This law would unduly impede the transition to citizenship, because deficient educational opportunities might permanently subordinate this group. While some permanent resident children could attend private schools or otherwise make up the deficiency, the general effect on the permanent resident population would be an enduring disadvantage.

This example also reminds us that transition is not just formal naturalization. To be sure, the denial of public education might mean more permanent residents fail the civics and English language tests for naturalization. But more significantly, and looking at the problem more broadly, the denial of public education will impede their economic and social integration into American society.

Would the contract model suggest the same constraint? It tells us that we may not bar permanent residents from public education if it was part of the immigration bargain when they arrived. But the contract model allows us to tell new permanent residents not to expect access to public education. If there are constraints on denial of public education to new permanent residents, the transition or affiliation models must supply them.

Does the affiliation model also suggest that all permanent resident children must have access to public education? Perhaps. While the transition model views public education as a key part of a permanent resident's transition to citizenship, the affiliation model would take a different approach. The argument would be that education is so basic to American society that even the newest newcomer begins with enough affiliation to demand it. This argument seems weaker than the transition model argument, for under the affiliation model newcomers' lack of tangible and intangible stake may justify some waiting period before they gain access to public education. Under the transition model, however, newcomers must have access to public education from the very beginning, or else their ability to become fuller members of American society will be injured irreparably.

If we shift momentarily from policy constraints to constitutional law, we can find support for the view that denial of public education to permanent resident children would be not only bad policy but also unconstitutional. In *Plyler v. Doe*,[36] a 1982 decision, the Supreme Court struck down a Texas law that effectively barred undocumented alien children from public schools. Of course, *Plyler* involved a state measure, so I do not suggest that it necessarily compels the same finding of unconstitutionality for a *federal* measure with the same prohibition.[37] What is significant for our attempt to give content to the transition model is that the court was deeply troubled by a denial of public education even to the undocumented, whether as a matter of state or federal law. Quoting the passage from *Brown v. Board of Education*[38] that "it is doubtful that any child may reasonably be expected to succeed in life if he is denied the opportunity of an education," the court expressed fear that the result would be to create an underclass that would be permanently denied full participation in American society.[39] These concerns would undoubtedly be heightened if permanent resident children were targeted. Given one prevailing national self-image as a society of upward mobility in which education counts more than family wealth, restrictions on access to education seem especially permanent and objectionable.[40]

Welfare Benefits

What is enough like public education to suggest similar public policy constraints? A strong candidate is welfare benefits, at least those that are basic "safety-net" benefits. These are core financial protections and social services that help guarantee noncitizens a minimum socioeconomic position, from which they can make a transition to citizenship through formal naturalization and socioeconomic integration.

Identifying these core protections is an imprecise task, but welfare benefits generally should count, to the extent that they guard against the most abject forms of poverty. The transition model cautions strongly against any withdrawing of the safety net from permanent residents, should they fall into dire circumstances due to causes arising after admission.[41] Especially if we view the acquisition of citizenship not only as a formal legal act but also as a socioeconomic process, withdrawing the safety net unduly impedes the transition.

Does the contract model suggest the same constraints? As with public education, it says that we may not bar permanent residents from welfare if they arrived when access to welfare was part of the immigration bargain. But the contract model lets us tell new permanent residents that they should not expect access. Indeed, this is part of the thinking behind the current welfare scheme, which adopts quite different regimes for permanent residents before and after August 1996.

Does the affiliation model support the argument that as a matter of public policy, *all* permanent residents must have access to welfare benefits? As with public education, the affiliation model might do so, on the ground that the safety net is so basic to American society that even the newest newcomer should have it. But new permanent residents have a weaker argument than long-term permanent residents that they have acquired a stake in American society, especially without having contributed economically through tax payments. Thus, as with public education, the affiliation model gives newer permanent residents a weaker argument for immediate welfare than the transition model does. For long-term permanent residents, in contrast, the affiliation model offers considerable protection.

The transition and affiliation models of permanent residence combine to argue that new restrictions on SSI and food stamps for permanent residents are unwise as a policy matter. A contract model is consistent with both bars with regard to future permanent residents. But for noncitizens who are already permanent residents, the bar on long-term permanent residents is inconsistent with the affiliation model. The bar on those who have been permanent residents for a shorter period is inconsistent with the transition model.

The next question is whether policy constraints suggested by the transition and affiliation models also suggest that the new restrictions are unconstitutional. Here we come to two landmark Supreme Court cases: *Graham v. Richardson*[42] and *Mathews v. Diaz*.[43] *Graham* struck down Arizona and Pennsylvania state laws that conditioned welfare eligibility on citizenship or length of permanent residence. The court first discussed equal protection and concluded that "classifications based on alienage, like those based on nationality or race, are inherently suspect and subject to close judicial scrutiny. Aliens as a class are a prime example of a 'discrete and insular minority' . . . for whom such heightened judicial solicitude is appropriate."[44] The second part of *Graham* offered federal preemption as an additional reason for its holding.[45] *Diaz* upheld a federal law that allowed permanent residents access to Medicare only if they had resided in the United States for five years. The court reasoned that "in the exercise of its broad power over naturalization and immigration, Congress regularly makes rules that would be unacceptable if applied to citizens."[46]

Graham calls for close judicial scrutiny of alienage classifications, even calling them "inherently suspect." In contrast, *Diaz* suggests that the political branches' plenary power over immigration includes the power to adopt alienage classifications as part of immigration law and that this power is subject to few if any constitutional constraints. The obvious difference is that *Graham* struck down state statutes, while *Diaz* upheld a federal statute. But this explanation needs to go beyond simple federal preemption, especially since the court's primary approach in both cases was equal protection.

The best explanation of *Graham* is that Arizona and Pennsylvania could not justify their welfare bars as alienage classifications intended to play a role in national self-definition.[47] This was also the problem with the Texas statute in *Plyler.* In *Diaz,* Justice Stevens explained: "a division by a State of the category of persons who are not citizens of that State into subcategories of United States citizens and aliens has no apparent justification, whereas, a comparable classification by the Federal Government is a routine and normally legitimate part of its business."[48]

Diaz characterized federal alienage classifications as part of federal power over immigration and naturalization. *Diaz is* right to treat immigration and naturalization as closely linked; both contribute to national self-definition. But does *Diaz* also say that the plenary power doctrine—often thought to exempt the political branches' immigration decisions from serious constitutional judicial review—also immunizes alienage classifications?

I think the answer is no. The noncitizens lost in *Diaz,* but the court stopped well short of suggesting that constitutional challenges to federal alienage classifications are never taken seriously or that aliens do not acquire a constitutionally recognized stake through residence in this country.[49] Instead, the court began: "The Fifth Amendment, as well as the Fourteenth Amendment, protects every one of these persons from deprivation of life, liberty, or property without due process of law."[50] The court focused on the noncitizen's functional attachment to the national community, not on formal citizenship. So viewed, *Diaz is* consistent with earlier cases that vindicated aliens' constitutional rights in alienage matters.[51] I doubt that the *Diaz* court would have upheld the Medicare restriction had it classified not only by alienage, but also by gender or legitimacy, as did the immigration statute that the court upheld in *Fiallo v. Bell,*[52] exercising minimal, if any, constitutional judicial review.

None of this suggests directly that the new welfare restrictions are unconstitutional, but it does suggest that courts should take a constitutional challenge seriously. Most policy and constitutional discussion of the new restrictions proceeds from an affiliation model. Thus, the question is whether permanent residents are close enough to citizens that they should have equal access to welfare. So viewed, the question seems to pose the type of balancing of political interests that makes courts understandably reluctant to intervene with a finding of unconstitutionality. In contrast, the transition model suggests that there is a minimum standard of protection rather than a balancing of interests. For support, consider this passage from *Graham:* "In the ordinary case an alien, becoming indigent and unable to work, will be unable to live where, because of discriminatory denial of public assistance, he cannot 'secure the necessities of life, including food, clothing and shelter.' "[53] In short, the transition model may provide a new basis for courts to find that the 1996 immigrant welfare restrictions go so far as to be unconstitutional.

Petitioning for Family Members to Immigrate

What about family reunification opportunities, which are considerably fewer for permanent residents than for citizens? As a policy matter, the long wait before spouses and minor children may join permanent residents is highly problematic. The transition model explains why in a way that the contract and affiliation models do not.

When someone qualifies to immigrate as a permanent resident, he or she may be accompanied or followed by spouses and minor children.[54] But individuals who later become spouses or children of a permanent resident must wait in the second family-based preference category. So must adult sons and daughters. In October 1997, spouses and minor children of permanent residents who receive immigrant visas have been waiting since June 1993 or earlier.

Under a transition model, this is problematic because long waits for relatives of permanent residents seriously hinder the formation of a functioning family unit. Close relatives do not come to the United States at all, or they come unlawfully. Either way, both formal naturalization and socioeconomic integration are severely impaired. We need not entirely eliminate the difference between citizens and permanent residents. For example, the transition model does not constrain rules that make more distant relatives wait or even make them ineligible to immigrate. Also, we need not entirely exempt permanent residents' spouses and minor children from numerical limitations. The problem is not that all relatives of permanent residents face some waiting period, but rather that for some close relatives, the period is so long that it is inconsistent with the transition model.

The gap between permanent residents and citizens is an incentive to naturalize, since the five years required for naturalization is shorter than the waiting period for the second family-based preference.[55] Would closing this gap remove an incentive to naturalize? Literally, yes. But because the long wait causes hardships that are suffered primarily while naturalization is not an option, it is hard to view this alienage classification as a benign incentive. More prominent is its inconsistency with the transition model of permanent residence.

Analysis would be different under the contract model, which suggests that permanent residents must accept any family reunification disadvantages that they knew about before they became permanent residents. The affiliation model suggests that newer permanent residents are insufficiently affiliated to demand similar family reunification rights. After some period of years, however, the affiliation model suggests similar family reunification opportunities for permanent residents and citizens. This happens currently, since the second preference waiting period functions as the affiliation period. Note, however, that once the permanent resident has been here for five years, closing the gap between permanent residents and citizens would remove an incentive to naturalize.

If the transition model suggests policy constraints on a long waiting period, does it also suggest that a long waiting period is unconstitutional? Some Supreme Court decisions outside the immigration and alienage context discuss a constitutional interest in family reunification. Prominent is *Moore v. City of East Cleveland*,[56] which struck down a zoning ordinance that prohibited a homeowner and one of her grandsons from living in her house at the same time. The court found the ordinance unconstitutional because it interfered excessively with the integrity of the family unit. Another important case is *Stanley v. Illinois*,[57] which struck down an Illinois statute that made the children of unwed fathers wards of the state upon the death of the mother. In so holding, the Supreme Court recognized a father's constitutional interest in custody of his child born out of wedlock.

Does any such constitutional interest limit the government's power to make the rules governing family-based immigration? Perhaps not. Courts are likely to rule that the plenary power doctrine trumps *Moore* and similar precedents, especially where, as here, the constitutional challenge is directed against substantive admission rules rather than the procedures by which those rules are applied. A leading example of the plenary power doctrine in a family reunification context is the court's 1977 decision in *Fiallo v. Bell*.[58] In general, the constitutional basis for family unity has only weakly supported constitutional challenges to the admission categories and numerical limits established by Congress.[59]

Notice, however, that this outcome depends entirely on characterizing the issue as admission of new immigrants, which would place it squarely within the "immigration law" sphere in which the plenary power doctrine operates to limit. If we characterize the issue as involving the family reunification opportunities of permanent residents, the constitutionality of the long second preference waiting period becomes more questionable.

Politics

Other alienage classifications limit political activity by permanent residents. We should consider three general types: voting, political speech, and public employment.

1. Voting. Is limiting voting in public elections to citizens inconsistent with the transition model? Probably not. To be sure, one can argue that political participation through voting can foster some aspects of the transition to citizenship.[61] Yet, the argument seems unpersuasive that it unduly impedes the transition if permanent residents are ineligible to vote. Voting ineligibility does not directly impede formal naturalization and socioeconomic integration. But arguably, permanent residents who may not vote are vulnerable to other measures that do impede their transition. Citizens or interest groups who have similar political aims may represent noncitizens during the transition period. This protection may be incomplete, but if it is, the resulting inconsistency with the transition model is attributable to those measures themselves—not to the voting bar.

The contract model also suggests that noncitizens may be denied the vote. Alien suffrage ended as a general practice in the 1920s, so no one who has become a permanent resident recently can argue that denial of suffrage would be inconsistent with the immigration bargain.

Is limiting voting in public elections to citizens inconsistent with the affiliation model? Most arguments in favor of alien suffrage are based on an affiliation model. The idea is that noncitizens, by virtue of a period of affiliation with American society, should have the right to vote. The incentive problem reappears here. For permanent residents who have not been here long enough to naturalize, the affiliation model lends much less support. Long-term permanent residents have a stronger affiliation-based argument for the right to vote, but they are eligible to naturalize by the same measure. For them, naturalization is the simple way to acquire the franchise, assuming that faithful adherence to the transition model has indeed made naturalization routine.

Interestingly, some proponents of alien suffrage point to Europe, where noncitizen voting is under more serious discussion. The crucial difference between Europe and the United States is that naturalization is generally more difficult in Europe. Where naturalization is more difficult, the affiliation model supports alien suffrage more persuasively than it does where naturalization is routine.

The best response to the incentive problem is that the affiliation model may call for alien suffrage before the permanent resident becomes eligible to naturalize. The small size of a community and the nature of the issue may make it more important for sound governance to define the voting community without regard to U.S. citizenship. This explains why the strongest arguments in favor of alien suffrage concern local voting, as opposed to state and national voting.

2. *"Political speech."* What about political speech? As a matter of policy, should permanent residents enjoy the same First Amendment protections as citizens? Suppose the government tries to remove a noncitizen who has engaged in political speech or in an activity that would be protected by the First Amendment in a citizen's case. This is typically considered immigration law, not alienage law, because it concerns admission and expulsion. In fact, however, the potential exposure to removal regulates the lives of noncitizens in the United States just as surely as the other alienage classifications that we have examined.[61] Or suppose permanent residents were not allowed to contribute money to political campaigns.[62] Here again, the First Amendment comes into play, since the Supreme Court has recognized campaign contributions as a form of protected speech.[63]

How do our three models help us analyze these situations? Arguably, political activity is no different from voting, but in fact there are subtle but important differences, on which the transition model sheds the most light. An essential part of this model is that the transition period be a time of socioeconomic integration. Participating in American society while enjoying the same First Amendment protections as citizens is an essential part of this integration. One could counter that voting is equally important as a matter of socioeconomic integration, that only the permanent resident who votes during the transition period is fully able to both naturalize and integrate. But compare the effects of denying permanent residents voting and all political activity. Voting is a formal act, infrequently performed even by citizens, which is significant but not pervasively constitutive of an individual's life in a community. In stark contrast, exposure to removal from the United States for taking part in a demonstration or fundraising for or contributing financially to political candidates and groups is to regulate pervasively permanent residents' everyday lives in a way that unduly impedes the social aspects of their transition to citizenship.

Again, the transition model adds to the affiliation model's constraints by responding to the incentive problem. For long-term permanent residents, the naturalization option may be available, but for newer permanent residents who are as yet ineligible, prohibitions on political activity pose different, serious threats.

Are these not only policy constraints but also constitutional limitations on these alienage classifications? A confident answer is elusive, but on balance, the transition and affiliation models raise the type of concerns that have led one federal appeals court to find a First Amendment violation in this context.[64]

3. Public employment. Citizenship requirements for public employment pose issues similar to voting and political speech, but with interesting and significant differences. The thinking behind these requirements has been that public employment involves not mere participation in the political process, but rather something more central to politics—serving as a representative of government, as well as policymaking itself. Thus, even states and localities should be allowed to distinguish aliens from citizens when they are defining not national membership, but membership in smaller political communities.

The defect in this analysis is that public employment is *employment.* So viewed, it represents an economic good apart from its political implications. To bar noncitizens from all public employment is to erect a significant barrier to their participation in the labor market, particularly in localities where a large share of available employment is in the public sector. For this reason, the transition model of permanent residence suggests policy constraints on a citizenship requirement for *all* public employment. Such a requirement has reduced political aspects, while it has heightened economic impact. When citizenship requirements are more precisely focused on jobs that truly involve representing the government and/or policymaking, they more closely resemble citizenship requirements for voting, and they minimize the impediment to socioeconomic integration.

These policy considerations are also reflected in constitutional doctrine. In *Sugarman v. Dougall,*[65] the Supreme Court struck down a New York law that required U.S. citizenship for all state public employees. But in contrast to *Graham*'s much narrower view of state and local alienage classifications, *Sugarman* left the door open for citizenship requirements for any government employment that is closely related to "political functions."

The court applied this exception in *Cabell v. Chavez-Salido.*[66] A California law required U.S. citizenship for state probation officers. In upholding this statute, Justice White wrote for a majority of five that "although citizenship is not a relevant ground for the distribution of economic benefits, it is a relevant ground for determining membership in the political community."[67] He continued: "The exclusion of aliens from basic governmental processes is not a deficiency in the democratic system but a necessary consequence of the community's process of political self-definition."[68] The court has also used this "political functions" exception to uphold state citizenship requirements for public school teachers[69] and state troopers.[70]

The difficulties on both policy and constitutional levels lie not with principle, but with application. In *Cabell,* for example, differing characterizations of the facts explain the disagreement between the majority and dissent. The majority emphasized the representation and policymaking duties of probation officers. The dissent emphasized that the noncitizen applicants were being denied jobs.

IV. Conclusion

The contract, affiliation, and transition models have many more applications than I can discuss here. My goal has not been a comprehensive taxonomy of alienage classifications. Rather, I have tried to show that both policy and constitutional analysis of alienage classifications would profit from a more textured understanding of how alienage classifications define what permanent residence is. That understanding begins with the idea that analysis depends on whether we view permanent residence as an indefinite status to be compared to citizenship status, or as a contract with the new immigrant, or as a transition to naturalization. Each of these three models suggests different protections, which only in combination define the position of permanent residents in this nation of immigrants.

Notes

1. Section 402, Personal Responsibility and Work Opportunity Reconciliation Act, Pub. L. 104–93, 110 Stat. 2105 (1996). The bar does not apply to persons who worked in the United States for at least forty quarters without receiving federal means-tested benefits. It also does not apply to refugees, asylees, and persons granted withholding of deportation for their first five years in the United States. Soon after enactment, these restrictions were challenged on constitutional grounds in several federal lawsuits. See, e.g., *Abreu v. Callahan,* 971 F. Supp. 799 (S.D.N.Y. 1997) (granting government's motion to dismiss).

2. Future legal immigrants are formally barred for the first five years, after which most sponsored immigrants will remain ineligible under "deeming provisions" that attribute a sponsor's income to the immigrant.

3. Congress restored access to SSI benefits for blind or disabled noncitizens who were already permanent residents in August 1996. The bars remain for age-based SSI and food stamps, and for future permanent residents. See Balanced Budget Act of 1997, Pub. L. 105–33, 111 Stat. 251 (1997).

4. Aliens seeking admission must fit within one of the categories for immigrants in Immigration and Nationality Act [INA] § 203, 8 U.S.C. § 1153, or nonimmigrants in INA § 101(a)(15), 8 U.S.C. § 1101(a)(15). They must not be

"inadmissible"; see INA § 212(a), 8 U.S.C. § 1182(a). Admissions may be numerically limited; see INA §§ 201–04, 8 U.S.C. § 1151–54.

5. See *Ng Fung Ho v. White,* 259 U.S. 276 (1922).

6. See INA § 237, 8 U.S.C. § 1227.

7. See generally INA §§ 201–3, 8 U.S.C. §§ 1151–53.

8. Citizenship also matters for more than deciding the "rights" of citizens and noncitizens. For example, it can serve as the basis for extraterritorial application of domestic law. See, e.g., *Blackmer v. United States,* 284 U.S. 421 (1932).

9. See Michael Walzer, *Spheres of Justice: A Defense of Pluralism and Equality* (New York: Basic Books, 1983), 39, where he argues that the "distinctiveness of cultures and groups . . . depends on closure."

10. See *Schneider v. Rusk,* 377 U.S. 163 (1964).

11. Art. II, § 1, cl. 5.

12. INA § 201(b)(2)(A)(ii), 8 U.S.C. § 1151(b)(2)(A)(ii).

13. See *Newton v. INS,* 736 F.2d 336, 342–43 (6th Cir. 1984), quoting *Acosta v. Gaffney,* 558 F.2d 1153, 1157–58 (3d Cir. 1977).

14. Earlier versions of the 1996 welfare legislation would have restricted eligibility beyond naturalization, creating two groups of citizens for welfare purposes.

15. See Hiroshi Motomura, "Whose Immigration Law?: Citizens, Aliens, and the Constitution," *Columbia Law Review* 97 (1997): 1567, 1572; and Hiroshi Motomura, "Immigration and Alienage, Federalism and Proposition 187," *Virginia Journal of International Law* 35 (1994): 201, 202–3.

16. See *Chae Chan Ping v. United States* (Chinese Exclusion Case), 130 U.S. 581 (1889). For more modern articulations of the plenary power doctrine, see *Fiallo v. Bell,* 430 U.S. 787 (1977); *Kleindienst v. Mandel,* 408 U.S. 753 (1972). See generally Hiroshi Motomura, "Immigration Law After a Century of Plenary Power: Phantom Constitutional Norms and Statutory Interpretation," *Yale Law Journal* 100 (1990): 545–614; and Hiroshi Motomura, "The Curious Evolution of Immigration Law: Procedural Surrogates for Substantive Constitutional Rights," *Columbia Law Review* 92 (1992): 1625–704.

17. See *Wong Wing v. United States,* 163 U.S. 228, 234 (1896); *Yick Wo v. Hopkins,* 118 U.S. 356, 373–74 (1886).

18. See *Chy Lung v. Freeman,* 92 U.S. (2 Otto) 275 (1875).

19. For a full discussion, see Linda S. Bosniak, "Membership, Equality, and the Difference That Alienage Makes," *New York University Law Review* 69 (1994): 1047. See also Motomura, "Immigration and Alienage," 202–3.

20. See *Graham v. Richardson,* 403 U.S. 365, 376 (1971) ("Aliens like citizens pay taxes and may be called into the armed forces. . . . Aliens may live within a state for many years, work in the state and contribute to the economic growth of the state. . . . There can be no 'special public interest' in tax revenues to which aliens have contributed on an equal basis with the residents of the State").

21. *Mathews v. Diaz,* 426 U.S. 67, at 80.

22. *Mathews v. Diaz,* at 82–83.

23. *Johnson v. Eisentrager,* 339 U.S. 763, 770 (1950).

24. See T. Alexander Aleinikoff, "Theories of Loss of Citizenship," *Michigan Law Review* 84 (1986): 1471, 1494–98 ("Denationalization may grossly intrude upon a person's conception of self").

25. On aliens' versus citizens' rights, see Motomura, "Whose Immigration Law?" 1572; and Hiroshi Motomura, "Whose Alien Nation? Two Models of Constitutional Immigration Law," *Michigan Law Review* 94 (1996): 1927, 1942–45.

26. Walzer, *Spheres of Justice*, 52.

27. Walzer, *Spheres of Justice*, 52. See also at 61: "No democratic state can tolerate the establishment of a fixed status between citizen and foreigner (though there can be stages in the transition from one of these political identities to the other)."

28. William Rogers Brubaker, "Membership Without Citizenship: The Economic and Social Rights of Noncitizens," in *Immigration and the Politics of Citizenship in Europe and North America*, ed. William Rogers Brubaker (Lanham, Md.: German Marshall Fund and University Press of America, 1989), 145, 162: "Paradoxically, inclusion in the social and economic community may facilitate (self-) exclusion from the political community. Secure status as a denizen, a member of the outer circle, may dissuade an immigrant from becoming a citizen, a member of the inner circle."

29. In its recent report to Congress, the U.S. Commission on Immigration Reform's discussion of "Americanization and Integration of Immigrants" reflects much of this focus. See U.S. Commission on Immigration Reform, *Becoming an American: Immigration and Immigrant Policy* (Washington, D.C.: U.S. Government Printing Office, 1997), 25–45.

30. Cf. Tomas Hammar, "State, Nation, and Dual Citizenship," in *Immigration and the Politics of Citizenship*, 81, 93 (identifying two options for minimizing the harm to democracy if a large denizen population is excluded from the political process: to confer full political rights on denizens or to increase denizens' rates of naturalization).

31. Compare the idea that birthright citizenship to children of undocumented aliens avoids the creation of a permanent, subordinated caste of noncitizens.

32. This reasoning explains the definition of "protected individuals" under the antidiscrimination provisions of INA § 274B, 8 U.S.C. § 1324b, which includes permanent residents, refugees, and asylees, but not "an alien who fails to apply for naturalization within six months of the date the alien first becomes eligible . . . to apply for naturalization." This approach is more faithful to the transition model than the approach that Congress deleted from INA § 274A in 1990: relying on the filing of the optional "declaration of intention to become a citizen of the United States" under INA § 335, 8 U.S.C. 1446.

33. INA § 334, 8 U.S.C. § 1445.

34. "Report Card on INS Adjudications," *AILA Monthly Mailing* 16 (December 1997): 993. Congress acknowledged this processing problem when it extended welfare eligibility for refugees and asylum from five years after arrival to seven years after arrival. See H.R. Rep. 105–149, 105th Cong., 1st Sess., 1997 WL 353017, at 2399 (1997).

35. The availability of dual nationality for naturalized citizens may have the opposite effect under the affiliation model. Tolerating citizenship as a nonexclusive commitment to one nationality suggests that citizenship need not confer significant benefits over and above what permanent residence entails. This acceptance of a less precious and exclusive citizenship suggests, in turn, that affil-

iation through long-term permanent residence is worthy of recognition through the absence of alienage classifications. Under the affiliation model, dual citizenship may constrain alienage classifications.

36. *Plyler v. Doe,* 457 U.S. 202 (1982).

37. Recall that immigration and alienage law both contribute to national self-definition. This view of alienage classifications allows the federal government to justify them against an equal protection challenge in ways that states cannot. See Motomura, "Immigration and Alienage," 206–11. In *Plyler,* Texas could not justify its denial of education to undocumented children by suggesting that this measure was its contribution to the national self-definition project. If Congress rather than Texas had acted, the court could not have relied so heavily on uncertainty about the federal attitude toward undocumented aliens. See 457 U.S. at 219 n.19, 225.

38. *Brown v. Board of Education,* 347 U.S. 483 (1954).

39. *Plyler v. Doe,* 457 U.S. at 207–08, 218–19, 226.

40. *Plyler v. Doe,* 226 (referring to the "special constitutional sensitivity" of education). See also U.S. Commission on Immigration Reform, *Becoming an American,* 36–45.

41. INA § 237, 8 U.S.C. § 1227, provides: "Any alien who, within five years after the date of entry, has become a public charge from causes not affirmatively shown to have arisen since entry is deportable." My elaboration of the transition model is consistent with this deportability ground and with efforts to reduce welfare dependency generally. I only suggest that unforeseen poverty among new immigrants should elicit the same response by way of welfare benefits as poverty among citizens. The appropriate level of welfare benefits for citizens is a topic beyond the scope of this chapter.

42. *Graham v. Richardson,* 403 U.S. 365 (1971).

43. *Mathews v. Diaz,* 426 U.S. 67 (1976).

44. *Graham v. Richardson,* 403 U.S. at 371–72 (citing *United States v. Carolene Prods. Co.,* 304 U.S. 144, 152–53 n.4 [1938], and *Takahashi v. Fish & Game Commission,* 334 U.S. 410, 420 [1948]).

45. *Graham v. Richardson,* 403 U.S. at 376–77.

46. *Mathews v. Diaz,* 426 U.S. at 79–80.

47. According to the court, these are matters for the federal government: "State laws that restrict the eligibility of aliens for welfare benefits merely because of their alienage conflict with these overriding national policies in an area constitutionally entrusted to the Federal Government." *Graham v. Richardson,* 403 U.S. at 378. See also *Nyquist v. Mauclet,* 432 U.S. 1, 10 (1977) (encouraging naturalization is an exclusively federal interest).

48. *Mathews v. Diaz,* 426 U.S. at 85. See also 86–87: "The Fourteenth Amendment's limits on state powers are substantially different from the constitutional provisions applicable to the federal power over immigration and naturalization"; and 84–85: "The equal protection analysis also involves significantly different considerations because it concerns the relationship between aliens and the States rather than between aliens and the Federal Government."

49. See *Mathews v. Diaz,* 426 U.S. at 77, citing *Wong Yang Sung v. McGrath,*

339 U.S. 33, 48–51, modified, 339 U.S. 908 (1950); *Wong Wing v. United States,* 163 U.S. 228, 238 (1886); and *Russian Volunteer Fleet v. United States,* 282 U.S. 481, 489 (1931).

50. *Mathews v. Diaz,* 426 U.S. at 77.

51. See, e.g., *Wong Wing v. United States,* 163 U.S. 228, 234 (1896).

52. *Fiallo v. Bell,* 430 U.S. 787 (1977). *Fiallo* summarily rejected a constitutional challenge to the INA's definition of "child," which at that time recognized an illegitimate child's mother but not his or her father for immigration purposes.

53. *Graham v. Richardson,* 403 U.S. 365, 379–80 (1971). See also *Nyquist v. Mauclet,* 432 U.S. 1, 12–15 (1977) (Burger, J., dissenting) (strict scrutiny should apply to alienage classifications only when they deprive aliens of the basic necessities of life).

54. INA § 203(d), 8 U.S.C. § 1153(d).

55. See Reed Ueda, *Postwar Immigrant America: A Social History* (Boston: St. Martin's Press, 1994), 128 (discussing family reunification as an incentive to naturalize).

56. *Moore v. City of East Cleveland,* 431 U.S. 494 (1977).

57. *Stanley v. Illinois,* 405 U.S. 645 (1972).

58. *Fiallo v. Bell,* 430 U.S. 787 (1977).

59. See also *United States ex rel. Knauff v. Shaughnessy,* 338 U.S. 537 (1950) (alien spouse seeking initial entry has no procedural due process right to exclusion hearing).

60. See de la Garza and DeSipio, "Save the Baby, Change the Bathwater, and Scrub the Tub: Latino Electoral Participation After Seventeen Years of Voting Right Act Coverage," *Texas Law Review* 71 (1993): 1479, 1522–23, proposing that noncitizens be allowed to vote for five years while they are ineligible to naturalize, after which they could no longer vote but could naturalize; those who actually vote would be exempt from the naturalization exam.

61. See *Harisiades v. Shaughnessy,* 342 U.S. 580 (1952).

62. Several bills introduced in the 105th Congress would bar permanent residents from making campaign contributions. See, e.g., S.95, 105th Cong., 1st Sess., § 203 (1997); S.229, 105th Cong., 1st Sess., § 401 (1997).

63. See *Buckley v. Valeo,* 424 U.S. 1 (1976).

64. See *American-Arab Anti-Discrimination Committee v. Reno,* 70 F.3d 1045 (9th Cir. 1995).

65. *Sugarman v. Dougall,* 413 U.S. 634, 646 (1973).

66. *Cabell v. Chavez-Salido,* 454 U.S. 432, 433, 445–47 (1982).

67. *Cabell v. Chavez-Salido,* 454 U.S. at 438.

68. *Cabell v. Chavez-Salido,* 454 U.S. at 439.

69. See *Ambach v. Norwick,* 441 U.S. 68, 69–72 (1979).

70. See *Foley v. Connelie,* 435 U.S. 291, 297–300 (1978).

Membership and American Social Contracts: A Response to Hiroshi Motomura

Daniel J. Tichenor

Only a few years ago, it was no small feat to explain precisely how permanent resident aliens are treated differently from citizens in the United States. The *obligations* of U.S. citizenship and legal permanent residence—from paying taxes to serving in the military in times of war—were nearly identical and remain so today.[1] Likewise, an expansion of alien rights since the 1960s extended to legal permanent resident aliens (LPRs) most of the same social and economic entitlements and legal protections enjoyed by citizens at the start of the decade. How quickly this received wisdom has become quaint. Whereas the communal obligations of LPRs and citizens remain virtually indistinguishable, a great divide now separates citizens and noncitizens in their access to social welfare benefits and other individual rights.

This contemporary impoverishment of immigrant rights, the culmination of recent welfare and immigration reform,[2] deeply informs Hiroshi Motomura's incisive reflections on alienage classification. One of the most important contributions of his chapter is the set of conceptual models it offers for understanding the legal status of LPRs. The nature and meaning of permanent residence, Motomura observes, depends on whether we view the claims of legal immigrants in terms of their length of residence (affiliation model), the fixed bargains they have implicitly accepted upon admission (contract model), or their status as potential citizens (transition model).

This essay was written in response to a draft of Hiroshi Motomura's chapter, presented at the Duke University Workshop on Citizenship and Naturalization, October 30–November 1, 1997.

Yet Motomura is not merely concerned with expanding our theoretical framework for exploring the membership status of permanent resident aliens. At least implicitly, a normative concern for using the contract, affiliation, and transition models to recover many of the individual rights recently lost by LPRs pervades his chapter. Motomura observes that in different ways his "three models all protect permanent residents" as legal claimants; his expectation is that these models will provide "cumulative protections" for LPRs whose rights have found their way onto the legislative chopping-block several times since the 1994 election. Nevertheless, it is the *transition* model, one richly inspired by political theorist Michael Walzer's writings on permanent residents as "potential citizens" in modern liberal democracies,[3] that serves as Motomura's chief vehicle for vindicating LPR rights. By thinking about LPR status as but a transition to citizenship, he recognizes that differential treatment is only justified if it does not "unduly impede" the process by which legal immigrants "become full members easily." In this vein, for example, Motomura argues that limiting welfare benefits for LPRs is fundamentally suspect since the transition to citizenship includes a process of "socioeconomic integration" for which safety net protections may be crucial.

At a time when various political actors have declared open season on the legal rights of noncitizens, Motomura offers a compelling defense of welfare benefits, public education, family reunification, free political speech, and other basic membership goods for LPRs. For the purpose of stimulating debate, however, let me offer two distinctive critiques of his analysis. First, I would like to press him on the extent to which his three models of permanent residence might be interpreted in a manner that yields far fewer rights for legal immigrants than he intends. Indeed, Motomura's models can be turned on their head by others to justify significant limits on the rights of legal immigrants. Consider, for example, the potential vulnerabilities for LPRs that the contract model presents. Motomura suggests that the restoration of SSI benefits to those with LPR status as of August 1996 shows how a sense of contractual fairness toward newcomers who arrived before passage of recent welfare reform "protects [their] original expectations" of welfare eligibility. Of course, such a contractual resolution also assumes that all legal immigrants who arrive after this cutoff date have implicitly agreed to forego access to a panoply of public benefits. We are left, then, with two tiers of membership status for LPRs: alien-haves and alien-have-nots. And if future legislation modifies this "bargain" for newcomers even further, this model could underwrite additional gradations of membership among legal immigrants based on precisely when one gained LPR status.

There is another reason the contract model should give us pause: Migrants from poor countries are likely to accept any terms of admission that wealthy nations such as the United States dictate. As a result, they have about as much "bargaining power" as American workers possessed over labor contracts in the decades before the Wagner Act. The ignominious history of past U.S. guestworker programs, such as the Bracero Program with Mexico, should remind us of the enormous power imbalance in shaping contracts between government officials and citizens, on the one side, and noncitizens, on the other. Moreover, noncitizens have little or no ability to see that the fixed bargains they have accepted upon admission are enforced. Mexican *braceros*, for example, frequently endured substandard working conditions and wages that violated *explicit* contractual agreements during the postwar decades.[4] The capacity of noncitizens to garner protection from implicit bargains is at best an elusive goal.

Recognizing some of these concerns, Motomura asserts that the affiliation and transition models together fortify LPR rights where contractual protections are inadequate. Such analysis, however, may understate the degree to which the affiliation and transition models work at cross-purposes. At the heart of the transition model lies a celebration of immigrants who embrace U.S. citizenship. From this perspective, long-term affiliations with the United States are not sufficient to legitimize broad legal protections for LPRs. Rather, their legal and moral claims under the transition model most fundamentally derive from a willingness to be "potential citizens," an idealized devotion to American society. In turn, long-term LPRs who choose not to naturalize may be stigmatized as detached from, perhaps even disloyal to, the nation in which they live. By rejecting the status of potential citizen, these LPRs might well be cast by the transition model as undeserving of many rights reserved for citizens and earnest "citizens-in-training."

Finally, the transition model can be reinterpreted to justify a scant few rights for LPRs based on particular notions of virtuous citizenship. For example, many conservatives in American politics today celebrate new immigrants for possessing qualities straight out of a Horatio Alger novel: a stout work ethic, a passion for economic autonomy, and entrepreneurial success. It is primarily for this reason that many immigration defenders in the Republican party joined restrictionist colleagues in supporting welfare reform that denied basic public benefits for noncitizens. Desirable potential citizens, so the argument goes, exemplify the enormous opportunities available to those willing to ply themselves without public handouts. LPRs unable to resist welfare dependency might be viewed as poor future citizens. This conception of virtuous citizenship, then, would make economic self-sufficiency crucial to the integration of potential citizens (in stark contrast to the safety-net protections that Motomura and I believe should be extended to newcomers). In short, the transition model is potentially far more ubiquitous than Motomura suggests; it not only fails inherently to justify extensive rights for legal immigrants, but it also accommodates a draconian vision of LPR status.

A second critique of Motomura's essay is that its singular focus on the rights of legal immigrants obscures their entanglement, and perhaps their profound tension, with other egalitarian projects in the United States. Reflecting on how the logic of the transition model vindicates both negative and positive freedoms for LPRs, Motomura writes compellingly of the moral and practical necessities of assuring the socioeconomic integration of legal immigrants. What complicates this argument, however, is the fact that socioeconomic integration remains a pipedream for the millions of poor American citizens who constitute our indigenous economic "underclass."[5]

Deep economic inequality among American citizens captures not only the elusiveness of many positive freedoms in the United States, but raises important questions about whether immigration might limit, even imperil, the socioeconomic integration of the nation's poorest citizens. Existing research on the impact of immigration on economically marginalized citizens is limited and inconclusive. Nevertheless, many Americans long have found noncitizen rights irresistible, embracing the universality of U.S. liberal-egalitarian principles. A reverence for human equality, after all, demands that a person's life prospects and pursuits not be immutably shaped by where he or she is born.

At the same time, robust immigration and expansive noncitizen rights may undermine significant efforts to generate greater equality among citizens. Consider, for example, the rigorous economic and democratic projects that political scientist Jennifer Hochschild argues are necessary to salvage the American dream from formidable racial and class divisions. To restore faith in the American dream, she argues, all citizens must have "more than a formal chance to get ahead."[6] In her view, it demands government policies that ensure

> a good education through high school, enough shelter and sustenance that one can focus on how to define success rather than how to eat or stay warm, and neighborhoods that are safe and decent enough that one can focus on how to pursue success rather than how to make it home alive. It might imply the availability of jobs for all who seek them.[7]

But can these positive freedoms be sustained politically if they are extended to large numbers of newly arrived immigrants? Scholars like Joseph Carens remind us that a steady influx of poor immigrants erodes the communal bonds and mutual obligations that make the welfare state viable.[8] Unfortunately, expanding the rights of outsiders may very well undercut ambitious communal efforts to attack the most tenacious forms of poverty among disadvantaged citizens.

Motomura's three models of permanent residency invaluably expand our understanding of noncitizen rights. His engaging defense of LPR rights in terms of contractual obligations, social affiliation, and future citizenship challenges those who would limit the legal protections available for newcomers. Yet, as I have argued, we would do well to bear in mind that these models may be reinterpreted by restrictionists in a manner that justifies few rights for newcomers. Moreover, the entanglement of immigration and citizenship rights may pose disquieting tradeoffs for those of us who both welcome immigration and yearn to redress oppressive poverty in American society. Indeed, equality in our "nation of immigrants" appears to be far more contentious than most of us are willing to acknowledge.

Notes

1. Only such political tasks as voting stand out as special duties for citizens, although we know that many routinely ignore them.
2. I am referring primarily to Section 402 of the Personal Responsibility and Work Opportunity Reconciliation Act of 1996.
3. Michael Walzer, *Spheres of Justice* (New York: Basic Books, 1983), 31–63.
4. See, for example, Mark Reisler, *By the Sweat of their Brow: Mexican Immigrant Labor in the United States* (Westport, Conn.: Greenwood Press, 1976).
5. This concept is skillfully discussed by Ronald Mincy, "The Underclass: Concept, Controversy, and Evidence," in *Confronting Poverty: Prescriptions for Change*, ed. Sheldon Danziger, Gary Sandefur, and Daniel Weinberg (Cambridge: Harvard University Press, 1994), 109–46.
6. Jennifer Hochschild, *Facing Up to the American Dream: Race, Class, and the Soul of the Nation* (Princeton: Princeton University Press, 1995), xiv.
7. Hochschild, *American Dream*, xiv.
8. Joseph Carens, "Immigration and the Welfare State," in *Democracy and the Welfare State*, ed. Amy Gutmann (Princeton: Princeton University Press, 1988), 211.

Index

Abercrombie, Thomas, 78
Adams, John, 15
African Americans (blacks), 42, 53, 54, 111, 142; racism toward, 53
Afroyim v. Rusk, 160, 161–62, 168, 179–80
Aleinikoff, T. Alexander, 32, 92, 93, 115, 170–71, 183n27
Alien and Sedition Acts, 115, 120, 153
alienage classifications: legitimacy of, xxx, 114, 199–218
alienation: as challenge to democratic governance, xxix, 109
allegiance(s): multiple, xiii, 111. *See also* oath of allegiance
American Legion, 132, 133
Americanization: and American character, 17; of current citizens, 65, 77; in early twentieth century, xvii, xix, xxii, 51–52, 68–70, 77–81, 108, 130, 131–32; and incorporation, 120–21; as mutual and reciprocal process, xxiv, 63, 65, 66, 77, 80; and nativism, xvii, 68–70, 79, 132; original spirit of, 69–70, 80; and patriotism, 78, 119; and racism, xxi–xxii, 51–52, 55–58, 63, 68–70; revival of, xvii, xxii, 51–52, 62–70, 80–81, 108; role of government in, 63, 65; as way to undermine nativism, 63–64, 78, 80
Anti–Federalists, 17, 112, 116
Appiah, Kwame Anthony, xxi, 92, 93

Aristotle, 10–11, 12, 14, 23, 47n5
assimilation: and English instruction, 45, 52–53, 63, 65–68, 78, 121, 132, 144, 145, 152, 164, 186n58; and immigration, xvii, 44–45, 113–14; as threat to individual freedom, xxi, 46. *See also* Americanization, and incorporation; incorporation, and socioeconomic integration

Bible: injunction to welcome foreigners in, 77
Bosniak, Linda, xxv–xxvi
Bourne, Randolph, 92
Bracero Program, 58, 225
Brimelow, Peter, 60, 113, 114
Brown v. Board of Education, 210
Buchanan, Pat, xiii, 89, 113

Cabell v. Chavez-Salido, 217–18
Calhoun, John C., 31–32, 53
Carens, Joseph, xxv–xxvii, 41, 226
Changing Relation Project, 115–16
Cherokee. *See* Native Americans (Indians), Americanization of
Chinese Exclusion Act, 4, 54, 78, 115
Christianity, 12–15
citizen(s): formation of, xxiv, 11–12, 22–23, 110–11, 126–27, 128–29, 133; origin of concept, xii, 9; politicians' role in creating, xi–xv; responsibilities of, xi, 27, 63, 80, 111, 118, 174, 178–81

229

234 *Index*

Raskin, Jamin, 115
Rawls, John, xxi, 43
Rehnquist, William H., 125
Reich, Robert, 103
religion: American citizenship's influ-
    ence on, 22, 44; freedom of, 12, 13,
    43, 124; and problem of political ob-
    ligation, 12–15
republican government. *See* self-gov-
    ernment
republicanism, 5, 17, 18–19, 21, 22–23,
    51; role of majority rule in, 32
rights: affirmative action and, 24; cul-
    tural, 109; group, 23–25, 31–33, 80,
    109; individual, 15, 23, 86; language,
    25, 109; natural, 3, 13–15, 16, 21, 23,
    32–33, 50; of permanent residents,
    xxx–xxxi, 107, 114–15, 118, 145,
    165–66, 199–218, 223–27; political,
    24, 159–60; special, 24–25; welfare,
    114, 118, 165–66, 170–71, 199,
    203–4, 210–13, 221n47, 223–25
Roberts, Dorothy, 61
Rogers v. Bellei, 159, 185n45
Rosberg, Gerald, 122
Rotary Club, 133
Roybal, Edward, 123
Rubin, Gary, 126

Scheffler, Samuel, 87
Schneider v. Rusk, 160, 174
Schuck, Peter, xxvii–xxix, 114, 193
self-government, xx, xxiv–xxv, 21–22,
    33, 108, 110, 112, 116, 117, 118, 122,
    128–29, 131
slavery, 5, 7–9, 21; U.S. Constitution's
    position on, 7
Smith, Lamar, 107
Smith, Rogers M., 5, 50
social contract, 14, 15–16, 32, 44, 111
social justice, 24, 30

socialism, 5
solidarity: group, 85–87; national, 86–
    90, 92–93, 94–96, 101–104; posteth-
    nic, 94; "species–wide," 92–93, 102,
    104
Sons of the American Revolution, 79
Spiro, Peter, 165, 166, 167–68, 171–72,
    183n21, 184n31, 184n35
Stanley v. Illinois, 214
Stein, Dan, 171
Subversive Activities Control Act, 67
Sugarman v. Dougall, 217
Suny, Ronald Grigor, 91–92

Thirteenth Amendment, 4, 21
Tichenor, Daniel, xxxi
Tocqueville, Alexis de, 25

Ueda, Reed, 120, 130
universalism, xxiii, 92–93, 102
U.S. Commission on Immigration Re-
    form (CIR), xvii, xxi–xxii, xxiii, 63–
    68, 80, 108, 145–46, 190n108

values: American, xxii, 63–64, 103, 111,
    122, 123–24, 129, 133, 165, 169–74;
    common, xxiv, 111; inculcation of,
    xxv, 44, 174; liberal, 87, 94, 145–46,
    165, 168
Voting Rights Act, 67

Walzer, Michael, 110, 120, 205, 224
Washington, George, 3–4, 12, 17, 42, 50
Weltburgertum, 85, 92
West, Thomas G., 15
Wilson, Pete, 60, 168
Wolfe, Alan, 130
work ethic, 18, 23
Wright, Jim, 128, 131

Young, Iris Marion, 23–33

About the Contributors

Kwame Anthony Appiah is Professor of Afro-American Studies and Philosophy at Harvard University. Among his many published works are *Color Conscious: The Political Morality of Race*, with Amy Gutmann (Princeton University Press, 1996), *In My Father's House: Africa in the Philosophy of Culture* (Oxford University Press, 1992), and *Necessary Questions* (Prentice Hall, 1989).

Linda S. Bosniak is Professor of Law at Rutgers Law School-Camden. She has authored several articles on the subjects of immigration, citizenship, and nationalism.

Joseph H. Carens is Professor of Political Science at the University of Toronto. Among numerous other works, he is author of *Culture, Citizenship, and Community* (forthcoming, Oxford University Press). He is currently completing a book on the ethics of immigration.

David A. Hollinger is Professor of History at the University of California at Berkeley. His two most recent books are *Postethnic America: Beyond Multiculturalism* (Basic Books, 1995), and *Science, Jews, and Secular Culture: Studies in Mid-Twentieth Century American Intellectual History* (Princeton University Press, 1996).

Michael Jones-Correa is Assistant Professor of Government at Harvard University. He is the author of *Between Two Nations: The Political Predicament of Latinos in New York City* (forthcoming, Cornell University Press), and various articles on Latino identity and politics, the role of gender in shaping immigrant politics, and Hispanics as a foreign policy lobby.

Charles R. Kesler is Associate Professor of Government and Director of the Henry Salvatori Center at Claremont McKenna College. He is the editor of and a contributor to *Saving the Revolution: The Federalist Papers and the American Founding*, and is co-editor, with William F. Buckley, of *Keeping the Tablets: Modern American Conservative Thought*. He is currently writing a book on the political theory and practice of the American founders.

John J. Miller is National Political Reporter at *National Review* and a contributing editor at *Reason* magazine. His recent book is entitled *The Unmaking of Americans: How Multiculturalism Has Undermined America's Assimilation Ethic* (Free Press, 1998).

Hiroshi Motomura is Nicholas Doman Professor of International Law at the University of Colorado School of Law. In addition to publishing numerous articles on immigration law and policy, he is co-author, with Alex Aleinikoff and David Martin, of the casebook *Immigration: Process and Policy*, and is co-editor, with Kay Hailbronner and David Martin, of *Admission Policies: The Search for Workable Solutions in the United States and Germany*.

Juan F. Perea is University Research Foundation Professor of Law at the University of Florida College of Law. He has written extensively on issues of race, ethnicity, and the law, and is the editor of *Immigrants Out! The New Nativism and the Anti-Immigrant Impulse in the United States* (New York University Press, 1997). He is co-author, with Richard Delgado, Angela Harris, and Stephanie Wildman, of *Race and Races: Cases and Resources for a Multiracial America* (forthcoming, West Publishing Co.).

Noah M. J. Pickus is an Assistant Professor in the Terry Sanford Institute of Public Policy and the Department of Political Science at Duke University. His recent publications include essays on immigration and democracy and on citizenship in American political thought. He is the primary author of *Becoming American/America Becoming: The Final Report of the Duke Workshop on Immigration and Citizenship* (March, 1998) and is currently completing a book on immigration, citizenship, and nationhood.

Peter H. Schuck is Simeon E. Baldwin Professor of Law at Yale Law School. He is the author of *Suing Government: Citizen Remedies for Official Wrongs* (Yale University Press, 1983); *Agent Orange on Trial: Mass Toxic Disasters in the Courts* (Harvard University Press, 1987); and, with

Rogers M. Smith, *Citizenship Without Consent* (Yale University Press, 1985). He is also the editor of *Paths to Inclusion: The Integration of Migrants in the United States and Germany* (with Rainer Münz), and *Tort Law and the Public Interest: Competition, Innovation, and Consumer Welfare*, and *Foundations of Administrative Law*. His most recent book is *Citizens, Strangers, and In-Betweens: Essays on Immigration and Citizenship* (Westview Press, 1998).

Rogers M. Smith is Professor of Political Science at Yale University. His books include *Liberalism and American Constitutional Law* (Harvard University Press, 1985), *Citizenship Without Consent*, with Peter H. Schuck (Yale University Press, 1985), and *Civic Ideals: Conflicting Visions of Citizenship in U.S. History* (Yale University Press, 1997).

Daniel J. Tichenor is Assistant Professor of Political Science and a Faculty Associate of the Eagleton Institute of Politics at Rutgers University, New Brunswick. He has authored several articles on immigration, race, and American political development. He is completing a book on American immigration policy from the late 19th century to the present.